INTRODUCTION TO
PROJECT MANAGEMENT

INTRODUCTION TO PROJECT MANAGEMENT

Kathy Schwalbe, Ph.D., PMP
Augsburg College

THOMSON
COURSE TECHNOLOGY

Australia • Canada • Mexico • Singapore • Spain • United Kingdom • United States

THOMSON

COURSE TECHNOLOGY

Introduction to Project Management is published by Course Technology

Publisher
Bob Woodbury

Senior Acquisitions Editor
Maureen Martin

Senior Product Manager
Tricia Boyle

Associate Product Manager
Jennifer Smith

Developmental Editor
Betsey Henkels

Production Editor
Brooke Booth

Senior Marketing Manager
Karen Seitz

Manufacturing Coordinator
Justin Palmeiro

Text Designer
GEX Publishing Services

Cover Designer
Laura Rickenbach

Copyeditor
Green Pen Quality Assurance

Proofreader
Karen Annett

Indexer
Liz Cunningham

Some of the product names and company names used in this book have been used for identification purposes only and may be trademarks or registered trademarks of their respective manufacturers and sellers.

PMI, PMP, and PMBOK are registered marks of the Project Management Institute, Inc.

DILBERT: © Scott Adams/Dist. by United Feature Syndicate, Inc. No part of it may be reproduced or used in any form without prior written permission.

Disclaimer
Course Technology reserves the right to revise this publication and make changes from time to time in its content without notice.

ISBN-13: 978-1-4188-3559-0
ISBN-10: 1-4188-3559-5

For Dan, Anne, Bobby, and Scott

TABLE OF CONTENTS

The future of many organizations depends on their ability to manage projects, programs, and portfolios of projects. Skills in these areas continue to be in high demand. Colleges have responded to this need by establishing courses and degree programs in project management, and corporations are investing in continuing education to help develop effective project teams and project, program, and portfolio managers.

What makes this text different from other project management texts? First of all, people asked me to write it. They like the fact that I explain concepts in a way that enables readers to understand and apply them. I've taken some information and several features of my first book, *Information Technology Project Management*, now in its fourth edition, and adapted them to create a more general project management book that addresses the need for people in *all* industries to understand and use good project management. This book includes many real-world examples in the "What Went Right," "What Went Wrong," and "Media Snapshot" segments. People like to read about real projects that succeeded and those that failed to learn from the successes and failures of others. They also like to recognize that there are projects in all aspects of life, particularity in the media. Additional features of this text are listed under "Pedagogical Features."

I'm most excited about the fact that this book provides comprehensive samples of applying various tools and techniques to a realistic project. Many people learn best by example, so I've provided detailed examples of applying project management to a project everyone can relate to. I have never come across a textbook that presents project management concepts and then brings them to life in a fully developed sample project. I believe this approach will help many people truly understand and apply good project management.

Approach

Businesses change rapidly, and the project management field changes just as quickly to lead conceptual thinking and meet business needs. For this reason, you cannot assume that what worked even five years ago is still the best approach today. This text provides up-to-date information on how good project, program, and portfolio management can help you achieve organizational success. Five distinct features of this text include its:

- relationship to the Project Management Body of Knowledge

- bundling with Microsoft Project 2003, VPMi software, and Fissure simulation

- comprehensive samples of applying tools and techniques to a realistic project

- inclusion of templates and seamless integration of various software applications

- companion Web site

Use of *PMBOK® Guide 2004 Framework*

The Project Management Institute (PMI) created the *Guide to the Project Management Body of Knowledge* (the *PMBOK® Guide 2004*) as a framework and starting point for understanding project management. The *PMBOK® Guide 2004* is, however, just that—a guide. This text uses the

PMBOK® Guide 2004 as a foundation, but goes beyond it by providing more details, high-lighting additional topics, and providing a real-world context for project management. It also includes information and examples of applying project, program, and portfolio management as well as a summary of best practices in the field.

Inclusion of Microsoft Project 2003, VPMi Enterprise Project Management Software, and Fissure Simulation Software

Software has advanced tremendously in recent years, and it is important for project, program, and portfolio managers and their teams to use software to help manage projects. Each copy of *Introduction to Project Management* includes a 120-day trial version of the leading project management software on the market—Microsoft Project 2003. The companion Web site includes a 105-page document, *Guide to Using Microsoft Project 2003*, which teaches you to use this powerful software in a systematic way. You do not need to buy a separate book to learn how to use Project 2003 effectively, but suggested resources are provided if you want to learn even more about the software. You also get a 120-day free trial of VPMi, a Web-based enterprise project management software product from Virtual Communications Services (VCS). This software automates project, program, and portfolio management and includes Microsoft Project integration. Appendix B provides information on using a project management simulation tool developed by Fissure, a PMI Registered Education Provider. Fissure has used an expanded version of this simulation tool to help thousands of people learn how to apply various project management concepts.

Comprehensive Samples of Applying Tools and Techniques To A Realistic Project

Unlike other texts, this text shows the reader how an organization selected, initiated, planned, executed, monitored and controlled, and closed a realistic project, called the Just-In-Time Training project. It provides *over 50 sample applications* of documents, tools, and techniques such as a business case, project charter, project management plan, work breakdown structure, Gantt chart, cost baseline, Pareto chart, resource histogram, performance report, risk register, contract, lessons learned report, and so on for this project. You can also access all of these samples and the template files used to create them from the companion Web site for this text. As one reviewer of this text stated

> *It comprehensively communicates what it really takes to manage a large project, including required deliverables, work products, and documentation. I haven't seen either a text or documentation in industry which communicates this subject this comprehensively or this accurately.*

(Gilbert S. Leonard, Adjunct Professor and retired project manager, Exxon Mobil Corporation)

Provides Templates and Seamless Integration of Various Software Applications

Most organizations have learned by now that they do not have to reinvent the wheel when it comes to much of the documentation required for managing projects. This text uses over

50 templates for creating various documents, spreadsheets, diagrams, and charts, and you can download these templates from the companion Web site. Various software applications are used throughout the text in a seamless fashion. Let's face it—if you're involved in project, program, or portfolio management, you have to know how to use various software tools to do your job.

Includes a Companion Web Site (www.course.com/mis/pm/schwalbe)

A companion Web site provides you with a one-stop location to access informative links and tools to enhance your learning. Similar to other companion Web sites provided by Course Technology, this site will be a valuable resource as you access lecture notes, online quizzes, templates, student files, and links to references. You can also access the author's site to see real class syllabi, samples of student projects, and other helpful links. Please see the insert card at the front of this book for instructions on how to access the companion Web site for this book.

CoursePort: CoursePort provides a central location from which you can access Thomson Course Technology's online learning solutions with convenience and flexibility.

- Gain access to online resources including robust Student Online Companion Web sites.

- Simplify your course work by reducing human error and the need to keep track of multiple passwords.

- Take advantage of CoursePort's tailored services, including personalized homepages.

Please see the password card included in the front of this book for instructions on how to access the CoursePort site for this text.

Organization and Content

Introduction to Project Management is organized into eight chapters and two appendices. The first two chapters introduce project, program, and portfolio management and discuss different approaches for their selection. You'll read about Global Construction and how they decided to initiate the Just-In-Time Training project. The next six chapters follow the five process groups of project management: initiating, planning (broken down into two chapters), executing, monitoring and controlling, and closing. These six chapters apply various tools and techniques in each of these process groups to the Just-In-Time Training project. Best practices are described throughout the text, with a summary in the final chapter. Appendix A provides suggested resources to help you learn more about project management. It describes information provided on the companion Web site and a list of additional sites with useful information. Appendix B provides information on using Fissure project management simulation software.

Pedagogical Features

Several pedagogical features are included in this text to enhance presentation of the materials so that you can more easily understand the concepts and apply them. Throughout the text, emphasis is placed on applying concepts to up-to-date, real-world project management.

Learning Objectives, Chapter Summaries, Discussion Questions, Exercises, and Team Projects

Learning Objectives, Chapter Summaries, Quick Quizzes, Discussion Questions, Exercises, and Team Projects are designed to function as integrated study tools. Learning Objectives reflect what you should be able to accomplish after completing each chapter. Chapter Summaries highlight key concepts you should master. The Quick Quizzes help you reinforce your understanding of important concepts in each chapter. The Discussion Questions help guide critical thinking about those key concepts. Exercises provide opportunities to practice important techniques, as do the Team Projects. The companion Web site provides several additional study aids, such as lecture notes and interactive quizzes for each chapter.

Opening Case and Case Wrap-Up

To set the stage, each chapter begins with an opening case related to the materials in that chapter. These scenarios spark student interest and introduce important concepts in a real-world context. As project management concepts and techniques are discussed, they are applied to the opening case and other similar scenarios. Each chapter then closes with a Case Wrap-Up—some problems are overcome and some problems require more effort—to further illustrate the real world of project management.

What Went Right? and What Went Wrong?

Failures, as much as successes, can be valuable learning experiences. Each chapter of the text includes one or more examples of real projects that went right as well as examples of projects that went wrong. These examples further illustrate the importance of mastering key concepts in each chapter.

Media Snapshots

The world is full of projects. Several televisions shows, movies, newspapers, Web sites, and other media highlight project results, good and bad. Relating project management concepts to all types of projects, as highlighted in the media, will help you understand and see the importance of this growing field. Why not get people excited about studying project management by showing them how to recognize project management concepts in popular television shows, movies, or other media?

Cartoons

Each chapter includes a cartoon, some from Dilbert and some original ones, which use humor to illustrate concepts from the text.

Key Terms

The field of project management includes many unique terms that are vital to creating a common language and understanding of the field. Key terms are displayed in bold face and are defined the first time they appear. Definitions of key terms are provided in alphabetical order at the end of each chapter and in a glossary at the end of the text.

Application Software

Learning becomes much more dynamic with hands-on practice using the top project management software tool in the industry, Microsoft Project 2003, as well as other tools, such as spreadsheet software and Internet browsers. Each chapter offers you many opportunities to get hands-on experience and build new software skills that enable readers go move beyond reading by applying concepts to problems posed for them. In this way, the text accommodates both those who learn by reading and those who learn by doing. In addition to the exercises and team projects found at the end of chapters, several challenging projects are provided at the end of *Guide to Using Microsoft Project 2003*, available on the companion Web site.

SUPPLEMENTS

The following supplemental materials are available when this text is used in a classroom setting. All of the teaching tools available with this text are provided to the instructor on CD-ROM or from *www.course.com*.

- **Electronic Instructor's Manual:** The Instructor's Manual that accompanies this textbook includes additional instructional material to assist in class preparation, including suggestions for lecture topics and additional discussion questions.

- **ExamView®:** This textbook is accompanied by ExamView, a powerful testing software package that allows instructors to create and administer printed, computer (LAN-based), and Internet exams. ExamView includes hundreds of questions that correspond to the topics covered in this text, enabling students to generate detailed study guides that include page references for further review. The computer-based and Internet testing components allow students to take exams at their computers, and also save the instructor time by grading each exam automatically.

- **PowerPoint Presentations:** This text comes with Microsoft PowerPoint slides for each chapter. These are included as a teaching aid for classroom presentation, to be made available to students on the network for chapter review, or to be printed for classroom distribution. Instructors can modify slides or add their own slides for additional topics they introduce to the class.

- **Solution Files:** Solutions to end-of-chapter questions can be found on the Instructor Resource CD-ROM and may also be found on the Course Technology Web site at *www.course.com*. The solutions are password protected.

- **Distance Learning**: Course Technology offers online WebCT and Blackboard (versions 5.0 and 6.0) courses for this text to provide the most complete and dynamic learning experience possible. When you add online content to one of your courses, you're adding a lot: automated tests, topic reviews, quick quizes, and additional case projects with solutions. For more information on how to bring distance learning to your course, contact your local Course Technology sales representative.

- **Student Online Companion:** Visit the companion Web site for this text at *www. course.com/mis/pm/schwalbe* for links to lecture notes, template files, interactive quizzes, *Guide to Using Microsoft Project 2003*, information for accessing VPMi web-based project management software, and other helpful resources.

ACKNOWLEDGEMENTS

I never would have taken on another major book project without the help of many people. I would like to thank the staff at Course Technology for their dedication and hard work in helping me produce this book and in doing such an excellent job of marketing it. Maureen Martin, Tricia Boyle, Betsey Henkels, Brooke Booth, Karen Seitz, and many more people did a great job in planning and executing all of the work involved in producing this book. It's amazing how many little details are involved in writing a good book, and Course Technology worked effectively to produce a high quality text.

I thank my many colleagues and experts in the field who contributed information to this book. Paul Sundby provided information on the construction industry, Mike Vinje shared best practice information, Nick Matteucci provided VPMi access, Jesse Freese provided the Fissure simulation software, and many other people provided inputs and inspiration. I really enjoy the network of project managers, authors, and consultants in this field who are passionate about improving the theory and practice of project management.

I also want to thank my students and colleagues at Augsburg College and the University of Minnesota for providing input. I received many valuable comments from them on ways to improve my courses. I am also grateful for the examples students provide and the questions they ask in classes. I learn new aspects of project management and teaching all the time by interacting with students, faculty, and staff.

Five faculty reviewers provided excellent feedback for me in writing this book. Aileen Cater-Steel, University of Southern Queensland, Australia; Raffael Guidone, New York City College of Technology; Gilbert S. Leonard, Cy-Fair College; Linda Holcomb, Kingwood College; and Tom Norris, State University of New York at Cobleskill provided outstanding suggestions for improving the text.

Most of all, I am grateful to my family. Without their support, I never could have written this book. My wonderful husband, Dan, was very patient and supportive, as always. Our three children, Anne, Bobby, and Scott, continue to be very supportive of their mom's work. Our oldest, Anne, is now a college graduate and will be a teacher herself this fall. Bobby is in college now, and he actually thinks it's cool that his mom wrote a textbook. Scott is glad that I can work at home a lot and likes seeing his name in print. Our children all understand the main reason why I write—I have a passion for educating future leaders of the world, including them.

As always, I am eager to receive your feedback on this book. Please send all feedback to me at schwalbe@augsburg.edu

Kathy Schwalbe, Ph.D., PMP
Augsburg College

ABOUT THE AUTHOR

Kathy Schwalbe is an Associate Professor in the Department of Business Administration at Augsburg College in Minneapolis, where she teaches courses in project management, problem solving for business, systems analysis and design, information systems projects, and electronic commerce. Kathy is also an adjunct faculty member at the University of Minnesota, where she teaches a graduate-level course in project management in the engineering department. She also provides training and consulting services to several organizations and speaks at numerous conferences. Kathy's first job out of college was as a project manager in the Air Force. Kathy worked for ten years in industry before entering academia in 1991. She was an Air Force officer, project manager, systems analyst, senior engineer, and information technology consultant. Kathy is an active member of PMI, having served as the Student Chapter Liaison for the Minnesota chapter, VP of Education for the Minnesota chapter, Editor of the ISSIG Review, member of PMI's test-writing team, and member of the OPM3 update team. Kathy earned her Ph.D. in Higher Education at the University of Minnesota, her MBA at Northeastern University's High Technology MBA program, and her B.S. in mathematics at the University of Notre Dame.

CHAPTER **1**

AN INTRODUCTION TO PROJECT, PROGRAM, AND PORTFOLIO MANAGEMENT

LEARNING OBJECTIVES

After reading this chapter, you will be able to:

- Understand the growing need for better project, program, and portfolio management

- Explain what a project is, provide examples of projects, list various attributes of projects, and discuss the triple constraint of project management

- Describe project management and key elements of the project management framework, including project stakeholders, project management knowledge areas, common tools and techniques, and project success factors

- Discuss the relationship between project, program, and portfolio management and their contribution to enterprise success

- Describe the project management profession, including suggested skills for project, program, and portfolio managers, the role of professional organizations such as the Project Management Institute, the importance of certification and ethics, and the growth of project and portfolio management software

OPENING CASE

Doug Armbruster, the chief executive officer (CEO) of Global Construction, Inc., was summarizing annual corporate highlights to the board of directors. When one of the board members asked what he was most proud of that year, Doug thought for a few seconds and then replied,

"Excellent question, Gabe. Honestly, I think the main reason we had record-breaking profits this year was because we have truly embraced the fact that we are a project-based organization. We have dramatically improved our ability to select and implement projects that help our company succeed. Our projects align with our business strategies, and we have consistent processes in place for getting things done. Marie Scott, our director of the Project Management Office, has done an outstanding job in making this happen. And believe me, it was not easy. It's never easy to implement changes across an entire company. But with this new capability to manage projects across the organization, I am very confident that we will have continued success in years to come."

INTRODUCTION

Many people and organizations today have a new or renewed interest in project management. Until the 1980s, project management primarily focused on providing schedule and resource data to top management in the military and construction industries. Today's project management involves much more, and people in every industry and every country manage projects. New technologies have become a significant factor in many businesses, and the use of interdisciplinary and global work teams has radically changed the work environment.

The following statistics demonstrate the significance of project management in today's society:

- A 2001 report showed that the United States spends $2.3 trillion on projects every year, and the world as a whole spends nearly $10 trillion on projects of all kinds. Projects, therefore, account for about one-fourth of the United States' and the world's gross domestic product.[1]

- In 2003, the average senior project manager in the United States earned almost $90,000 per year. The average salary of a program manager was $103,464, just slightly less than the average chief information officer (CIO) salary of $103,925. The average salary for a project management office (PMO) director was $118,633.[2]

- Project management certification continues to be one of the most popular certifications throughout the world.

- In the United States, the number-one reality television show in 2004, *The Apprentice,* portrayed the important role project managers play in business. Each week of the show, teams selected a project manager to lead them in accomplishing that week's project. The project manager was held partly responsible for the team's success or failure. Whether you are trying to make money by selling lemonade, running a golf tournament, or developing a new product, project managers play a vital role to business success.

WHAT WENT WRONG?

In 1995, the Standish Group published an often-quoted study titled "The CHAOS Report" or simply "CHAOS." This prestigious consulting firm surveyed 365 information technology executive managers in the United States who managed more than 8,380 information technology application projects. As the title of the study suggests, the projects were in a state of chaos. United States companies spent more than $250 billion each year in the early 1990s on approximately 175,000 information technology application development projects. Examples of these projects included creating a new database for a state department of motor vehicles, developing a new system for car rental and hotel reservations, and implementing a client/server architecture for the banking industry. The study reported that the overall success rate of information technology projects was *only* 16.2 percent. The surveyors defined success as meeting project goals on time and on budget.

The study also found that more than 31 percent of information technology projects were canceled before completion, costing U.S. companies and government agencies more than $81 billion. The authors of this study were adamant about the need for better project management in the information technology industry. They explained, "Software development projects are in chaos, and we can no longer imitate the three monkeys—hear no failures, see no failures, speak no failures."[3]

Today's companies, governments, and nonprofit organizations are recognizing that to be successful, they need to be conversant with and use modern project management techniques. Individuals are realizing that to remain competitive, they must develop skills to become good project team members and project managers. They also realize that many of the concepts of project management will help them as they work with people and technology on a day-to-day basis.

Many organizations claim that using project management provides advantages, such as:

- Better control of financial, physical, and human resources
- Improved customer relations
- Shorter development times
- Lower costs
- Higher quality and increased reliability
- Higher profit margins
- Improved productivity
- Better internal coordination
- Higher worker morale

In addition to project management, organizations are embracing program and portfolio management to address enterprise-level needs. This chapter introduces projects and project management; describes the differences between project, program, and portfolio management; discusses the role of the project, program, and portfolio manager; and provides important background information on these growing professions.

To discuss project management, it is important to understand the concept of a project. A **project** is "a temporary endeavor undertaken to create a unique product, service, or result."[4] Operations, on the other hand, is work done in organizations to sustain the business. Projects are different from operations in that they end when their objectives have been reached or when the project has been terminated.

Examples of Projects

Projects can be large or small and involve one person or thousands of people. They can be done in one day or take years to complete. Examples of projects include the following:

- A young couple hires a firm to design and build them a new house.
- A retail store manager works with employees to display a new clothing line.
- A college campus upgrades its technology infrastructure to provide wireless Internet access.
- A construction company designs and constructs a new office building for a client.
- A television network develops a system to allow viewers to vote for contestants and provide other feedback on programs.
- The automobile industry develops standards to streamline procurement.
- A government group develops a program to track child immunizations.

Project Attributes

As you can see, projects come in all shapes and sizes. The following attributes help define a project further:

- *A project has a unique purpose.* Every project should have a well-defined objective. For example, many people hire firms to design and build a new house, but each house, like each person, is unique.
- *A project is temporary.* A project has a definite beginning and a definite end. For a home construction project, owners usually have a date in mind when they'd like to move into their new homes.
- *A project is developed using progressive elaboration or in an iterative fashion.* Projects are often defined broadly when they begin, and as time passes, the specific details of the project become clearer. For example, there are many decisions that must be made in planning and building a new house. It works best to draft plans for owners to approve before more detailed plans are developed.
- *A project requires resources, often from various areas.* Resources include people, hardware, software, or other assets. Many different types of people and resources are needed to build a home.
- *A project should have a primary customer or sponsor.* Most projects have many interested parties, but someone must take the primary role of sponsorship. The **project sponsor** usually provides the direction and funding for the project.

- *A project involves uncertainty.* Because every project is unique, it is sometimes difficult to define the project's objectives clearly, estimate exactly how long it will take to complete, or determine how much it will cost. External factors also cause uncertainty, such as a supplier going out of business or a project team member needing unplanned time off. This uncertainty is one of the main reasons project management is so challenging.

It should not be difficult to explain the goals or purpose of a project. Unlike Dilbert, the cartoon character shown in Figure 1-1 who provides many examples of how not to manage projects, you should not have to make up words to describe a project!

DILBERT: © Scott Adams/Dist. by United Feature Syndicate, Inc.

FIGURE 1-1 Lost for words

A good project manager is crucial to a project's success. **Project managers** work with the project sponsors, the project team, and the other people involved in a project to meet project goals.

The Triple Constraint

Every project is constrained in different ways by its scope, time, and cost goals. These limitations are sometimes referred to in project management as the **triple constraint**. To create a successful project, a project manager must consider scope, time, and cost, and balance these three often-competing goals. He must consider the following:

- *Scope:* What work will be done as part of the project? What unique product, service, or result does the customer or sponsor expect from the project?
- *Time:* How long should it take to complete the project? What is the project's schedule?
- *Cost:* What should it cost to complete the project? What is the project's budget?

Figure 1-2 illustrates the three dimensions of the triple constraint. Each area—scope, time, and cost—has a target at the beginning of the project. For example, a couple might initially plan to move into their new 2000-square-foot home in six months and spend $300,000 on the entire project. These goals can be viewed as the discrete target goals, or the bull's-eye on the target. The couple will have to make many decisions along the way that might affect meeting those goals. They might need to increase the budget to meet scope and time goals or decrease the scope to meet time and budget goals. Because projects

An Introduction to Project, Program, and Portfolio Management involve uncertainty and limited resources, projects rarely finish according to the discrete scope, time, and cost goals originally set. Instead of discrete target goals, it is often more realistic to set a range of goals, such as spending between $275,000 and $325,000 and having the home completed within five to seven months. These goals might mean hitting the target but not the bull's-eye.

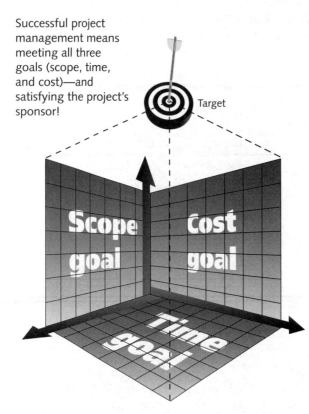

Successful project management means meeting all three goals (scope, time, and cost)—and satisfying the project's sponsor!

Target

Scope goal

Cost goal

Time goal

FIGURE 1-2 The triple constraint of project management

Experienced project managers know that you must decide which aspect or aspects of the triple constraint are most important. If time is most important, you must often change the initial scope and/or cost goals to meet the schedule. If scope goals are most important, you might need to adjust time and/or cost goals. If it is crucial to meet time and cost goals, the scope must be flexible. In any case, sponsors must provide some type of target goals for a project's scope, time, and cost.

Although the triple constraint describes how the basic elements of a project—scope, time, and cost—interrelate, other elements can also play significant roles. Quality is often a key factor in projects, as is customer or sponsor satisfaction. Some people, in fact, refer to the *"quadruple constraint"* of project management, including quality along with scope, time, and cost. Others believe that quality considerations, including customer satisfaction, must be inherent in setting the scope, time, and cost goals of a project. A project team may meet scope, time, and cost goals but fail to meet quality standards or satisfy their sponsor if they have not adequately addressed these concerns. The project manager should be communicating with the sponsor throughout the project to make sure the project meets her expectations.

How can you avoid the problems that occur when you meet scope, time, and cost goals but lose sight of quality or customer satisfaction? The answer is *good project management, which includes more than meeting the triple constraint.*

WHAT IS PROJECT MANAGEMENT?

Project management is "the application of knowledge, skills, tools, and techniques to project activities to meet project requirements."[5] Project managers must not only strive to meet specific scope, time, cost, and quality goals of projects, but also facilitate the entire process to meet the needs and expectations of the people involved in or affected by project activities.

Figure 1-3 illustrates a framework to help you understand project management. Key elements of this framework include the project stakeholders, project management knowledge areas, project management tools and techniques, project success, and contribution of a portfolio of projects to the success of the entire enterprise. Each of these elements of project management is discussed in more detail in the following sections.

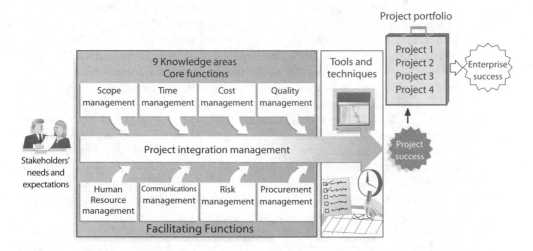

FIGURE 1-3   Project management framework

Project Stakeholders

Stakeholders are the people involved in or affected by project activities and include the project sponsor, project team, support staff, customers, users, suppliers, and even opponents to the project. These stakeholders often have very different needs and expectations. For example, there are several stakeholders involved in a home construction project.

- The project sponsors would be the potential new homeowners. They would be the people paying for the house and could be on a very tight budget, so they would expect the contractor to provide accurate estimates of the costs involved in building the house. They would also need a realistic idea of when they could move in and what type of home they could afford given their budget constraints. The new homeowners would have to make important decisions to keep the costs of the house within their budget. Can they afford to finish the basement right away? If they can afford to finish the basement, will it affect the projected move-in date? In this example, the project sponsors are also the customers and users for the product, which is the house.

- The project manager in this example would normally be the general contractor responsible for building the house. He would need to work with all the project stakeholders to meet their needs and expectations.

- The project team for building the house would include several construction workers, electricians, carpenters, and so on. These stakeholders would need to know exactly what work they must do and when they need to do it. They would need to know if the required materials and equipment will be at the construction site or if they are expected to provide the materials and equipment. Their work would need to be coordinated because there are many interrelated factors involved. For example, the carpenter cannot put in kitchen cabinets until the walls are completed.

- Support staff might include the employers of the homeowners, the general contractor's administrative assistant, and other people who support the stakeholders. The employers of the homeowners might expect their employees to complete their work but allow some flexibility so that they can visit the building site or take phone calls related to the building of the house. The contractor's administrative assistant would support the project by coordinating meetings between the buyers, contractor, suppliers, and so on.

- Building a house requires many suppliers. The suppliers would provide the wood, windows, flooring materials, appliances, and so on. Suppliers would expect exact details on what items they need to provide, where and when to deliver those items, and so on.

- There might or might not be opponents to a project. In this example, there might be a neighbor who opposes the project because the workers are making so much noise that she cannot concentrate on her work at home or her sleeping children might be woken up. She might interrupt the workers to voice her complaints or even file a formal complaint. Alternatively, the neighborhood might have association rules concerning new home design and construction. If the homeowners did not follow these rules, they might have to halt construction due to legal issues.

As you can see from this example, there are many different stakeholders on projects, and they all have different interests. Stakeholders' needs and expectations are important in the beginning and throughout the life of a project. Successful project managers develop good relationships with project stakeholders to understand and meet their needs and expectations.

Project Management Knowledge Areas

Project management knowledge areas describe the key competencies that project managers must develop. The center of Figure 1-3 shows the nine knowledge areas of project management. The four core knowledge areas of project management include project scope, time, cost, and quality management. These are core knowledge areas because they lead to specific project objectives. Brief descriptions of each core knowledge area are as follows:

- Project scope management involves defining and managing all the work required to complete the project successfully.
- Project time management includes estimating how long it will take to complete the work, developing an acceptable project schedule, and ensuring timely completion of the project.
- Project cost management consists of preparing and managing the budget for the project.
- Project quality management ensures that the project will satisfy the stated or implied needs for which it was undertaken.

The four facilitating knowledge areas of project management are human resource, communications, risk, and procurement management. These are called facilitating areas because they are the processes through which the project objectives are achieved. Brief descriptions of each facilitating knowledge area are as follows:

- Project human resource management is concerned with making effective use of the people involved with the project.
- Project communications management involves generating, collecting, disseminating, and storing project information.
- Project risk management includes identifying, analyzing, and responding to risks related to the project.
- Project procurement management involves acquiring or procuring goods and services for a project from outside the performing organization.

Project integration management, the ninth knowledge area, is an overarching function that affects and is affected by all of the other knowledge areas. Project managers must have knowledge and skills in all nine of these areas.

Project Management Tools and Techniques

Thomas Carlyle, a famous historian and author, stated, "Man is a tool-using animal. Without tools he is nothing, with tools he is all." As the world continues to become more complex, it is even more important for people to develop and use tools, especially for managing important projects. **Project management tools and techniques** assist project managers and their teams in carrying out work in all nine knowledge areas. For example, some popular time-management tools and techniques include Gantt charts, project network diagrams, and critical-path analysis. Table 1-1 lists some commonly used tools and techniques by knowledge area. Note that a tool or technique is much more than a software package. You will learn more about several of these tools and techniques throughout this text, and are examples of applying them are also provided.

TABLE 1-1 Common project management tools and techniques by knowledge area

Knowledge area/category	Tools and techniques
Integration management	Project selection methods, project management methodology, stakeholder analysis, project charters, project management plans, project management software, change control boards, project review meetings, lessons learned reports
Scope management	Scope statements, work breakdown structures, statements of work, scope management plans, scope verification techniques, scope change controls
Time management	Gantt charts, project network diagrams, critical-path analysis, crashing, fast tracking, schedule performance measurements
Cost management	Net present value, return on investment, payback analysis, earned value management, project portfolio management, cost estimates, cost management plans, cost baselines
Quality management	Quality metrics, checklists, quality control charts, Pareto diagrams, fishbone diagrams, maturity models, statistical methods
Human resource management	Motivation techniques, empathic listening, responsibility assignment matrices, project organizational charts, resource histograms, team building exercises
Communications management	Communications management plans, conflict management, communications media selection, status reports, virtual communications, templates, project Web sites
Risk management	Risk management plans, risk registers, probability/impact matrices, risk rankings
Procurement management	Make-or-buy analyses, contracts, requests for proposals or quotes, source selections, supplier evaluation matrices

WHAT WENT RIGHT?

Follow-up studies done by the Standish Group (see the previously quoted "CHAOS" study in the What Went Wrong? passage) showed some improvement in the statistics for information technology projects in the past decade:

- The number of successful IT projects has more than doubled, from 16 percent in 1994 to 34 percent in 2002, although that number dropped to 29 percent based on the 2004 third quarter research report.
- The number of failed projects was cut in half, from 31 percent in 1994 to 15 percent in 2002. The number of failed projects increased, however, from 15 percent in 2002 to 18 percent in 2004, based on the 2004 third quarter research report.
- The United States spent about the same amount of money on IT projects in 1994 and 2002 ($250 billion and $255 billion, respectively), but the amount of money wasted on challenged projects (those that did not meet scope, time, or cost goals, but were completed) and failed projects was down to $55 billion in 2002 compared to $140 billion in 1994.[6]

Even though there have been significant improvements in managing information technology projects, there is still much room for improvement in that industry as well as in many other industries. The best news is that project managers are learning how to succeed more often. "The reasons for the increase in successful projects vary. First, the average cost of a project has been more than cut in half. Better tools have been created to monitor and control progress and better skilled project managers with better management processes are being used. The fact that there are processes is significant in itself."[7]

Despite its advantages, project management is not a silver bullet that guarantees success on all projects. Project management is a very broad, often complex discipline. What works on one project might not work on another, so it is essential for project managers to continue to develop their knowledge and skills in managing projects. It is also important to learn from the mistakes and successes of others.

Project Success

How do you define the success or failure of a project? There are several ways to define project success. The following list outlines a few common criteria for measuring project success as applied to the sample project of building a new 2,000-square-foot home within six months for $300,000:

- The project met scope, time, and cost goals. If the home was 2,000 square feet and met other scope requirements, was completed in six months, and cost $300,000, we could call it a successful project based on these criteria. Note that the "CHAOS" studies mentioned in the What Went Wrong? and What Went Right? examples used this definition of success.

- The project satisfied the customer/sponsor. Even if the project met initial scope, time, and cost goals, the couple paying for the house might not be satisfied. Perhaps the project manager never returned their calls and was rude to them or made important decisions without their approval. If the customers were not happy about important aspects of the project, it would be deemed a failure based on this criterion. Many organizations implement a customer satisfaction rating system for projects to measure project success.
- The results of the project met its main objective, such as making or saving a certain amount of money, providing a good return on investment, or simply making the sponsors happy. If the couple liked their new home and neighborhood after they lived there for a while, even if it cost more or took longer to build or the project manager was rude to them, it would be a successful project based on this criterion. As another example, suppose the owners actually wanted to keep the house for just a few years and then sell it for a good return. If that happened, the couple would deem the project a success, regardless of other factors involved.

Project managers play a vital role in helping projects succeed. Project managers work with the project sponsors, the project team, and the other people involved in a project to meet project goals. They also work with the sponsor to define success for that particular project. Good project managers do not assume that their definition of success is the same as the sponsor's. They take the time to understand their sponsor's expectations. For example, if you are building a home for someone, find out what is most important:

- Meeting scope, time, and cost goals of the project to build the home
- Satisfying other needs, such as communicating in a certain way
- Being sure the project delivers a certain result, such as providing the home of the owner's dreams or a good return on investment.

The success criterion should help you develop key performance indicators needed to track project success.

PROGRAM AND PROJECT PORTFOLIO MANAGEMENT

As mentioned earlier, about one-quarter of the world's gross domestic product is spent on projects. Projects make up a significant portion of work in most business organizations or enterprises, and successfully managing those projects is crucial to enterprise success. Two important concepts that help projects meet enterprise goals are the use of programs and project portfolio management.

Programs

A **program** is "a group of related projects managed in a coordinated way to obtain benefits and control not available from managing them individually."[8] As you can imagine, it is often more economical to group projects together to help streamline management, staffing, purchasing, and other work. The following are examples of programs (Figure 1-4 illustrates the first program in the list).

- A construction firm has a program for building one hundred residential single-family homes in a particular neighborhood. Each home is a separate project for a specific homeowner—the sponsor—but the entire development is a program. A similar scenario applies to a program involving several apartment-building projects in a particular region. There would be several benefits to managing these projects under one program, such as getting planning approvals for all the homes at once, hiring workers who could work on more than one home, and purchasing common materials in bulk to earn discounts.
- A clothing firm has a program to analyze customer buying patterns. Projects under this program might include one to send out and analyze electronic surveys, one to conduct several focus groups in different geographic locations with different types of buyers, and one to develop an information system to help collect and analyze current customers' buying patterns.
- A government agency has a program for children's services, which includes a project to provide prenatal care for expectant mothers, a project to immunize newborns and young children, and a project for developmental testing for preschool children.

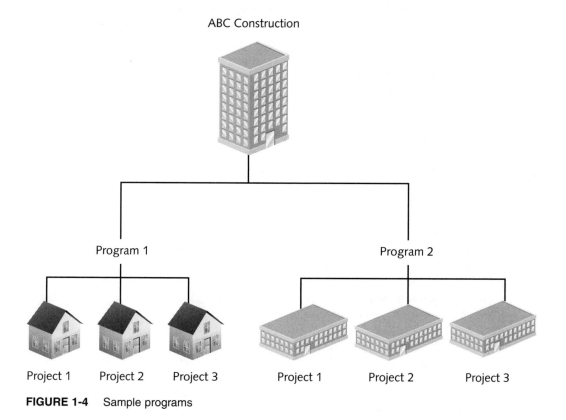

FIGURE 1-4   Sample programs

A **program manager** provides leadership and direction for the project managers heading the projects within the program. Program managers also coordinate the efforts of project teams, functional groups, suppliers, and operations staff supporting the projects to ensure that project products and processes are implemented to maximize benefits. Program managers are responsible for more than the delivery of project results; they are change agents responsible for the success of products and processes produced by those projects.

Program managers often have review meetings with all their project managers to share important information and coordinate important aspects of each project. Many program managers worked as project managers earlier in their careers, and they enjoy sharing their wisdom and expertise with their project managers. Effective program managers recognize that managing a program is much more complex than managing a single project. They know that technical and project management skills are not enough. In addition to skills required for project managers, program managers must also possess strong business knowledge, leadership capability, and communication skills.

Project Portfolio Management

In many organizations, project managers also support an emerging business strategy of **project portfolio management** (also called **portfolio management** in this text), in which organizations group and manage projects and programs as a portfolio of investments that contribute to the entire enterprise's success. Pacific Edge Software's product manager, Eric Burke, defines project portfolio management as "the continuous process of selecting and managing the optimum set of project initiatives that deliver maximum business value."[9]

The Project Management Institute (PMI) published the *Organizational Project Management Maturity Model (OPM3): Knowledge Foundation* in 2003, which describes the importance not only of managing individual projects or programs well, but also of following organizational project management to align projects, programs, and portfolios with strategic goals. OPM3 is a standard organizations can use to measure their organizational project management maturity against a comprehensive set of best practices, as described in more detail in Chapter 8 of this text.

Portfolio managers need to understand how projects fit into the bigger picture of the organization, especially in terms of finances and business risks. They create portfolios based on meeting specific organizational goals, such as maximizing the value of the portfolio or making effective use of limited resources. Portfolio managers help their organizations make wise investment decisions by helping to select and analyze projects from a strategic perspective. Portfolio managers might or might not have previous experience as project or program managers. It is most important that they have strong financial and analytical skills and understand how projects and programs can contribute to meeting strategic goals.

Figure 1-5 illustrates the differences between project management and project portfolio management. Notice that the main distinction is a focus on meeting tactical or strategic goals. Tactical goals are generally more specific and short-term than strategic goals, which emphasize long-term goals for an organization. Individual projects often address tactical goals, whereas project portfolio management addresses strategic goals. Project management addresses questions related to how well projects are managed in terms of meeting scope, time, and costs goals and stakeholder expectations. Project portfolio management addresses questions related to what projects are being done and how well they meet organizational goals, such as making good investments and being competitive.

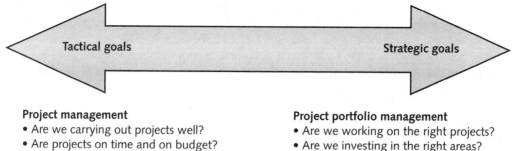

Project management
- Are we carrying out projects well?
- Are projects on time and on budget?
- Do project stakeholders know what they should be doing?

Project portfolio management
- Are we working on the right projects?
- Are we investing in the right areas?
- Do we have the right resources to be competitve?

FIGURE 1-5   Project management compared to project portfolio management

There can be portfolios for all types of projects. The following list outlines a few examples:

- In a construction firm, strategic goals might include increasing profit margins on large projects, decreasing costs on supplies, and improving skill levels of key workers. Projects could be grouped into these three categories for portfolio management purposes.
- In a clothing firm, strategic goals might include improving the effectiveness of information technology, introducing new clothing lines, reducing inventory costs, and increasing customer satisfaction. These might be the main categories for the the firm's portfolio of projects.
- A government agency for children's services could group projects into a portfolio based on such key strategies as improving health and providing education to help make decisions on the best way to use available funds and resources.

Organizations group projects into portfolios to help them make better investment decisions, such as increasing, decreasing, discontinuing, or changing specific projects or programs based on financial performance, risks, resource utilization, and similar factors that affect business value and strategy. For example, if a construction firm has much higher profit margins on apartment buildings than single-family homes, it might choose to pursue more apartment-building projects. The firm might also create a new project to investigate ways to increase profits for single-family-home projects. On the other hand, if the company has too many projects focused on financial performance and not enough focused on improving its workforce, the portfolio manager might suggest initiating more projects to support that strategic goal.

By grouping projects into portfolios, organizations can better tie their projects to meeting strategic goals. Portfolio management can also help an organization do a better job of managing its human resources by hiring, training, and retaining workers to support the projects in the organization's portfolio. For example, if the construction firm needs more people with experience in building apartment buildings, it can make necessary adjustments by hiring or training current workers in the necessary skills.

As you can imagine, good project managers should have many skills. Good program and portfolio managers often need additional skills and experience in managing projects and understanding organizational strategies. This section describes some of the skills that will help you manage projects, and you will learn many more throughout this text. If you are serious about considering a career in project management, you should consider becoming a certified project management professional. You should also be familiar with some of the many project management software products available on the market today.

Suggested Skills for Project, Program, and Portfolio Managers

Project managers and their teams must develop knowledge and skills in the following areas:

- All nine project management knowledge areas
- The application area, including specific standards and regulations
- The project environment
- General management
- Human relations

An earlier section of this chapter introduced the nine project management knowledge areas, as well as some tools and techniques that project managers use. The application area refers to the application to which project management is applied. For example, a project manager responsible for building houses or apartment buildings should understand the construction industry, including standards and regulations important to that industry and those types of construction projects. A project manager in a clothing firm or government agency must understand those application areas.

The project environment differs from organization to organization and from project to project, but there are some skills that will help in most project environments. These skills include change management and understanding how organizations work within their social, political, and physical environments. Project managers must be comfortable leading and handling change, because most projects introduce changes in organizations and involve changes within the projects themselves. Project managers need to understand the organizations they work in and how products are developed and how services are provided. For example, it takes different skills and behaviors to manage a project for a Fortune 100 company in the United States than it does to manage a government project for a new business in Poland.

Project managers should also possess general management knowledge and skills. They should understand important topics related to financial management, accounting, procurement, sales, marketing, contracts, manufacturing, distribution, logistics, the supply chain, strategic planning, tactical planning, operations management, organizational structures and behavior, personnel administration, compensation, benefits, career paths, and health and safety practices. On some projects, it will be critical for the project manager to have substantial experience in one or several of these general management areas. On other projects, the project manager can delegate detailed responsibility for some of these areas to a team member, support staff, or even a supplier. Even so, the project managers must be intelligent and experienced enough to know which of these areas are most important and who is qualified to do the work. They must also make and/or take responsibility for all key project decisions.

Achieving high performance on projects requires human relations—or soft—skills. Some of these soft skills include effective communication, influence within the organization to get things done, leadership, motivation, negotiation, conflict management, and problem solving. Project managers must lead their project teams by providing vision, delegating work, creating an energetic and positive environment, and setting an example of appropriate and effective behavior. Project managers must focus on teamwork skills to use their people effectively. They need to be able to motivate different types of people and develop esprit de corps within the project team and with other project stakeholders.

MEDIA SNAPSHOT

In 2004, millions of people in the United States watched the first season of the reality television show called *The Apprentice,* in which contestants vied for a high-level position working for Donald Trump. Each week, Trump fired one contestant and told them bluntly why they were fired or why they were spared. Trump's reasons provide insight into improving project management skills, as follows:

- Leadership and professionalism are crucial. No matter how smart you are (the first candidate fired had degrees in medicine and business), you must be professional in how you deal with people and display some leadership potential.
- Know what your sponsor expects from the project, and learn from your mistakes. Jason, the second person and first project manager fired, decided not to take the time to meet with his project sponsors, causing his team to fail their assignment. Mr. Trump wanted everyone to remember that crucial mistake.
- Trust your team and delegate decisions. Sam had several problems as a team member and project manager, but his lack of trust in and respect for and from his teammates led to his downfall.
- Know the business. Restaurants often have the highest profit margins on certain items, such as drinks. Find out what's most important to your business when running projects. One team focused on increasing bar sales and easily won the competition that week.
- Stand up for yourself. When Trump fired Kristi over two other candidates, he explained his decision by saying that Kristi didn't fight for herself, whereas the other two women did.
- Be a team player. Tammy clearly did not get along with her team, and no one supported her in the boardroom when her team lost.

continued

- Don't be overly emotional and always stay organized. Erika had a difficult time leading her team in selling Trump Ice, and she became flustered when they did not get credit for sales because their paperwork was not done correctly. Her emotions were evident in the boardroom when she was fired.
- Work on projects and for people you believe in. Kwame's team selected an artist based on her profit potential even though he and other teammates disliked her work. The other team picked an artist they liked, and they easily outsold Kwame's team.
- Think outside the box. Troy led his team in trying to make the most money selling rickshaw rides. The other team brainstormed ideas and decided to sell advertising space on the rickshaws, which was a huge success.
- There is some luck involved in project management, and you should always aim high. Nick and Amy were teamed against Bill, Troy, and Kwame to rent out a party room for the highest price. Troy's team seemed very organized and did get a couple of good bids, but Nick and Amy didn't seem to have any real prospects. They got lucky when one potential client came back at the last minute and agreed to a much higher than normal price.

Importance of Leadership Skills

In a recent study, one hundred project managers listed the characteristics they believed were critical for effective project management and the characteristics that made project managers ineffective. Table 1-2 lists the results. The study found that effective project managers provide leadership by example, and are visionary, technically competent, decisive, good communicators, and good motivators. They also stand up to top management when necessary, support team members, and encourage new ideas. The study also found that respondents believed that *positive leadership contributes the most to project success.* The most important characteristics and behaviors of a positive leader include being a team builder and communicator, having high self-esteem, focusing on results, demonstrating trust and respect, and setting goals.

TABLE 1-2 Most significant characteristics of effective and ineffective project managers

Effective project managers	Ineffective project managers
Lead by example	Set bad examples
Are visionaries	Are not self-assured
Are technically competent	Lack technical expertise
Are decisive	Avoid or delay making decisions
Are good communicators	Are poor communicators
Are good motivators	Are poor motivators

Zimmerer, Thomas W., and Mahmoud M. Yasin. "A Leadership Profile of American Project Managers." *Project Management Journal* (March 1998), 31–38.

Leadership and *management* are terms often used interchangeably, although there are differences. Generally, a **leader** focuses on long-term goals and big-picture objectives while inspiring people to reach those goals. A **manager** often deals with the day-to-day details of meeting specific goals. People have expressed the difference in various ways: "Managers do things right, and leaders do the right things"; "Leaders determine the vision, and managers achieve the vision"; "You lead people and manage things."

However, project managers often take on the role of both leader and manager. Good project managers know that people make or break projects, so they must set a good example to lead their team to success. They are aware of the greater needs of their stakeholders and organizations, so they are visionary in guiding their current projects and in suggesting future ones.

As mentioned earlier, program managers need the same skills as project managers. They often rely on their past experience as project managers, strong business knowledge, leadership capability, and communication skills to handle the responsibility of overseeing the multiple projects that make up their programs. It is most important that portfolio managers have strong financial and analytical skills and understand how projects and programs can contribute to meeting strategic goals.

Companies that excel in project, program, and portfolio management grow project leaders, emphasizing development of business and communication skills. Instead of thinking of leaders and managers as specific people, it is better to think of people as having leadership skills—such as being visionary and inspiring—and management skills—such as being organized and effective. Therefore, the best project, program, and portfolio managers have leadership and management characteristics; they are visionary yet focused on the bottom line. Above all else, they focus on achieving positive results.

Project Management Certification

Professional certification is an important factor in recognizing and ensuring quality in a profession. The Project Management Institute (PMI) is a global professional society. PMI provides certification as a **Project Management Professional (PMP)**—someone who has documented sufficient project experience, agreed to follow the PMI code of professional conduct, and demonstrated knowledge of the field of project management by passing a comprehensive examination.

The number of people earning PMP certification continues to increase. In 1993, there were about 1000 certified project management professionals. By the end of December 2004, there were 102,047 certified project management professionals.[10] Figure 1-6 shows the rapid growth in the number of people earning project management professional certification from 1993 to 2004. Although most PMPs are in the United States and Canada, the PMP credential is growing in popularity in several countries, such as Japan, China, and India.

Some companies are requiring that all project managers be PMP certified. Project management certification is also enabling professionals throughout the world to share a common base of knowledge. For example, any person with PMP certification can list, describe, and use the nine project management knowledge areas, as described in PMI's *Guide to the Project Management Body of Knowledge (PMBOK® Guide)*. Sharing a common base of knowledge is important because it helps advance the theory and practice of project management. Consult PMI's Web site at *www.pmi.org* for more information on PMP certification.

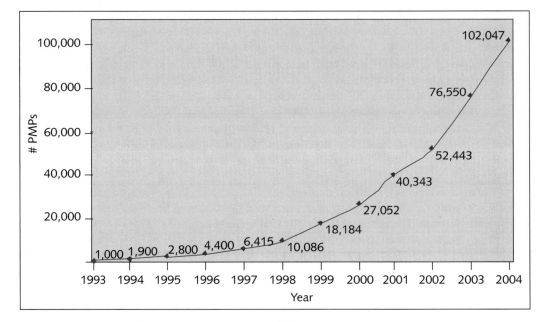

FIGURE 1-6 Growth in PMP certification, 1993–2004

Ethics in Project Management

Ethics is an important part of all professions. Project managers often face ethical dilemmas. For example, several projects involve different payment methods. If a project manager can make more money by doing a job poorly, should he do the job poorly? If a project manager is personally opposed to the development of nuclear weapons, should he refuse to manage a project that helps produce them? It is important for project managers to make decisions in an ethical manner.

PMI developed a PMP code of professional conduct that all applicants must sign to become certified PMPs. PMI states that it is vital for all PMPs to conduct their work in an ethical manner. Conducting work in an ethical manner helps the profession earn the confidence of the public, employers, employees, and project team members. The PMP code of professional conduct lists responsibilities of the project manager to the profession, such as compliance with all organizational rules and policies, professional practice, and advancement of the profession. It also lists responsibilities to customers and the public, such as qualifications, experience, and performance of professional services, as well as conflict-of-interest situations. For example, one of the responsibilities to customers and the public includes refraining "from offering or accepting inappropriate payments, gifts or other forms of compensation for personal gain, unless in conformity with applicable laws or customs of the country where project management services are being provided."[11]

Project Management Software

Unlike the cobbler neglecting to make shoes for his own children, the project management and software development communities have definitely responded to the need to provide more software to assist in managing projects. The Project Management Center, a Web site for people involved in project management, provides an alphabetical directory of more than three hundred project management software solutions (*www.infogoal.com/pmc*). This site and others demonstrate the growth in available project management software products, especially Web-based tools. Deciding which project management software to use has become a project in itself. This section provides a summary of the basic types of project management software available and references for finding more information.

> As mentioned on the resources page in the front of this text, a 120-day evaluation copy of Microsoft Project 2003 is included on the CD-ROM provided with this text. The companion Web site includes a *Guide to Using Microsoft Project 2003*, which will help you develop hands-on skills using this most popular project management software tool today. You can also access a 120-day trial version of VPMi—a Web-based product from VCS (*www.vcsonline.com*)—by following the information provided on the resources page in the front of this text and on the companion Web site. You will see example screens from both of these products in this text.

Many people still use basic productivity software, such as Microsoft Word or Microsoft Excel, to perform many project management functions, such as determining project scope, time, and cost; assigning resources; and preparing project documentation. People often use productivity software instead of specialized project management software because they already have it and know how to use it. However, there are hundreds of project management software tools that provide specific functionality for managing projects. These project management software tools can be divided into three general categories based on functionality and price:

- *Low-end tools:* These tools provide basic project management features and generally cost less than $200 per user. They are often recommended for small projects and single users. Most of these tools allow users to create Gantt charts, which cannot be done easily using current productivity software. For example, Milestones Simplicity by KIDASA Software, Inc., has a Schedule Setup Wizard that walks users through simple steps to produce a Gantt chart. For $49 per user, this tool also includes a large assortment of symbols, flexible formatting, an outlining utility, and an Internet Publishing Wizard. Several companies provide add-on features to Excel or Microsoft Access to provide basic project management functions using familiar software products.

- *Midrange tools:* A step up from low-end tools, midrange tools are designed to handle larger projects, multiple users, and multiple projects. All of these tools can produce Gantt charts and network diagrams, and can assist in critical-path analysis, resource allocation, project tracking, status reporting, and so on. Prices range from about $200 to $500 per user, and several tools require additional server software for using work-group features. Microsoft Project is still the most widely used project management software today, and Microsoft Project 2003 includes an enterprise version. Other companies that sell midrange project management tools include Artemis, PlanView, Primavera, and Welcom, to name just a few.

- *High-end tools:* Another category of project management software is high-end tools, sometimes referred to as enterprise project management software. These tools provide robust capabilities to handle very large projects, dispersed work groups, and enterprise functions that summarize and combine individual project information to provide project portfolio management information. These products are generally licensed on a per-user basis, integrate with enterprise database management software, and are accessible via the Internet. In 2003, Microsoft introduced its Enterprise Project Management Solution. Several companies that provide midrange tools now offer enterprise versions of their software. There are also several inexpensive, Web-based products on the market. For example, VCS's VPMi Enterprise Online (*www. vcsonline.com*) is available for only $12 per user per month.

Figures 1-7 and 1-8 provide sample screens from two different project management software tools. Figure 1-7 shows a sample screen from Microsoft's Enterprise Project Management Solution, displaying all published projects in a company's portfolio sorted by country. This particular view shows red, yellow, or green symbols (shown in different shades of gray in the figure) indicating the status of each project in terms of meeting schedule and budget goals.

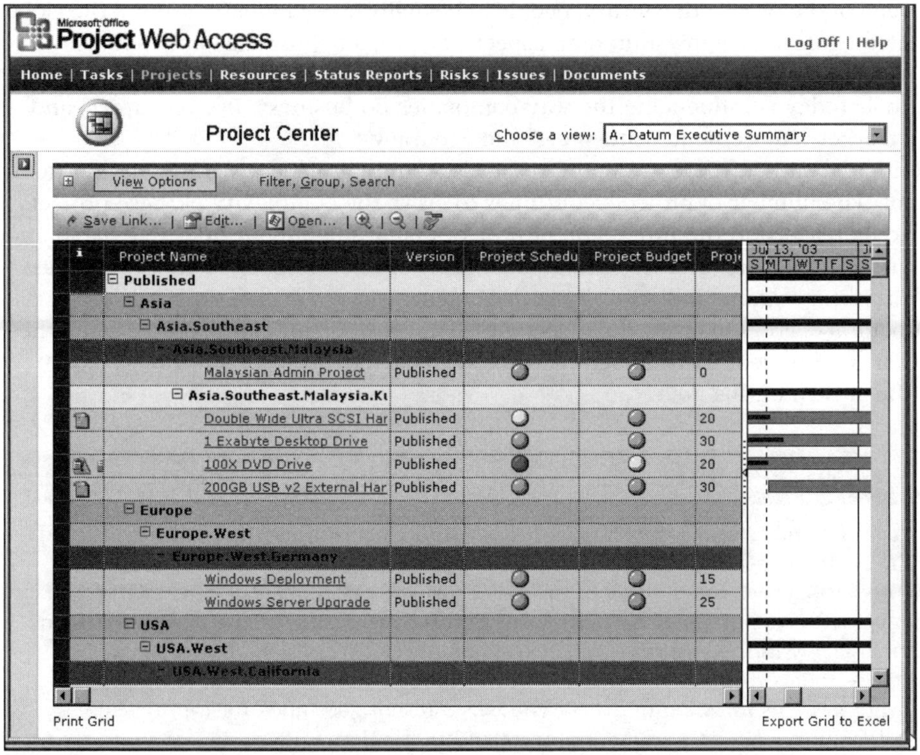

FIGURE 1-7 Sample screen from the Microsoft Enterprise Project Management Solution

Figure 1-8 shows a sample screen from VCS's VPMi Portfolio Management Software, displaying a process map. Users can quickly see projects in various stages of their life cycles, such as pending projects, active projects, and closed/canceled projects. You will learn more about using project management software and portfolio management features in later chapters.

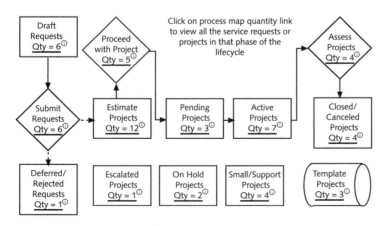

FIGURE 1-8 Sample screen from VPMi Portfolio Management Software by VCS

By the end of the twentieth century, people in virtually every industry around the globe began to investigate and apply different aspects of project, program, and portfolio management. The sophistication and effectiveness with which organizations use these concepts and tools today is influencing the way companies do business, use resources, and respond to market requirements with speed and accuracy.

As mentioned earlier, there are many reasons to study project, program, and portfolio management. The number of projects continues to grow, the complexity of these projects continues to increase, and the profession of project management continues to expand and mature. Many colleges, universities, and companies now offer courses related to various aspects of project, program, and portfolio management. You can even earn bachelor's, master's, and doctoral degrees in project management. The growing number of projects and the evidence that good project management can really make a difference continue to contribute to the growth of this field.

CASE WRAP-UP

Another board member asked the CEO to describe more about what the PMO director did to help the company become more successful at managing projects. Doug explained how Marie Scott worked with him and all of the vice presidents to reorganize several parts of the company to support their new emphasis on project, program, and project portfolio management. They formed a project team to implement a Web-based project management software tool across the enterprise. They formed another team to develop project-based reward systems for all employees. They also authorized funds for a project to educate all employees in project management and to develop a mentoring program for project, program, and project portfolio managers. Doug and Marie had successfully convinced everyone that effectively selecting and managing projects was crucial to their company's future. The board and the company's shareholders were very pleased with the results.

Chapter Summary

There is a new or renewed interest in project management today as the number of projects continues to grow and their complexity continues to increase. The success rate of information technology projects has more than doubled since 1995, but still only about one-third are successful in meeting scope, time, and cost goals. Using a more disciplined approach to managing all types of projects can help organizations succeed.

A project is a temporary endeavor undertaken to create a unique product, service, or result. Projects are unique, temporary, and developed incrementally; they require resources, have a sponsor, and involve uncertainty. The triple constraint of project management refers to managing the scope, time, and cost dimensions of a project.

Project management is the application of knowledge, skills, tools, and techniques to project activities to meet project requirements. Stakeholders are the people involved in or affected by project activities. A framework for project management includes the project stakeholders, project management knowledge areas, and project management tools and techniques. The nine knowledge areas are project integration management, scope, time, cost, quality, human resource, communications, risk, and procurement management.

A program is a group of related projects managed in a coordinated way to obtain benefits and control not available from managing them individually. Project portfolio management involves organizing and managing projects and programs as a portfolio of investments that contribute to the entire enterprise's success. Portfolio management emphasizes meeting strategic goals, whereas project management focuses on tactical goals.

The profession of project management continues to grow and mature. Project, program, and portfolio managers play key roles in helping projects and organizations succeed. They must perform various duties; possess many skills; and continue to develop skills in project management, general management, and their particular application area. Soft skills, especially leadership, are particularly important for project, program, and portfolio managers. The Project Management Institute (PMI) is an international professional society that provides Project Management Professional (PMP) certification and upholds a code of ethics. Today, hundreds of project management software products are available to assist people in managing projects.

Quick Quiz

1. Approximately what percentage of the world's gross domestic product is spent on projects?
    a. 10 percent
    b. 25 percent
    c. 50 percent
    d. 75 percent

2. Which of the following is not a potential advantage of using good project management?

   a. shorter development times

   b. higher worker morale

   c. lower cost of capital

   d. higher profit margins

3. A _____ is a temporary endeavor undertaken to create a unique product, service, or result.

   a. program

   b. process

   c. project

   d. portfolio

4. Which of the following is not an attribute of a project?

   a. Projects are unique.

   b. Projects are developed using progressive elaboration.

   c. Projects have a primary customer or sponsor.

   d. Projects involve little uncertainty.

5. Which of the following is not part of the triple constraint of project management?

   a. meeting scope goals

   b. meeting time goals

   c. meeting communications goals

   d. meeting cost goals

6. _____ is the application of knowledge, skills, tools, and techniques to project activities to meet project requirements.

   a. Project management

   b. Program management

   c. Project portfolio management

   d. Requirements management

7. Project portfolio management addresses _____ goals of an organization, whereas project management addresses _____ goals.

   a. strategic, tactical

   b. tactical, strategic

   c. internal, external

   d. external, internal

8. Several individual housing projects done in the same area by the same firm might best be managed as part of a _____ .

   a. portfolio

   b. program

   c. investment

   d. collaborative

9. The most significant characteristic or attribute of an effective project manager is that he or she _____ .

   a. is a strong communicator

   b. is decisive

   c. is visionary

   d. leads by example

10. What kind of certification does the Project Management Institute provide?

   a. Microsoft Certified Project Manager (MCPM)

   b. Project Management Professional (PMP)

   c. Project Management Expert (PME)

   d. Project Management Mentor (PMM)

Quick Quiz Answers

1. B; 2. C; 3. C; 4. D; 5. C; 6. A; 7. A; 8. B; 9. D; 10. B

Discussion Questions

1. Why is there a new or renewed interest in the field of project management?

2. What is a project, and what are its main attributes? How is a project different from what most people do in their day-to-day jobs? What is the triple constraint?

3. What is project management? Briefly describe the project management framework, providing examples of stakeholders, knowledge areas, tools and techniques, and project success factors.

4. Discuss the relationship between projects, programs, and portfolio management, and their contribution to enterprise success.

5. What are the roles of the project, program, and portfolio managers? What are suggested skills for project managers? What additional skills do program and portfolio managers need?

6. What role does the Project Management Institute play in helping the profession? What functions can you perform with project management software? What are some popular names of low-end, midrange, and high-end project management tools?

Exercises

Note: These exercises can be done individually or in teams in class, as homework, or in a virtual environment. Students can either write their results in a paper or prepare a short presentation to show their results.

1. Search the Internet for the terms *project management, program management,* and *project portfolio management.* Write down the number of hits that you received for each of these phrases. Find at least three Web sites that provide interesting information on one of the topics, including the Project Management Institute's Web site (*www.pmi.org*). Write a one-page paper or prepare a short presentation summarizing key information about these three Web sites.

2. Find an example of a real project with a real project manager. Feel free to use projects in the media (the Olympics, television shows, movies, and so on) or a project from work, if applicable. Write a one-page paper or prepare a short presentation describing the project in terms of its scope, time, and cost goals and each of the project's attributes. Try to include information describing what went right and wrong on the project and the role of the project manager and sponsor. Also describe whether you consider the project to be a success, and why or why not. Include at least one reference and proper citations.

3. Visit the Project Management Center (*www.infogoal.com/pmc*) and at least three of its links to project management software providers. Write a one-page paper or prepare a short presentation summarizing your findings.

Team Projects

1. Find someone who works as a project manager or is a member of a project team. Prepare several interview questions, and then ask him your questions in person, via the phone, or via the Internet. Discuss the results with your team, and then prepare a one- to two-page paper or prepare a short presentation summarizing your findings.

2. Go to *www.monster.com* and search for jobs as a "project manager" or "program manager" in three geographic regions of your choice. Write a one- to two-page paper or prepare a short presentation summarizing what you found.

3. As a team, discuss projects that you are currently working on or would like to work on to benefit yourself, your employers, your family, or the broader community. Come up with at least 10 projects, and then determine if they could be grouped into programs. Write a one- to two-page paper or prepare a short presentation summarizing your results.

Companion Web Site

Visit the companion Web site for this text (*www.course.com/mis/pm/schwalbe*) to access:

- Lecture notes
- Interactive quizzes
- Template files
- Sample documents
- Guide to Using Microsoft Project 2003

- VPMi enterprise project management software
- More ideas for team projects, including real projects and case studies
- Links to additional resources related to project management

Key Terms

leader — A person who focuses on long-term goals and big-picture objectives, while inspiring people to reach those goals.

manager — A person who deals with the day-to-day details of meeting specific goals.

portfolio — A collection of projects or programs and other work that are grouped together to facilitate effective management of that work to meet strategic business objectives.

program — A group of projects managed in a coordinated way to obtain benefits and control not available from managing them individually.

program manager — The person who provides leadership and direction for the project managers heading the projects within a program.

project — A temporary endeavor undertaken to create a unique product, service, or result.

project management — The application of knowledge, skills, tools, and techniques to project activities to meet project requirements.

project management knowledge areas — The scope, time, cost, quality, human resource, communications, risk, procurement management, and project integration management.

Project Management Professional (PMP) — The certification provided by PMI that requires documenting project experience, agreeing to follow the PMI code of ethics, and passing a comprehensive exam.

project management tools and techniques — The methods available to assist project managers and their teams; some popular tools in the time-management knowledge area include Gantt charts, network diagrams, critical-path analysis, and project management software.

project manager — The person responsible for working with the project sponsor, the project team, and the other people involved in a project to meet project goals.

project portfolio management — The grouping and managing of projects and programs as a portfolio of investments that contribute to the entire enterprise's success.

project sponsor — The person who provides the direction and funding for a project.

stakeholders — The people involved in or affected by project activities.

triple constraint — The balancing of scope, time, and cost goals

End Notes

[1] Project Management Institute, Inc., *The PMI Project Management Fact Book, Second Edition,* 2001.

[2] Project Management Institute, Inc., *Project Management Salary Survey, Third Edition,* 2003.

[3] The Standish Group, "The CHAOS Report" (*www.standishgroup.com*) (1995).

[4] Project Management Institute, Inc., *A Guide to the Project Management Body of Knowledge (PMBOK® Guide)* (2004), p. 5.

[5] Ibid, p. 16.

[6] The Standish Group, "Latest Standish Group CHAOS Report Shows Project Success Rates Have Improved by 50%," (March 25, 2003) and "CHAOS Demographics and Project Resolution" (2004).

[7] The Standish Group, "CHAOS 2001: A Recipe for Success" (2001).

[8] Project Management Institute, Inc., *A Guide to the Project Management Body of Knowledge (PMBOK® Guide)* (2004), p. 8.

[9] Eric Burke, "Project Portfolio Management," PMI Houston Chapter Meeting (July 10, 2002).

[10] Project Management Institute, Inc., "PMI Today" (February 2005).

[11] Project Management Institute, Inc., "Project Management Institute Certification Handbook" (January 2003), p. 22.

CHAPTER 2

PROJECT, PROGRAM, AND PORTFOLIO SELECTION

LEARNING OBJECTIVES

After reading this chapter, you will be able to:

- Describe the importance of aligning projects with business strategy, the strategic planning process, and using a SWOT analysis
- Explain the four-stage planning process for project selection and provide examples of applying this model to ensure the strategic alignment of projects
- Summarize the various methods for selecting projects and demonstrate how to calculate net present value, return on investment, payback, and the weighted score for a project
- Discuss the program selection process and distinguish the differences between programs and projects
- Describe the project portfolio selection process and the five levels of project portfolio management

OPENING CASE

Marie Scott, the director of the Project Management Office for Global Construction, was facilitating a meeting with several senior managers throughout the company. The purpose of the meeting was to discuss a process for selecting projects, grouping them into programs, and determining how they fit into the organization's portfolio of projects. She had invited an outside consultant to the meeting to provide an objective view of the theory and practice behind project, program, and portfolio selection.

She could see that several managers were getting bored with the presentation, while others looked concerned that their projects might be cancelled if the company implemented a new approach for project selection. After the consultant's presentation, Marie had each participant write down his or her questions and concerns and hand them in anonymously for her group to review. She was amazed at the obvious lack of understanding of the need for projects to align with business strategy. How should her group respond?

ALIGNING PROJECTS WITH BUSINESS STRATEGY

Most organizations face hundreds of problems and opportunities for improvement and consider potential projects to address them. These organizations—both large and small—cannot undertake most of the potential projects identified because of resource limitations and other constraints. Therefore, an organization's overall business strategy should guide the project selection process and management of those projects.

WHAT WENT WRONG?

Unfortunately, when deciding to approve projects, many organizations lack a structured process. Mike Peterson, project management professional (PMP) and director with PricewaterhouseCoopers' Advisory Services, described an organization that decided it needed to implement a new financial system, which is often a very expensive, challenging project. "With little in the way of analysis, they selected a big-name enterprise resource planning package, and hired a boutique firm to assist with the implementation. At no time did they formally define the benefits the new system was meant to usher in; nor did they decide, exactly, which processes were to be redesigned. Their own assumptions were not articulated, timelines were never devised, nor were the key performance indicators needed to track success ever established."[1]

What was the result of this project? It was completed over budget and behind schedule, and instead of helping the company, it prevented it from closing its books for over twelve months. The company undertook a long and costly project, and ultimately failed to improve the organization's effectiveness. The company could have avoided many of the problems it encountered if it had followed a formal, well-defined process to identify and select projects.

Strategic Planning

Successful leaders look at the big picture or strategic plan of the organization to determine what projects will provide the most value. The same can be said for successful individuals. No one person can do everything, so individuals must pick projects to pursue based on their talents, interests, limitations, and so on. **Strategic planning** involves determining long-term objectives by analyzing the strengths and weaknesses of an organization, studying opportunities and threats in the business environment, predicting future trends, and projecting the need for new products and services. Strategic planning provides important information to help organizations identify and then select potential projects.

SWOT Analysis

Many people are familiar with **SWOT analysis**—analyzing **S**trengths, **W**eaknesses, **O**pportunities, and **T**hreats—which is used to aid in strategic planning. For example, a group of four people who want to start a new business in the film industry could perform a SWOT analysis to help identify potential projects. They might determine the following based on a SWOT analysis:

- Strengths:
  - As experienced professionals, we have numerous contacts in the film industry.
  - Two of us have strong sales and interpersonal skills.
  - Two of us have strong technical skills and are familiar with several film-making software tools.
  - We all have impressive samples of completed projects.
- Weaknesses:
  - None of us have accounting/financial experience.
  - We have no clear marketing strategy for products and services.
  - We have little money to invest in new projects.
  - We have no company Web site and limited use of technology to run the business.
- Opportunities:
  - A current client has mentioned a large project she would like us to bid on.
  - The film industry continues to grow.
  - There are two major conferences this year where we could promote our company.
- Threats:
  - Other individuals or companies can provide the services we can.
  - Customers might prefer working with more established individuals/organizations.
  - There is high risk in the film business.

Based on their SWOT analysis, the four entrepreneurs outline potential projects as follows:

- Find an external accountant or firm to help run the business
- Hire someone to develop a company Web site, focusing on our experience and past projects
- Develop a marketing plan
- Develop a strong proposal to get the large project the current client mentioned
- Plan to promote the company at two major conferences this year

FOUR-STAGE PLANNING PROCESS FOR PROJECT SELECTION

One of the most important factors in project success is selecting the best projects to undertake. In additional to using a SWOT analysis, organizations often follow a detailed planning process for project selection. Figure 2-1 shows a four-stage planning process for selecting projects. Note the hierarchical structure of this model and the results produced from each stage. *It is very important to start at the top of the pyramid to select projects that support the organization's business strategy:*

1. *Strategic planning*: The first step of the project selection process is to determine the organization's strategy, goals, and objectives. This information should come from the strategic plan or strategy planning meetings. For example, if a firm's competitive strategy is cost leadership, it should focus on projects that will help it retain its position as a low-cost producer.

2. *Business area analysis*: The second step is to analyze business processes that are central to achieving strategic goals. For example, could the organization make improvements in sales, manufacturing, engineering, information technology (IT), or other business areas to support the strategic plan?

3. *Project planning*: The next step is to start defining potential projects that address the strategies and business areas identified. Managers should discuss the potential projects' scope, time, and cost goals; projected benefits; and constraints as part of this process.

4. *Resource allocation*: The last step in the project planning process is choosing which projects to do and assigning resources for working on them. The amount of resources the organization has available or is willing to acquire will affect resource-allocation decisions.

FIGURE 2-1   Pyramid for the project planning process

METHODS FOR SELECTING PROJECTS

Although people in organizations identify many potential projects as part of their strategic planning process, they also identify projects by working on day-to-day operations. For example, a project manager overseeing an apartment building project might notice that some workers are much more efficient than others. She might suggest a project to provide standardized training on specific skills. A marketing analyst might notice that competitors are using new forms of advertising and suggest a project to respond to this competition. It is important for organizations to encourage workers at all levels to submit project ideas because they know firsthand what problems they are encountering and what opportunities might be available.

How do senior managers decide which of the many potential projects their organization should pursue? Some projects directly support competitive strategy and are easy choices, but other project ideas require additional thought and analysis. However, organizations need to narrow down the list of potential projects to those projects that will be most beneficial. If people choose projects haphazardly (see Figure 2-2), the results might be as random as the choice.

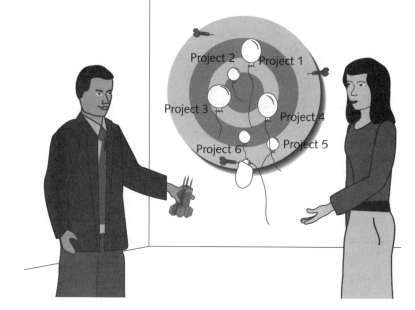

FIGURE 2-2 Choosing projects the wrong way

Selecting projects is not an exact science, but it is a critical part of project, program, and project portfolio management. Many methods exist for selecting from among possible projects. Common techniques are listed here and explained in the following sections:

- Focusing on competitive strategy and broad organizational needs
- Performing net present value analysis or other financial projections
- Using a weighted scoring model
- Implementing a balanced scorecard
- Addressing problems, opportunities, and directives
- Considering project time frame
- Considering project priority

In practice, organizations usually use a combination of these approaches to select projects. Each approach has advantages and disadvantages, and it is up to management to decide the best approach for selecting projects based on their particular organization. In any case, projects should first and foremost address business needs.

Focusing on Competitive Strategy and Broad Organizational Needs

When deciding what projects to undertake, when to undertake them, and to what level, top managers must focus on meeting their organization's many needs. Projects that address competitive strategy are much more likely to be successful because they will be important to the organization's competitive position.

For example, a company might have a competitive strategy of cost leadership, meaning that it attracts customers primarily because its products or services are inexpensive. Wal-Mart and Cub Foods fit into this category; a project to help reduce inventories and, thereby, costs would fit their competitive strategies. Other companies might have a particular focus for their competitive strategies, meaning that they develop products for a particular market niche. Babies"R"Us and Ron Jon Surf Shop fit into this category; a project to help attract new customers (new parents for Babies"R"Us and new surfers for Ron Jon Surf Shop) would fit their competitive strategies.

In addition to projects that directly tie to competitive strategy, organizations might pursue projects that everyone agrees will meet broad organizational needs. These needs might involve improving the firm's IT infrastructure, improving safety, or providing faster customer service. It is often impossible to estimate the financial value of such projects, but everyone agrees that they do have a high value. As the old proverb says, "It is better to measure gold roughly than to count pennies precisely."

One method for selecting projects based on broad organizational needs is to first determine whether they meet three important criteria: need, funding, and will. Do people in the organization agree that the project needs to be done? Does the organization have the capacity to provide adequate funds to perform the project? Is there a strong will to make the project succeed? For example, many visionary chief executive officers (CEOs) can describe a broad need to improve certain aspects of their organizations, such as communications. Although they cannot specifically describe how to improve communications, they might allocate funds to projects that address this need. As projects progress, the organization must reevaluate the need, funding, and will for each project to determine if the projects should be continued, redefined, or terminated.

Performing Financial Projections

Financial considerations are often an important aspect of the project selection process, especially during tough economic times. As authors Dennis Cohen and Robert Graham put it, "Projects are never ends in themselves. Financially they are always a means to an end, cash."[2] Many organizations require an approved business case before pursuing projects, and financial projections are a critical component of the business case. Three primary methods for determining the projected financial value of projects include net present value analysis, return on investment, and payback analysis. Because project managers often deal with business executives, they must understand how to speak their language, which often boils down to understanding these important financial concepts.

Net Present Value Analysis

Net present value (NPV) analysis is a method of calculating the expected net monetary gain or loss from a project by discounting all expected future cash inflows and outflows to the present point in time. (Detailed steps to walk you through the calculation are outlined in the following paragraphs.) An organization should consider only projects with a positive NPV if financial value is a key criterion for project selection. This is because a positive NPV means the return from a project exceeds the **opportunity cost of capital**—the return available by investing the capital elsewhere. Projects with higher NPVs are preferred to projects with lower NPVs if all other factors are equal.

Figure 2-3 illustrates the NPV concept for two different projects. Note that this example starts discounting right away in Year 1 and uses a 10 percent discount rate for both projects. (The paragraphs that follow explain the discount rate.) You can use the NPV function in Microsoft Excel to calculate the NPV quickly. Detailed steps on performing this calculation manually are provided in Figure 2-4. Note that Figure 2-3 lists the projected benefits first, followed by the costs, and then the calculated cash flow amount. Notice that the sum of the **cash flow**—benefits minus costs, or income minus expenses—is the same for both projects at $5,000. The net present values are different, however, because they account for the time value of money. Money earned today is worth more than money earned in the future, primarily due to inflation. Project 1 had a negative cash flow of $5,000 in the first year, whereas Project 2 had a negative cash flow of only $1,000 in the first year. Although both projects had the same total cash flows without discounting, these cash flows are not of comparable financial value. NPV analysis, therefore, is a method for making equal comparisons between cash flow for multiyear projects.

	A	B	C	D	E	F	G
1	Discount rate	10%					
2							
3	**PROJECT 1**	YEAR 1	YEAR 2	YEAR 3	YEAR 4	YEAR 5	**TOTAL**
4	Benefits	$0	$2,000	$3,000	$4,000	$5,000	$14,000
5	Costs	$5,000	$1,000	$1,000	$1,000	$1,000	$9,000
6	Cash flow	($5,000)	$1,000	$2,000	$3,000	$4,000	**$5,000**
7	NPV ——→	**$2,316**					
8		Formula =npv(b1,b6:f6)					
9							
10	**PROJECT 2**	YEAR 1	YEAR 2	YEAR 3	YEAR 4	YEAR 5	**TOTAL**
11	Benefits	$1,000	$2,000	$4,000	$4,000	$4,000	$15,000
12	Costs	$2,000	$2,000	$2,000	$2,000	$2,000	$10,000
13	Cash flow	($1,000)	$0	$2,000	$2,000	$2,000	**$5,000**
14	NPV ——→	**$3,201**					
15		Formula =npv(b1,b13:f13)					
16							
17							

Note that totals are equal, but NPVs are not because of the time value of money

FIGURE 2-3 Net present value example

Discount rate	10%					
PROJECT 1	**1**	**2**	**3**	**4**	**5**	**TOTAL**
Costs	$5,000	$1,000	$1,000	$1,000	$1,000	$9,000
Discount factor*	0.91	0.83	0.75	0.68	0.62	
Discounted costs	$4,545	$826	$751	$683	$621	**$7,427**
Benefits	$0	$2,000	$3,000	$4,000	$5,000	$14,000
Discount factor*	0.91	0.83	0.75	0.68	0.62	
Discounted benefits	0	$1,653	$2,254	$2,732	$3,105	**$9,743**
Discounted benefits - discounted costs, or NPV ⟶						**$2,316**
*Note: The discount factors are NOT rounded to two decimal places.						
They are calculated using the formula discount factor = 1/(1+discount rate)`year.						
You can access this spreadsheet on the companion Web site.						

FIGURE 2-4   Detailed NPV calculations

There are some items to consider when calculating NPV. Some organizations refer to the investment year(s) for project costs as Year 0 instead of Year 1 and do not discount costs in Year 0. Other organizations start discounting immediately based on their financial procedures; it is simply a matter of preference for the organization. The discount rate can also vary, based on the prime rate and other economic considerations. You can enter costs as negative numbers instead of positive numbers, and you can list costs first and then benefits. For example, Figure 2-5 shows the financial calculations a consulting firm provided in a business case for an intranet project. Note that the discount rate is 8 percent, costs are listed first, and costs are entered as positive numbers. The NPV and other calculations are still the same; only the format is different. A project manager must be sure to check with his organization to find out its guidelines for when discounting starts, what discount rate to use, and what format the organization prefers.

Discount rate	8%					
Assume the project is completed in Year 0			Year			
	0	1	2	3	Total	
Costs	140,000	40,000	40,000	40,000		
Discount factor	1	0.93	0.86	0.79		
Discounted costs	140,000	37,200	34,400	31,600	243,200	
Benefits	0	200,000	200,000	200,000		
Discount factor	1	0.93	0.86	0.79		
Discounted benefits	0	186,000	172,000	158,000	516,000	
Discounted benefits - costs	(140,000)	148,800	137,600	126,400	272,800	←NPV
Cumulative benefits - costs	(140,000)	8,800	146,400	272,800		
ROI ──────────────→	112%					
		Payback in Year 1				

FIGURE 2-5 Intranet project NPV example

To determine NPV, follow these steps:

1. Determine the estimated costs and benefits for the life of the project and the products it produces. For example, the intranet project example assumed the project would produce a system in about six months that would be used for three years, so costs are included in Year 0, when the system is developed, and ongoing system costs and projected benefits are included for Years 1, 2, and 3.
2. Determine the discount rate. A **discount rate** is the rate used in discounting future cash flows. It is also called the capitalization rate or opportunity cost of capital. In Figures 2-3 and 2-4, the discount rate is 10 percent per year, and in Figure 2-5, the discount rate is 8 percent per year.
3. Calculate the net present value. There are several ways to calculate NPV. Most spreadsheet software has a built-in function to calculate NPV. For example, Figure 2-3 shows the formula that Excel uses: =npv(discount rate, range of cash flows), where the discount rate is in cell B1 and the range of cash flows for Project 1 are in cells B6 through F6. To use the NPV function, there must be a row in the spreadsheet (or column, depending on how it is organized) for the cash flow each year, which is the benefit amount for that year minus the cost amount. The result of the formula yields an NPV of $2,316 for Project 1 and an NPV of $3,201 for Project 2. Because both projects have positive NPVs, they are both good candidates for selection. However, because Project 2 has a higher NPV than Project 1 (38 percent higher), it would be the better choice between the two. If the two numbers are close, other methods should be used to help decide which project to select.

The mathematical formula for calculating NPV is:

$$NPV = \Sigma_{t=0...n} \ A_t/(1+r)^t$$

where t equals the year of the cash flow, n is the last year of the cash flow, A is the amount of cash flow each year, and r is the discount rate. If you cannot enter the data into spreadsheet software, you can perform the calculations by hand or with a simple calculator. First, determine the annual **discount factor**——a multiplier for each year based on the discount rate and year——and then apply it to the costs and benefits for each year. The formula for the discount factor is $1/(1+r)^t$, where r is the discount rate, such as 8 percent, and t is the year. For example, the discount factors used in Figure 2-5 are calculated as follows:

Year 0: discount factor = $1/(1+0.08)^0$ = 1
Year 1: discount factor = $1/(1+0.08)^1$ = .93
Year 2: discount factor = $1/(1+0.08)^2$ = .86
Year 3: discount factor = $1/(1+0.08)^3$ = .79

After determining the discount factor for each year, multiply the costs and benefits by the appropriate discount factor. For example, in Figure 2-5, the discounted cost for Year 1 is $40,000 * .93 = $37,200. Next, sum all of the discounted costs and benefits each year to get a total. For example, the total discounted costs in Figure 2-5 are $243,200. To calculate the NPV, take the total discounted benefits and subtract the total discounted costs. In this example, the NPV is $516,000 – $243,200 = $272,800.

Return on Investment

Another important financial consideration is return on investment. **Return on investment (ROI)** is the result of subtracting the project costs from the benefits and then dividing by the costs. For example, if you invest $100 today and next year your investment is worth $110, your ROI is ($110 – 100)/100, or 0.10 (10 percent). Note that the ROI is always a percentage. It can be positive or negative. It is best to consider discounted costs and benefits for multiyear projects when calculating ROI. Figure 2-5 shows an ROI of 112 percent. You calculate this number as follows:

ROI = (total discounted benefits – total discounted costs)/discounted costs

ROI = (516,000 – 243,200) / 243,200 = 112%

The higher the ROI, the better; an ROI of 112 percent is outstanding. Many organizations have a required rate of return for projects. The **required rate of return** is the minimum acceptable rate of return on an investment. For example, an organization might have a required rate of return of at least 10 percent for projects. The organization bases the required rate of return on what it could expect to receive elsewhere for an investment of comparable risk.

You can also determine a project's **internal rate of return (IRR)** by finding what discount rate results in an NPV of zero for the project. You can use the Goal Seek function in Excel (use Excel's Help function for more information on Goal Seek) to determine the IRR quickly. Simply set the cell containing the NPV calculation to zero while changing the cell containing the discount rate. For example, in Figure 2-3, you could set cell B7 to zero while changing cell B1 to find that the IRR for Project 1 is 27 percent. (Note: The Excel file for Figure 2-3 is provided on the companion Web site if you want to try this out.)

Payback Analysis

Payback analysis is another important financial tool to use when selecting projects. **Payback period** is the amount of time it will take to recoup—in the form of net cash inflows—the total dollars invested in a project. In other words, payback analysis determines how much time will lapse before accrued benefits overtake accrued and continuing costs. Payback occurs in the year when the cumulative benefits minus costs reach zero. Figure 2-5 shows how to find the payback period. The cumulative benefits minus costs for Year 0 are ($140,000). Adding that number to the discounted benefits minus costs for Year 1 results in $8,800. Because that number is positive, the payback occurs in Year 1. Note that the year the project was undertaken in this example was called Year 0.

Creating a chart helps illustrate more precisely when the payback period occurs. Figure 2-6 charts the cumulative discounted costs and cumulative discounted benefits each year using the numbers from Figure 2-5. Note that the lines cross a little after Year 1 starts (assuming the project was done in Year 0). The cumulative discounted benefits and costs are equal to zero where the lines cross. A template file charting the payback period is provided on the companion Web site for this text. See Appendix A for a list of all template files.

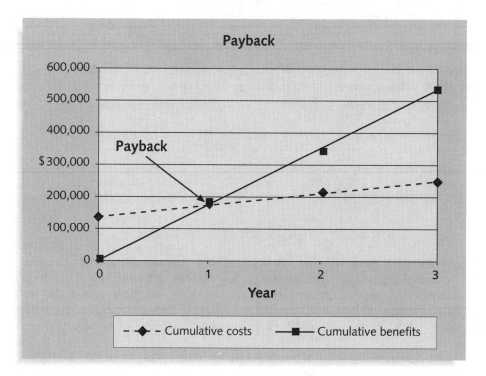

FIGURE 2-6   Charting the payback period

Many organizations have certain recommendations for the length of the payback period of an investment. For example, they might require all IT projects to have a payback period of less than two years or even one year, regardless of the estimated NPV or ROI. Rhonda Hocker, CIO at San Jose–based BEA Systems, Inc., notes that the general rule at the company is that its IT projects should have a payback period of less than one year. The company also tries to limit project teams to no more than 12 people, who perform the work within four months. Given the economic climate and rapid pace of change in businesses and technology, the company has to focus on delivering positive financial results quickly. [3] However, organizations must also consider long-range goals when making major investments. Many crucial projects, such as drug development or major transportation projects, cannot achieve a payback that quickly or be completed in such a short time period.

To aid in project selection, it is important for project managers to understand the organization's financial expectations for projects. It is also important for top management to understand the limitations of financial estimates, because they are just estimates.

Using a Weighted Scoring Model

A **weighted scoring model** is a tool that provides a systematic process for selecting projects based on many criteria. These criteria include such factors as meeting strategic goals or broad organizational needs; addressing specific problems or opportunities; the amount of time it will take to complete the project; the overall priority of the project; and the projected financial performance of the project.

The first step in creating a weighted scoring model is to identify criteria important to the project selection process. It often takes time to develop and reach agreement on these criteria. Holding facilitated brainstorming sessions or using software to exchange ideas can aid in developing these criteria. Some possible criteria for projects include the following:

- Supports key business objectives
- Has a strong internal sponsor
- Has strong customer support
- Uses a realistic level of technology
- Can be implemented in one year or less
- Provides a positive NPV
- Has low risk in meeting scope, time, and cost goals

Next, you assign a weight to each criterion. Once again, determining weights requires consultation and final agreement. These weights indicate how much you value each criterion or how important each criterion is. You can assign weights based on percentage, and the sum of all the criteria's weights must total 100 percent. You then assign numerical scores to each criterion (for example, 0 to 100) for each project. The scores indicate how much each project meets each criterion. At this point, you can use a spreadsheet application to create a matrix of projects, criteria, weights, and scores. Figure 2-7 provides an example of a weighted scoring model to evaluate four different projects. After assigning weights for the criteria and scores for each project, you calculate a weighted score for each project by multiplying the weight for each criterion by its score and adding the resulting values. For example, you calculate the weighted score for Project 1 in Figure 2-7 as:

$$25\%*90 + 15\%*70 + 15\%*50 + 10\%*25 + 5\%*20 + 20\%*50 + 10\%*20 = 56$$

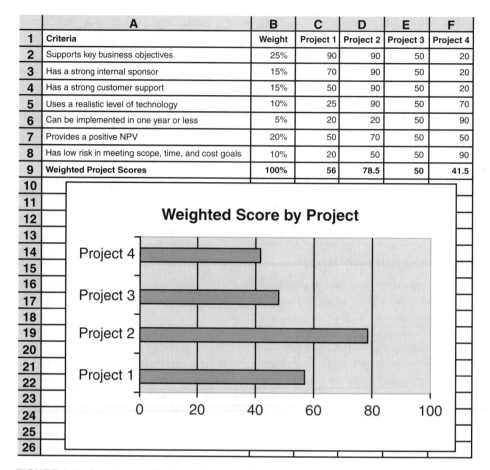

	A	B	C	D	E	F
1	Criteria	Weight	Project 1	Project 2	Project 3	Project 4
2	Supports key business objectives	25%	90	90	50	20
3	Has a strong internal sponsor	15%	70	90	50	20
4	Has a strong customer support	15%	50	90	50	20
5	Uses a realistic level of technology	10%	25	90	50	70
6	Can be implemented in one year or less	5%	20	20	50	90
7	Provides a positive NPV	20%	50	70	50	50
8	Has low risk in meeting scope, time, and cost goals	10%	20	50	50	90
9	**Weighted Project Scores**	100%	56	78.5	50	41.5

FIGURE 2-7   Sample weighted scoring model for project selection

Note that in this example, Project 2 is the obvious choice for selection because it has the highest weighted score. Creating a bar chart to graph the weighted scores for each project allows you to see the results at a glance. If you create the weighted scoring model in a spreadsheet, you can enter the data, create and copy formulas, and perform a "what-if" analysis. For example, suppose you change the weights for the criteria. By having the weighted scoring model in a spreadsheet, you can easily change the weights to update the weighted scores and charts automatically. This capability allows you to investigate various options for different stakeholders quickly. Ideally, the result should be reflective of the group's consensus, and any major disagreements should be documented. A template file for creating a weighted scoring model is provided on the companion Web site for this text.

Many readers of this text are probably familiar with a weighted scoring model because teachers often use them to determine grades. Suppose grades for a class are based on two homework assignments and two exams. To calculate final grades, the teacher would assign a weight to each of these items. Suppose Homework One is worth 10 percent of the grade, Homework Two is worth 20 percent of the grade, Test One is worth 20 percent of the grade, and Test Two is worth 50 percent of the grade. Students would want to do well on each of these items, but they would focus on performing well on Test Two because it is 50 percent of the grade.

You can also establish weights by assigning points. For example, a project might receive 100 points if it definitely supports key business objectives, 50 points if it somewhat supports them, and 0 points if it is totally unrelated to key business objectives. With a point model, you can simply add all the points to determine the best projects for selection without having to multiply weights and scores and sum the results.

You can also determine minimum scores or thresholds for specific criteria in a weighted scoring model. For example, suppose an organization decided that it should not consider a project if it does not score at least 50 out of 100 on every criterion. The organization can build this type of threshold into the weighted scoring model to automatically reject projects that do not meet these minimum standards. As you can see, weighted scoring models can aid in project selection decisions.

Implementing a Balanced Scorecard

Dr. Robert Kaplan and Dr. David Norton developed another approach to help select and manage projects that align with business strategy. A **balanced scorecard** is a methodology that converts an organization's value drivers—such as customer service, innovation, operational efficiency, and financial performance—to a series of defined metrics. Organizations record and analyze these metrics to determine how well projects help them achieve strategic goals.

The Balanced Scorecard Institute, which provides training and guidance to organizations using this methodology, quotes Kaplan and Norton's description of the balanced scorecard as follows:

> The balanced scorecard retains traditional financial measures. But financial measures tell the story of past events, an adequate story for industrial age companies for which investments in long-term capabilities and customer relationships were not critical for success. These financial measures are inadequate, however, for guiding and evaluating the journey that information age companies must make to create future value through investment in customers, suppliers, employees, processes, technology, and innovation.[4]

Visit *www.balancedscorecard.org* for more information on using this approach to project selection.

Problems, Opportunities, and Directives

Another method for selecting projects is based on their response to a problem, an opportunity, or a directive, as described in the following list:

- **Problems** are undesirable situations that prevent an organization from achieving its goals. These problems can be current or anticipated. For example, users of an information system at a large construction firm might be having trouble logging on to the system or getting information in a timely manner because the system has reached its capacity. In response, the company could initiate a project to enhance the current system by adding more access lines or upgrading the hardware with a faster processor, more memory, or more storage space.
- **Opportunities** are chances to improve the organization. For example, a large construction firm could implement a project to train workers on important construction skills.
- **Directives** are new requirements imposed by management, government, or some external influence. For example, many projects involving construction must meet rigorous building codes or government requirements.

Organizations select projects for any of these reasons. It is often easier to get approval and funding for projects that address problems or directives because the organization must respond to these categories of projects to avoid hurting the business. Many problems and directives must be resolved quickly, but managers must also consider projects that seek opportunities for improving the organization.

Project Time Frame

Another approach to project selection is based on the time it will take to complete a project or the date by which it must be done. For example, some potential projects must be finished within a specific time period. If they cannot be finished by this set date, they are no longer valid projects. Some projects can be completed very quickly—within a few weeks, days, or even minutes. However, even though many projects can be completed quickly, it is still important to prioritize them.

Project Priority

Another method for project selection is the overall priority of the project. Many organizations prioritize projects as being high, medium, or low priority based on the current business environment. For example, if it were crucial to cut operating costs quickly, projects that have the most potential to do so would be given a high priority. The organization should always complete high-priority projects first, even if a low- or medium-priority project could be finished in less time. Usually, there are many more potential projects than an organization can undertake at any one time, so it is very important to work on the most important ones first.

As you can see, organizations of all types and sizes can use many approaches to select projects. Many project managers have some say in which projects their organization selects for implementation. Even if they do not, they need to understand the motive and overall business strategy for the projects they are managing. Project managers and team members are often asked to justify their projects, and understanding many of these project selection methods can help them to do so.

PROGRAM SELECTION

After deciding which projects to pursue, organizations need to decide if it is advantageous to manage several projects together as part of a program. There might already be a program that a new project would logically fall under, or the organization might initiate a program and then approve projects for it. Recall that a program is a group of projects managed in a coordinated way to obtain benefits and control not available from managing them individually.

Focusing on Coordination and Benefits

What does it mean to manage a group of projects in a coordinated way? Project managers focus on managing individual projects. Project managers and their teams have to do many things to achieve individual project success. For example, if a project manager is in charge of building a new house for a sponsor, she must perform the following tasks, just to name a few:

- Work with local government groups to obtain permits
- Find and manage a land excavation firm to prepare the land
- Work with an architect to understand the house design
- Screen and hire various construction workers
- Find appropriate suppliers for the materials

If a construction firm is in charge of developing several houses in the same geographic area, it makes sense to coordinate these and other tasks for all the housing projects.

What benefits and control would be possible by managing projects as part of a program? There are several. For example, potential benefits in the housing program scenario include the following:

- *Saving money*: The construction firm can often save money by using economies of scale. It can purchase materials, obtain services, and hire workers for less money if it is managing the construction of one hundred houses instead of just one house.
- *Saving time*: Instead of each project team having to perform similar work, by grouping the projects into a program, one person or group can be responsible for similar work, such as obtaining all the permits for all the houses. This coordination of work usually saves time as well as money.
- *Increasing authority*: A program manager responsible for building one hundred houses will have more authority than a project manager responsible for building one house. The program manager can use this authority in multiple situations, such as negotiating better prices with suppliers and obtaining better services in a more timely fashion.

Approaches to Creating Programs

Some new projects naturally fall into existing programs, such as houses being built in a certain geographic area. As another example, many companies use IT, and they usually have a program in place for IT infrastructure projects. Projects might include purchasing new hardware, software, and networking equipment, or determining standards for IT. If a new office opens up in a new location, the project to provide the hardware, software, and networks for that office would logically fall under the infrastructure program.

Other projects might spark the need for developing a new program. For example, Global Construction from the opening case might win a large contract to build an office complex in a foreign country. Instead of viewing the contract as either one huge project or part of an existing program, it would be better to manage the work as its own program that comprises several smaller projects. For example, there might be separate project managers for each building. Grouping related projects into programs helps improve coordination through better communications, planning, management, and control. Organizations must decide when it makes sense to group projects together. When too many projects are part of one program, it might be wise to create a new program to improve their management. Remember that the main goal of programs is to obtain benefits and control not available from managing projects separately.

MEDIA SNAPSHOT

Many people enjoy watching the extra features on a DVD that describe the creation of a movie. For example, the extended edition DVD for *Lord of the Rings: The Two Towers* includes detailed descriptions of how the script was created, how huge structures were built, how special effects were made, and how talented professionals overcame numerous obstacles to complete the three movies. Instead of viewing each movie as a separate project, the producer, Peter Jackson, decided to develop all three movies as part of one program.

"By shooting all three films consecutively during one massive production and postproduction schedule, New Line Cinema made history. Never before had such a monumental undertaking been contemplated or executed. The commitment of time, resources, and manpower were unheard of as all three films and more than 1,000 effects shots were being produced concurrently with the same director and core cast." [5] At three years in the making, *The Lord of the Rings* trilogy was the largest production ever to be mounted in the Southern Hemisphere. The production assembled an international cast, employed a crew of 2,500, used over 20,000 days of extras, featured 77 speaking parts, and created 1,200 state-of-the-art computer-generated effects shots. Jackson said that doing detailed planning for all three movies made it much easier than he imagined to produce them, and the three movies were completed in less time and for less money by grouping them together. The budget for the three films was reported to be $270 million, and they grossed over $1 billion before the end of 2004.

PROJECT PORTFOLIO SELECTION

Projects and programs have existed for a long time, as has some form of project portfolio management. There is no simple process for deciding how to create project portfolios, but the goal of project portfolio management is clear: to help maximize business value to ensure enterprise success. You can measure business value in several ways, such as in market share, profit margins, growth rates, share prices, and customer or employee satisfaction ratings. Many factors are involved in ensuring enterprise success. Organizations cannot only pursue projects that have the best financial value. They must also consider resource availability (including people, equipment, and cash); risks that could affect success; and other concerns (potential mergers, public relations, balancing investments, and so on) that affect enterprise success.

Focusing on Enterprise Success

Project managers strive to make their projects successful and naturally focus on doing whatever they can to meet the goals of their particular projects. Likewise, program managers focus on making their programs successful. Project portfolio managers and other senior managers, however, must focus on how all of an organization's projects fit together to help the entire enterprise achieve success. That might mean canceling or putting several projects on hold, reassigning resources from one project to another, suggesting changes in project leadership, or taking other actions that might negatively affect individual projects or programs to help the organization as a whole. For example, a university might have to close a campus in order to provide quality services at other campuses. Running any large organization is complex, as is project portfolio management.

WHAT WENT RIGHT?

Many companies have seen great returns on investment after implementing basic ideas of project portfolio management. For example, Jane Walton, the project portfolio manager for IT projects at Schlumberger, saved the company $3 million in one year by simply organizing the organization's 120 IT projects into one portfolio. Before then, all IT projects and their associated programs were managed separately, and no one looked at them as a whole. Manufacturing companies used project portfolio management in the 1960s, and Walton anticipated the need to justify investments in IT projects just as managers have to justify capital investment projects. She found that 80 percent of the organization's projects overlapped, and 14 separate projects were trying to accomplish the same thing. By simply looking at all IT projects and programs together, Schlumberger could make better strategic business decisions. The company canceled several projects and merged others to reduce the newly obvious redundancy.[6]

Mercy Health Partners' chief information officer, Jim Albin, says project portfolio management helped his company improve its IT services and reduce costs by $4 million. It also helped encourage business area leaders to make decisions about how IT resources were used, not the IT department.[7] A crucial part of project portfolio management is looking at the big picture and not focusing on individual departments. Strategic business needs must drive portfolio management.

Recall that project portfolio management focuses on strategic issues while individual projects often focus on tactical issues. Portfolios should be formed and continuously updated to help the organization as a whole make better strategic decisions. Organizations normally put all projects into one portfolio, but then often break it down into more detailed sub-portfolios, often set up by major departments or other categories. Several companies create a separate portfolio for IT projects. It is often difficult to measure the financial value of many IT projects, yet these projects are often a large investment and have a strong effect on other business areas. For example, if you have to update your financial system to meet new government regulations, such as the 2002 Sarbanes-Oxley Act, where would it fit in your enterprise project portfolio? (After several major corporate scandals, the Sarbanes-Oxley Act was passed to help restore public confidence in the financial reporting of publicly traded companies in the United States. Companies have spent millions of dollars to be compliant with this act.) You have to do it to stay in business, but you can't generate a positive return on investment from that particular project.

Sample Approach for Creating a Project Portfolio

Figure 2-8 illustrates one approach for project portfolio management in which there is one large portfolio for the entire organization. Sections of the portfolio are then broken down to improve the management of projects in each particular sector. For example, Global Construction might have the main portfolio categories shown in the left part of Figure 2-8 (marketing, materials, IT, and HR [human resources]) and divide each of those categories further to address their unique concerns. The right part of this figure shows how the IT projects could be categorized in more detail to assist in their management. For example, there are three basic IT project portfolio categories:

1. *Venture*: Projects in this category would help transform the business. For example, Global Construction might have an IT project to provide Webcams and interactive Web-based reporting on construction sites that would be easily accessible by its customers and suppliers. This project could help transform the business by developing more trusting partnerships with customers and suppliers, who could know exactly what is happening with their construction projects.

2. *Growth*: Projects in this category would help the company grow in terms of revenue. For example, Global Construction might have an IT project to provide information on its corporate Web site in a new language, such as Chinese or Japanese. This capability could help the company grow its business in those countries.

3. *Core*: Projects in this category must be accomplished to run the business. For example, an IT project to provide computers for new employees would fall under this category.

Note that the core category of IT projects is labeled as nondiscretionary costs. This means that the company has no choice in whether to fund these projects; it must fund them to stay in business. Projects that fall under the venture or growth category would be discretionary costs because the company can use its own discretion in deciding whether to fund them. Also note the arrow in the center of Figure 2-8. This arrow indicates that the risks, value, and timing of projects normally increase as you go from core to growth to venture projects. However, some core projects can also be high risk, have high value, and require good timing.

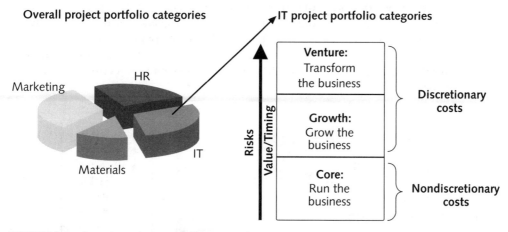

FIGURE 2-8   Sample project portfolio approach

Five Levels of Project Portfolio Management

As you can imagine, it takes time to understand and apply project portfolio management. You can develop and manage a project portfolio in many ways. Just as projects are unique, so are project portfolios.

An organization can view project portfolio management as having five levels, from simplest to most complex, as follows:

1. Put all of your projects in one list. Many organizations find duplicate or unneeded projects after they identify all the projects on which they are working.
2. Prioritize the projects in your list. It's important to know which projects are most important to an organization so that resources can be applied accordingly.
3. Divide your projects into several categories based on types of investment. Categorizing projects helps you see the big picture, such as how many projects are supporting a growth strategy, how many are helping to increase profit margins, how many relate to marketing, and how many relate to materials. Organizations can create as many categories as they need to help understand and analyze how projects affect business needs and goals.
4. Automate the list. Managers can view project data in many different ways by putting key information into a computerized system. You can enter the project information in spreadsheet software such as Excel. You might have headings for the project name, project manager, project sponsor, business needs addressed, start date, end date, budget, risk, priority, key deliverables, and so on. You can also use more sophisticated tools to help perform project portfolio management, such as enterprise project management software, as described in Chapter 1.

5. Apply modern portfolio theory, including risk-return tools that map project risks. Figure 2-9 provides a sample map to assist in evaluating project risk versus return, or business value. Each bubble represents a project, and the size of the bubble relates to its approved budget (that is, the larger bubbles have larger budgets). Notice that there are not and should not be projects in the lower-right quadrant, which is the location of projects that have low relative value and high risk. As described in Chapter 1, many project portfolio management software products are available on the market today to help analyze portfolios. Consult references on portfolio theory and project portfolio management software for more details on this topic.

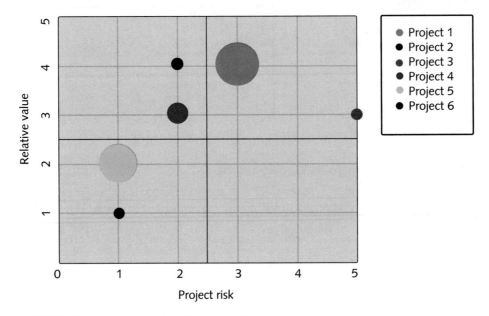

FIGURE 2-9 Sample project portfolio risk map

It is important for organizations to develop a fair, consistent, and logical process for selecting projects, programs, and portfolios. Studies show that one of the main reasons people quit their jobs is because they feel they do not make a difference. After employees understand how their work fits into the big picture, they can work more effectively to help themselves and their entire organizations succeed.

CASE WRAP-UP

Marie and her team summarized the inputs from the meeting and discussed them with their CEO, Doug Armbruster, and other senior managers. They felt people were nervous that the company might not be doing well and that their jobs were in jeopardy. They discussed options for how to proceed and decided that it was important for the CEO to explain the importance of aligning projects with business strategy. Doug and his staff put together a memo and presentation to explain that the company was doing very well, and that they had no intentions of either letting anyone go or cutting major programs. On the contrary, they had far more projects to pursue than they possibly could, and they believed that using project portfolio management would help them select and manage projects better. After everyone heard this information, they were much more open to working with Marie's group to improve their project, program, and portfolio management processes.

Chapter Summary

An organization's overall business strategy should guide the project selection process and management of those projects. Many organizations perform a SWOT analysis to help identify potential projects based on their strengths, weaknesses, opportunities, and threats.

The four-stage planning process helps organizations align their projects with their business strategy. The four stages of this model, from highest to lowest, are strategic planning, business area analysis, project planning, and resource allocation.

Several methods are available for selecting projects. Financial methods include calculating and analyzing the net present value, return on investment, and payback period for projects. You can also use a weighted scoring model; implement a balanced scorecard; address problems, opportunities, and directives; or consider project time frame or project priority to assist in project selection.

After determining what projects to pursue, it is important to decide if projects should be grouped into programs. The main criteria for program selection are the coordination and benefits available by grouping projects together into a program.

There is no simple process for deciding how to create project portfolios, but the goal of project portfolio management is to help maximize business value to ensure enterprise success. There are five levels of complexity for project portfolio managing, ranging from simply putting all projects in one list to applying modern portfolio theory to analyze risks and returns of a project portfolio.

Quick Quiz

1. Which of the following is not part of a SWOT analysis?
   a. strengths
   b. weaknesses
   c. opportunities
   d. tactics

2. A large company continues to be successful by providing new products and services for its market niche of brides. What is its main competitive strategy?
   a. cost leadership
   b. differentiation
   c. focus
   d. customer service

3. The last step in the four-stage planning process for projects is _____ .
   a. resource allocation
   b. project planning
   c. business area analysis
   d. strategic planning

4. It is very important to start at the top of the four-stage planning process pyramid to select projects that support the organization's _____ .

a. vision

b. business strategy

c. financial position

d. culture

5. Which of the following statements is false concerning the financial analysis of projects?

a. The higher the net present value the better.

b. A shorter payback period is better than a longer one.

c. The required rate of return is the discount rate that results in an NPV of zero for the project.

d. ROI is the result of subtracting the project costs from the benefits and then dividing by the costs.

6. A _____ is a methodology that converts an organization's value drivers—such as customer service, innovation, operational efficiency, and financial performance—into a series of defined metrics.

a. balanced scorecard

b. weighted scoring model

c. net present value analysis

d. directive

7. Which of the following is not a major benefit of grouping projects into programs?

a. increasing revenues

b. increasing authority

c. saving money

d. saving time

8. A college approved a project to provide discounts for faculty, students, and staff to use the city's new light-rail system. Under what existing program might this project naturally fit?

a. academic enrichment program

b. fund-raising program

c. entertainment program

d. transportation program

9. The goal of project portfolio management is to help maximize business value to ensure _____ .

a. profit maximization

b. enterprise success

c. risk minimization

d. competitive advantage

10. Many organizations find duplicate or unneeded projects after they perform which step in project portfolio management?

   a. prioritizing the projects in their list

   b. dividing the projects into several categories based on type of investment

   c. putting all projects in one list

   d. applying modern portfolio theory, including risk-return tools that map project risk

Quick Quiz Answers

1. D; 2. C; 3. A; 4. B; 5. C; 6. A; 7. A; 8. D; 9. B; 10. C

Discussion Questions

1. Why is it important to align projects to business strategy? What is SWOT analysis?

2. What are the stages called in the four-stage planning process for project selection? How does following this process assist in selecting projects that will provide the most benefit to organizations?

3. When should you use net present value analysis to evaluate projects? How do you decide which projects to pursue using net present value analysis? How do return on investment and payback period relate to net present value?

4. What are three main benefits of grouping projects into programs?

5. What are the five levels of project portfolio management?

Exercises

Note: These exercises can be done individually or in teams, in class, as homework, or in a virtual environment. Students can either write their results in a paper or prepare a short presentation to show their results.

1. Perform a financial analysis for a project using the format provided in Figure 2-5. Assume the projected costs and benefits for this project are spread over four years as follows: Estimated costs are $100,000 in Year 1 and $25,000 each year in Years 2, 3, and 4. Estimated benefits are $0 in Year 1 and $80,000 each year in Years 2, 3, and 4. Use an 8 percent discount rate. Create a spreadsheet (or use the business case financials template provided on the companion Web site) to calculate and clearly display the NPV, ROI, and year in which payback occurs. In addition, write a paragraph explaining whether you would recommend investing in this project based on your financial analysis.

2. Create a weighted scoring model to determine grades for a course. Final grades are based on three exams worth 15 percent, 20 percent, and 25 percent; homework worth 20 percent; and a group project worth 20 percent. Enter scores for three students. Assume Student 1 earns 100 percent (or 100) on every item. Assume Student 2 earns 80 percent on each of the exams, 90 percent on the homework, and 95 percent on the group project. Assume Student 3 earns 90 percent on Exam 1, 75 percent on Exam 2, 80 percent on Exam 3, 90 percent on the homework, and 70 percent on the group project. You can use the weighted scoring model template, create your own spreadsheet, or make the matrix by hand.

3. Search the Internet to find a real example of how a company or organization uses a structured process to aid in project, program, and/or project portfolio selection. Write a one-page paper or prepare a short presentation summarizing your findings.

Team Projects

1. Find someone who has been involved in the project selection process within an organization. Prepare several interview questions, and then ask him your questions in person, via the phone, or via the Internet. Be sure to ask if he uses any of the project selection tools discussed in this chapter (that is, financial analysis, weighted scoring models, balanced scorecard, and so on). Discuss the results with your team, and then prepare a one- to two-page paper or prepare a short presentation summarizing your findings.

2. Search the Internet to find two good examples of how organizations group projects into programs and two examples of how they create project portfolios. Write a one- to two-page paper or prepare a short presentation summarizing your results, being sure to cite your references.

3. Develop criteria that your class could use to help select what projects to pursue for implementation by your class or another group. For example, criteria might include benefits to the organization, interest level of the sponsor, interest level of the class, and fit with class skills and timing. Determine a weight for each criterion, and then enter the criteria and weights into a weighted scoring model, similar to that shown in Figure 2-7. (You can use the template for a weighted scoring model provided on the companion Web site.) Then review the list of projects you prepared in Chapter 1, Team Project 3, and enter scores for at least five of those projects. Calculate the weighted score for each project. Write a one- to two-page paper or prepare a short presentation summarizing your results.

Companion Web Site

Visit the companion Web site for this text (www.course.com/pm/intro) to access:

- Lecture notes
- Interactive quizzes
- Template files
- Sample documents
- Guide to Using Microsoft Project 2003
- VPMi enterprise project management software
- More ideas for team projects, including real projects, and case studies
- Links to additional resources related to project management

Key Terms

balanced scorecard — A methodology that converts an organization's value drivers to a series of defined metrics.

cash flow — Benefits minus costs, or income minus expenses.

directives — The new requirements imposed by management, government, or some external influence.

discount factor — A multiplier for each year based on the discount rate and year.

discount rate — The rate used in discounting future cash flows.

internal rate of return (IRR) — The discount rate that results in an NPV of zero for a project.

net present value (NPV) analysis — A method of calculating the expected net monetary gain or loss from a project by discounting all expected future cash inflows and outflows to the present point in time.

opportunities — Chances to improve the organization.

opportunity cost of capital — The return available by investing the capital elsewhere.

payback period — The amount of time it will take to recoup, in the form of net cash inflows, the total dollars invested in a project.

problems — Undesirable situations that prevent the organization from achieving its goals.

required rate of return — The minimum acceptable rate of return on an investment.

return on investment (ROI) — (Benefits minus costs) divided by costs.

strategic planning — The process of determining long-term objectives by analyzing the strengths and weaknesses of an organization, studying opportunities and threats in the business environment, predicting future trends, and projecting the need for new products and services.

SWOT analysis — Analyzing **S**trengths, **W**eaknesses, **O**pportunities, and **T**hreats.

weighted scoring model — A technique that provides a systematic process for basing project selection on numerous criteria.

End Notes

[1] Mike Peterson, "Why Are We Doing This Project?" Projects@Work (*www.projectsatwork. com*) (February 22, 2005).

[2] Dennis J. Cohen and Robert J. Graham, *The Project Manager's MBA* (San Francisco: Jossey-Bass), 2001, 31.

[3] Marc L. Songini, "Tight Budgets Put More Pressure on IT," *Computer World* (December 2, 2002).

[4] The Balanced Scorecard Institute, "What Is a Balanced Scorecard?" (*www.balancedscorecard. org*) (February 2003).

[5] The Compleat Sean Bean Web Site, "Lord of the Rings" (February 23, 2004).

[6] Scott Berinato, "Do the Math," *CIO Magazine* (October 1, 2001).

[7] Joshua Weinberger, "Voice of Experience: Mercy Health Partners CIO Jim Albin," *Baseline Magazine* (October 1, 2003).

CHAPTER **3**

INITIATING PROJECTS

LEARNING OBJECTIVES

After reading this chapter, you will be able to:

- Describe the five project management process groups, map them to the project management knowledge areas, discuss why organizations develop their own project management methodologies, and understand the importance of top management commitment and organizational standards in project management

- Discuss the initiating process used by Global Construction, including pre-initiating tasks, breaking large projects down into smaller projects, and initiating tasks

- Identify project stakeholders and perform a stakeholder analysis

- Prepare a business case to justify the need for a project

- Create a project charter to formally initiate a project

- Describe the importance of holding a good project kick-off meeting

- Develop a preliminary project scope statement to help understand project requirements

OPENING CASE

Marie Scott worked with other managers at Global Construction to decide what projects their firm should undertake to meet business needs. Construction is a low-margin, very competitive industry, and productivity improvements are crucial to improving shareholder returns. After participating in several strategic planning and project selection workshops, one of the opportunities the company decided to pursue was just-in-time training. Several managers pointed out that Global Construction was spending more than the industry average on training its employees, especially in its sales, purchasing, engineering, and information technology departments, yet productivity for those workers had not improved much in recent years. They also knew that they needed to transfer knowledge from many of their retiring workers to their younger workers. Global Construction still offered most courses during work hours using an instructor-led format, and the course topics had not changed in years. Several managers knew that their competitors had successfully implemented just-in-time training programs so that their workers could get the type of training they needed when they needed it. For example, much of the training was provided over the Internet, so employees could access it anytime, anywhere. Employees were also able to ask questions of instructors as well as experts within the company at any time via the Internet to help them perform specific job duties. In addition, experts documented important knowledge and let other workers share their suggestions. Management believed that Global Construction could reduce training costs and improve productivity by successfully implementing a project to provide just-in-time training on key topics and promote a more collaborative working environment.

Mike Sundby, the vice president of human resources, was the project's champion. After successfully completing a Phase I Just-In-Time Training study to decide how they should proceed with the overall project, Mike and his directors selected Kristin Maur to lead Phase II of the project. Kristin suggested partnering with an outside firm to help with some of the project's technical aspects. Mike asked Kristin to start forming her project team and to prepare important initiating documents, including a business case, a stakeholder analysis, a project charter, and a preliminary scope statement for the project. He was also looking forward to participating in the official kick-off meeting.

PROJECT MANAGEMENT PROCESS GROUPS

Recall from Chapter 1 that project management consists of nine project management knowledge areas: project integration, scope, time, cost, quality, human resource, communications, risk, and procurement management. Another important concept to understand is that projects involve five project management process groups: initiating, planning, executing, monitoring and controlling, and closing. Applying these process groups in a consistent, structured fashion increases the chance of project success. This chapter briefly describes each project management process group and then describes the initiating process in detail through a case study based on Global Construction's Just-In-Time Training project. Subsequent chapters describe the other process groups and apply them to the same project.

Project management process groups progress from initiating activities to planning activities, executing activities, monitoring and controlling activities, and closing activities. A **process** is a series of actions directed toward a particular result. All projects use the five process groups as outlined in the following list:

- **Initiating processes** include actions to begin or end projects and project phases. To initiate a project such as the Just-In-Time Training project, someone must develop a project charter and hold a kick-off meeting to officially start the project. This chapter will describes these and other initiating tasks in detail.

- **Planning processes** include devising and maintaining a workable scheme to ensure that the project meets its scope, time, and cost goals as well as organizational needs. There are often many different plans to address various project needs as they relate to each knowledge area. For example, as part of project scope management for the Just-In-Time Training project, the project team will develop a scope statement to plan the work that needs to be done to develop and provide the products and services produced as part of the project. As part of project time management, the project team will create a detailed schedule that lets everyone know when specific work will start and end. As part of procurement management, the project team will plan for work that will be done by external organizations to support the project. Chapters 4 and 5 describe the planning tasks in detail.

- **Executing processes** include coordinating people and other resources to carry out the project plans and produce the deliverables of the project or phase. A **deliverable** is a product or service produced or provided as part of a project. For example, a project to construct a new office building would include deliverables such as blueprints, cost estimates, progress reports, the building structure, windows, plumbing, and flooring. The Just-In-Time Training project would include deliverables such as a training needs survey, training materials, and classes. Chapter 6 describes executing tasks in detail.

- **Monitoring and controlling processes** measure progress toward achieving project goals, monitor deviation from plans, and take corrective action to match progress with plans and customer expectations. For example, the main objective of the Just-In-Time Training project is to provide training to help employees be more productive. If the first training course does not improve productivity or meet other customer expectations, the project team should take corrective action to deliver more suitable training courses. As another example, if the project team continues to miss deadlines in the schedule for the Just-In-Time Training project, the project manager should lead the team in taking corrective action, such as developing a more realistic schedule or securing additional resources to help meet deadlines. Chapter 7 describes monitoring and controlling tasks in detail.

- **Closing processes** include formalizing acceptance of the project or phase and bringing it to an orderly end. Administrative tasks are often involved in this process group, such as archiving project files, closing out contracts, documenting lessons learned, and receiving formal acceptance of the deliverables. It is also important to plan for a smooth transition of the results of the project to the responsible operational group. For example, after the Just-In-Time Training project is completed, the training department will need to schedule and provide courses developed as part of the project. The planning for this transition should be done as part of the closing process group. Chapter 8 describes closing tasks in detail.

The process groups are not isolated events. For example, project managers must perform monitoring and controlling processes throughout the project's life span. The level of activity and length of each process group varies for every project. Normally, executing tasks require the most resources and time, followed by planning tasks. Initiating and closing tasks are usually the shortest (at the beginning and end of a project or phase, respectively), and they require the least amount of resources and time. However, every project is unique, so there can be exceptions. You can apply the process groups for each major phase of a project, or you can apply the process groups to an entire project, as the Just-In-Time Training project case study does in this chapter.

Note that process groups apply to entire projects as well as to project phases. A **phase** is a distinct stage in project development, and most projects have distinct phases. For example, the Just-In-Time Training project includes phases called study or feasibility, course design and development, course administration, and course evaluation. In this case, the study or feasibility phase is done as a separate project. The other phases were done in a second, larger project. To ensure that they continue to meet current organizational needs, projects should successfully pass through each phase before continuing.

Mapping the Process Groups to the Knowledge Areas

You can map the process group into the nine project management knowledge areas. For example, project integration management includes the following seven processes:

- Develop a project charter and develop a preliminary project scope statement (during the initiating process group).
- Develop a project management plan (during the planning process group).
- Develop and manage project execution (during the executing process group).
- Monitor and control project work and integrated change control (during the monitoring and controlling process group).
- Close the project (during the closing process group).

Based on the *PMBOK® Guide*, 2004, there are 44 total processes in project management. Table 3-1 provides a big-picture view of the relationships among these processes, the time in which they are typically completed, and the knowledge areas into which they fit.

TABLE 3-1 Project management process groups and knowledge area mapping

Knowledge area	Project management process groups				
	Initiating	Planning	Executing	Monitoring and Controlling	Closing
Project integration management	Develop project charter; develop preliminary project scope statement	Develop project management plan	Direct and manage project execution	Monitor and control project work; integrate change control	Close project
Project scope management		Plan scope; define scope; create WBS		Verify scope; control scope	
Project time management		Define activity; sequence activity; estimate activity resources; estimate activity duration; develop schedule		Control schedule	
Project cost management		Estimate cost; plan cost budget		Control cost	
Project quality management		Plan for quality assurance	Perform quality assurance	Perform quality control	
Project human resource management		Develop human resources plan	Acquire project team; develop project team	Manage project team	
Project communications management		Plan for communications	Distribute information	Report performance; manage stakeholders	

TABLE 3-1 Project management process groups and knowledge area mapping (continued)

Knowledge area	Project management process groups				
	Initiating	Planning	Executing	Monitoring and Controlling	Closing
Project risk management		Develop risk management plan; identify risks; perform qualitative risk analysis; perform quantitative risk analysis; plan risk response		Monitor and control risk	
Project procurement management		Plan purchases and acquisitions; plan contracting	Request seller responses; select sellers	Administer contracts	Close contracts

PMBOK® Guide, *2004, p. 70*

This chapter describes in detail the processes followed and the outputs produced while initiating the Just-In-Time Training project. For example, key outputs of initiating described in this chapter include the following:

- Stakeholder analysis
- Business case for the project
- Project charter
- Kick-off meeting
- Preliminary scope statement

You can also access templates to help create these and other documents on the companion Web site for this text, as summarized in Appendix A. The remaining chapters of this text follow a similar format to describe the processes and outputs used for the Just-In-Time Training project for planning, executing, monitoring and controlling, and closing. To help you visualize outputs for each process group, Figure 3-1, shown later in the chapter, summarizes the outputs for the initiating process group. Similar figures or tables are provided in the following chapters as well.

Several organizations use PMI's information as a foundation for developing their own project management methodologies, as described in the next section. Notice in Table 3-1 that the majority of project management processes occur as part of the planning process group. Because each project is unique, project teams are always trying to do something that has not been done before. To succeed at unique and new activities, project teams must do a fair amount of planning. Recall, however, that the most time and money is normally spent on executing because that is where the project's products and/or services (for example, the buildings for a construction project, the training courses for a training project, and so on) are produced. It is good practice for organizations to determine how project management will work best in their own organizations.

Developing a Project Management Methodology

Some organizations spend a great deal of time and money on training efforts for general project management skills, but after the training, a project manager might still not know how to tailor their project management skills to the organization's particular needs. Because of this problem, some organizations develop their own internal project management methodologies. The *PMBOK® Guide* is a **standard** that describes best practices for what should be done to manage a project. A **methodology** describes *how* things should be done, and different organizations often have different ways of doing things.

For example, the *PMBOK® Guide* lists information that a project charter, as described later in this chapter, should address:

- Requirements that satisfy customer, sponsor, and other stakeholder needs, wants, and expectations
- Business needs, a high-level project description, or product requirements that the project is undertaken to address
- Project purpose or justification
- Assignment of a project manager and designation of his authority level
- Summary milestone schedule
- Stakeholder influences
- Identification of functional organizations and their participation
- Organizational, environmental, and external assumptions
- Organizational, environmental, and external constraints
- Business case justifying the project, including return on investment
- Summary budget or money allocated for the project

However, the *PMBOK® Guide* does not provide information on how the previously listed project charter requirements should be created, when, or by whom. For example, many organizations prefer that project charters be fairly short documents. They create a separate document, for example, with the business case information instead of including it in a project charter. (As the name implies, a **business case** is a document that provides justification for investing in a project.) Successful organizations have found that they need to develop and follow a customized, formal project management process that describes not only what needs to be done, but also how it should be done. They also must involve key stakeholders and ensure that projects are aligned with organizational needs.

WHAT WENT RIGHT?

William Ibbs and Justin Reginato completed a five-year study to help quantify the value of project management. Among their findings are the following points:

- Organizations with more mature project management practices have better project performance, which result in projects completed on time and within budget much more often than most projects.
- Project management maturity is strongly correlated with more predictable project schedule and cost performance.
- Organizations that follow good project management methodologies have lower direct costs of project management (6–7 percent) than those that do not (11–20 percent).[1]

Another study published by the Centre for Business Practices shows that creating value for stakeholders is the key to project and organizational success. Organizations that stress shareholders, customers, and employees outperform those that do not. "Over an 11-year period, the former increased revenues by an average of 682% versus 166% for the latter, expanded their workforces by 282% versus 36%, grew their stock prices by 901% versus 74%, and improved their net incomes by 756% versus 1%."[2]

Part of creating and following a project management methodology includes the creation and use of templates. A **template** is a file with a preset format that serves as a starting point for creating various documents so that the format and structure do not have to be re-created. Companies that excel in project management know that it does not make sense to reinvent the wheel by having every project manager decide how to create standard documents, such as project charters and business cases. They also know that top management commitment and organizational standards are crucial for project success.

The Importance of Top Management Commitment

Without top management commitment, many projects will fail. Some projects have a senior manager called a **champion** who acts as a key proponent for a project. Projects are part of the larger organizational environment, and many factors that might affect a project are out of the project manager's control. Top management commitment is crucial for the following reasons:

- Project managers need adequate resources. The best way to kill a project is to withhold the required money, human resources, and/or visibility for the project. If project managers have top management commitment, they will also have adequate resources and be able to focus on completing their specific projects.
- Project managers often require approval for unique project needs in a timely manner. For example, a project team might have unexpected problems and need additional resources halfway through the project, or the project manager might need to offer special pay and benefits to attract and retain key project personnel. With top management commitment, project managers can meet these specific needs in a timely manner.

- Project managers must have cooperation from people in other parts of the organization. Because most projects cut across functional areas, top management must help project managers deal with the political issues that often arise in these types of situations. If certain functional managers are not responding to project managers' requests for necessary information, top management must step in to encourage functional managers to cooperate.
- Project managers often need someone to mentor and coach them on leadership issues. Many project managers come from technical positions and are inexperienced as managers. Senior managers should take the time to pass on advice on how to be good leaders. They should encourage new project managers to take classes to develop leadership skills and allocate the time and funds for them to do so.

The Need for Organizational Standards

Another problem in most organizations is not having standards or guidelines to follow that could help in performing project management functions. These standards or guidelines might be as simple as providing standard forms or templates for common project documents, examples of good project documentation, or guidelines on how the project manager should perform certain tasks, such as holding a kick-off meeting or providing status information. Providing status information might seem like common sense to senior managers, but many new project managers have never given a project status report and are not used to communicating with a wide variety of project stakeholders. Top management must support the development of these standards and guidelines and encourage or even enforce their use.

Some organizations invest heavily in project management by creating a project management office or center of excellence. A **project management office (PMO)** is an organizational entity created to assist project managers in achieving project goals. Some organizations develop career paths for project managers. Some require that all project managers have project management professional (PMP) certification and that all employees have some type of project management training. The implementation of all of these standards demonstrates an organization's commitment to project management and helps them ensure project success.

Many people learn best by example. The following section describes an example of how Global Construction applied initiating processes to the Just-In-Time Training project. It uses some of the ideas from the *PMBOK® Guide* and additional ideas to meet the unique needs of this project and organization. Several templates illustrate how project teams prepare various project management documents. You can download these templates from the companion Web site for this text.

INITIATING PROCESS FOR GLOBAL CONSTRUCTION'S JUST-IN-TIME TRAINING PROJECT

Figure 3-1 illustrates the process that Global Construction will follow for initiating the Just-in-Time Training project. Notice that several tasks are completed *before* the project initiation starts. First, the project is approved through a formal project selection process and is given the go-ahead. Second, senior managers perform several activities as part of pre-initiating, as described in the following section. Finally, initiating begins as the project manager works with the team and other stakeholders to hold a kick-off meeting for the project and produce a stakeholder analysis, a business case, a project charter, and a preliminary scope statement.

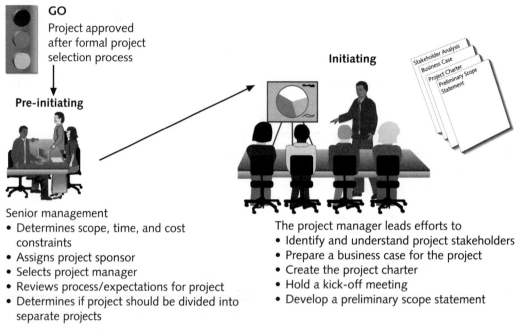

GO
Project approved after formal project selection process

Pre-initiating

Senior management
• Determines scope, time, and cost constraints
• Assigns project sponsor
• Selects project manager
• Reviews process/expectations for project
• Determines if project should be divided into separate projects

Initiating

Stakeholder Analysis
Business Case
Project Charter
Preliminary Scope Statement

The project manager leads efforts to
• Identify and understand project stakeholders
• Prepare a business case for the project
• Create the project charter
• Hold a kick-off meeting
• Develop a preliminary scope statement

FIGURE 3-1 Initiating process summary

Pre-initiating Tasks

It is good practice to lay the groundwork for a project before it officially starts. After a project is approved, senior managers should meet to accomplish the following tasks:

- Determine the scope, time, and cost constraints for the project
- Identify the project sponsor (the person who provides high-level direction and often the funding for the project)
- Select the project manager
- Meet with the project manager to review the process and expectations for managing the project
- Determine if the project should be divided into two or more smaller projects

Why is it necessary to perform these last two tasks? Many organizations have organizational processes and procedures in place for managing projects. It is very important for project managers to understand them as well as the expectations for the project. For example, will there be formal management reviews for the project, and if so, how often will they be held? Are there any regulations, standards, or guidelines related to the project? Is there historical information or are there reports on lessons from past projects that might apply to the project? Senior managers should also share their wisdom with project managers to get the project off to a good start. For example, they might recommend key people who would be good team members for the project or offer suggestions based on personal experiences.

Many people know from experience that it is easier to successfully complete a small project than a large one. It often makes sense to break large projects down into two or more smaller projects. For Global Construction's Just-In-Time Training project, senior management decided to use this approach. They knew that when scope, time, and cost goals for a large project were unclear, it would help to have a Phase I project to clarify the situation. For a large training project, there is often a study project done first before investing in a larger project.

Lucy Camarena, training director, would sponsor the study project, called the Just-In-Time Training Phase I project. Mike Sundby, the vice president of human resources, would act as the project champion. Lucy assigned one of her senior staff members, Ron Ryan, to manage the project. The scope, time, and cost goals and a summary of the approach and assumptions are provided in Table 3-2.

TABLE 3-2 Summary information for Just-In-Time Training Phase I project

Scope Goals

- Investigate and document the training taken in the last two years by all internal employees.
- Determine what courses were taken, the cost of all training, the process for approving/assigning training, and the evaluation of the training by participants, if available.
- Survey employees to get their input on what training they believe they'll need in the next two years, and how they want to receive that training (instructor-led in-house; instructor-led through a local college, university, or training company; Web-based; CD-ROM). Also hold focus groups to verify training needs.
- Recommend how to provide the most valuable training for Global Construction employees in the next two years.
- Determine the scope, time, and cost goals for the following project to develop and implement a Just-In-Time Training Phase II project.

Time Goals: Three months
Cost Goals: **$50,000**

  Approach/Assumptions:
- All of the costs would be for internal labor.
- All managers and employees would receive information about this study project.
- A response rate of 30 percent would be acceptable for the survey.
- The project team would do extensive research to back up their recommendations.
- The team would also provide detailed monthly reports and presentations to a steering committee.
- The final deliverables would include a one-hour final presentation and a comprehensive project report documenting all of the information and recommendations.

Senior managers were satisfied with the results of the Phase I project, but they realized that they did not want someone from the HR department to lead the Phase II project. Instead, they wanted a manager from one of their key operating divisions—such as sales, engineering, or purchasing—to lead the project. It was important to have buy-in for this new training program from the operating groups, and a strong project manager from one of those areas would likely have more respect and influence than one from HR. Someone from operations would also know firsthand what type of training people in operations would need. HR posted the position internally, and a selection committee decided that Kristin Maur, a former purchasing specialist and now a sales manager, was the best person to lead the Just-In-Time Training Phase II project.

Senior managers at Global Construction knew that it was good practice to have experienced managers from operations lead projects that were critical to the operational areas. They also knew that they needed support from several senior managers in the operating divisions as well as other areas, such as IT. So they asked key managers from several divisions to be on a project steering committee to oversee the project.

Now that important pre-initiating tasks were completed, Kristin Maur was ready to tackle important tasks to initiate the Just-In-Time Training project.

Initiating Tasks

The main tasks normally involved in project initiation are as follows:

- Identifying and understanding project stakeholders
- Preparing a business case for the project
- Creating the project charter
- Holding a kick-off meeting
- Developing a preliminary scope statement

For the Just-In-Time Training Phase I project, Ron Ryan led his small team in doing all of the initiating activities except for creating a business case. Global Construction only requires a formal business case for projects over a certain dollar amount (over $50,000 in this case) or when the sponsor requests it. The company also requires a stakeholder analysis and a project kick-off meeting as outputs of the initiating process. The following sections of this chapter describe each of these outputs in detail for the larger Just-In-Time Training Phase II project.

IDENTIFYING AND UNDERSTANDING PROJECT STAKEHOLDERS

Recall from Chapter 1 that project stakeholders are the people involved in or affected by project activities. Stakeholders can be internal to the organization or external.

- Internal project stakeholders generally include the project sponsor, project team, support staff, and internal customers for the project. Other internal stakeholders include top management, other functional managers, and other project managers. Because organizations have limited resources, projects affect top management, other functional managers, and other project managers by using some of the organization's limited resources.

- External project stakeholders include the project's customers (if they are external to the organization), competitors, and suppliers, and other external groups that are potentially involved in or affected by the project, such as government officials and concerned citizens.

Because the purpose of project management is to meet project requirements and satisfy stakeholders, it is critical that project managers take adequate time to identify, understand, and manage relationships with all project stakeholders. A tool to help accomplish these tasks is a stakeholder analysis.

Preparing a Stakeholder Analysis

A **stakeholder analysis** provides information on key stakeholders to help manage relationships with them. The type of information included in a stakeholder analysis includes the following:

- Names and organizations of key stakeholders
- Their roles on the project
- Unique facts about each stakeholder
- Their level of interest in the project
- Their influence on the project
- Suggestions for managing relationships with each stakeholder

It is helpful to start preparing a stakeholder analysis during initiation and adding information to it during the planning process.

How does a project manager identify key project stakeholders and find out more about them? The best way is by asking around. There might be formal organizational charts or biographies that can provide some information, but the main goal of the stakeholder analysis is to help project managers manage relationships with key stakeholders. Talking to other people who have worked with those stakeholders usually provides the best information. For example, in this case, Kristin Maur knew who some of the key stakeholders were but did not know any of them well. It did not take her long, however, to get the information she needed.

Because a stakeholder analysis often includes sensitive information, it should *not* be part of the official project plans, which are normally available for all stakeholders to review. In many cases, only project managers and a few other team members should be involved in preparing the stakeholder analysis. In most cases, the analysis is not even written down, and if it is, its distribution is strictly limited.

Sample Stakeholder Analysis

Table 3-3 provides an example of a stakeholder analysis that Kristin Maur could use to help her manage the Just-In-Time Training Phase II project (referred to without the Phase II from now on). It is important for project managers to take the time to perform a stakeholder analysis of some sort to identify and try to meet stakeholder needs and expectations. In addition, as new stakeholders are added to the project and more information is provided, the analysis should be updated. Early in this project, for example, all of the stakeholders are internal to the company; later on, however, there will be external stakeholders as well.

TABLE 3-3 Sample stakeholder analysis

Stakeholder Analysis
July 3, 2007

Project Name: Just-In-Time Training Project

	Mike Sundby	Lucy Camarena	Ron Ryan	Mohamed Abdul	Julia Portman
	KEY STAKEHOLDERS				
Organization	VP of HR	Training director	Senior HR staff member	Senior programmer/ analyst	VP of IT
Role on project	Project champion	Project sponsor	Led the Phase I project	Project team member	Project steering committee member
Unique facts	Outgoing, demanding, focuses on the big picture; MBA with emphasis on organizational design	Very professional, easy to work with but can stretch out discussions; Ph.D. in education	Old-timer; jealous that he wasn't asked to lead Phase II project	Excellent technical skills, English his second language, weak people skills, not excited about a training project	Thinks the company is way behind in applying IT, especially for training; wary of many suppliers
Level of interest	Very high	Very high	High	Medium	High
Level of influence	Very high; can call the shots	Very high; subject matter expert	Medium; he could sabotage the project	High; needs strong IT support for project to succeed	High; people listen to her at steering committee meetings
Suggestions on managing relationship	Keep informed, ask for advice as often as needed	Make sure she reviews work before showing to managers	Ask Lucy to talk to him to avoid problems, ask him to be available for advice	Help him see the project's importance, encourage his creativity	Compliment her a lot, ask for additional IT support as needed

PREPARING A BUSINESS CASE FOR THE PROJECT

Successful organizations initiate projects to meet business needs, and a common business need is to spend money wisely. As stated previously, a business case is a document that provides justification for investing in a project. As described in the opening case, Global Construction believed they could reduce training costs and improve productivity by successfully implementing a project to provide just-in-time training on key topics.

The Phase I project provided a wealth of information to help write a business case for the Phase II project. Kristin and Lucy reviewed this information carefully and worked together to create the business case. They also had one of the company's financial managers review the information for accuracy.

Contents of a Business Case

Like most project documents, the contents of a business case will vary to meet individual project needs. Typical information included in a business case includes the following:

- Introduction/Background
- Business Objective
- Current Situation and Problem/Opportunity Statement
- Critical Assumptions and Constraints
- Analysis of Options and Recommendation
- Preliminary Project Requirements
- Budget Estimate and Financial Analysis
- Schedule Estimate
- Potential Risks
- Exhibits

Because this project is relatively small and is for an internal sponsor, the business case is not as long as many other business cases. The following section shows the initial business case for the Just-In-Time Training project.

Sample Business Case

Kristin reviewed all of the information created from the Phase I project and drafted a business case. She reviewed it with her sponsor, Lucy (the training director) and had Peter from finance review the financial section. Peter told Kristin to be very conservative by not including any benefit projections that were based on productivity improvements. She still estimated that the project would have a 27 percent discounted return on investment and payback in the second year after implementing the new training program. The resulting business case is provided in Table 3-4.

TABLE 3-4 Sample business case

Business Case
July 11, 2007

Project Name: Just-In-Time Training Project

1.0 Introduction/Background

Global Construction employs 10,000 full-time employees in 10 different counties and 15 states in the United States. They spend an average of $1000 per employee for training (not including tuition reimbursement), which is higher than the industry average. However, the productivity of workers—especially in the sales, purchasing, engineering, and information technology departments—has not improved much in recent years. In the fast-paced, ever-changing construction market, training employees about new products, new technologies, and soft skills across a globally dispersed company with different populations is a challenge. By redesigning training, Global Construction can reduce training costs and improve productivity.

2.0 Business Objective

Global Construction's strategic goals include continuing growth and profitability. The company must have a highly skilled workforce to continue to compete in a global environment. Current training programs, however, are expensive and outdated. We can reduce costs by providing more targeted and timely training to our employees and by taking advantage of new technologies and business partnerships. Global Construction can also increase profits by improving productivity, especially by improving supplier management and negotiation skills.

3.0 Current Situation and Problem/Opportunity Statement

Global Construction has not updated its training approach or course offerings in the past five years. Most training is provided on-site during business hours and uses a traditional instructor-led approach with little or no technology involved. Department managers often request slots for various courses, but then they send whoever is available to the course because the department has already paid for it. Therefore, there is often a mismatch between skills needed by employees and the skills taught in a course. Our current training is expensive and ineffective. Many employees would like training in key subjects that are currently not provided and that would use more modern approaches and technologies. If the training is directly related to their jobs or interests, employees are willing to take it on their own time, if needed. Survey results indicated that employees are most in need of training in supplier management, negotiating skills, project management, Six Sigma (a quality management methodology), and software applications (for example, spreadsheet and Web development tools).

4.0 Critical Assumptions and Constraints

This project requires strong participation and cooperation from a wide variety of people. A project steering committee will be formed to provide close oversight and guidance. Some of the requested training will be outsourced, as will development of unique courses. The project will include investigating and taking advantage of new training technologies, such as multimedia and Web-based

TABLE 3-4 Sample business case (continued)

courses that workers can take on their own time. Employees will also be able to contact instructors and internal experts via the Internet for guidance in performing current work tasks as part of this project.

5.0 Analysis of Options and Recommendation

There are three options for addressing this opportunity:

1. Do nothing. The business is doing well, and we can continue to conduct training as we have in the past.

2. Instead of providing any internal training, give each employee up to $1000 to spend on outside training as approved by her supervisor. Require employees to stay with the company for one year after using training funds or return the money.

3. Design and implement a new training program as part of this project.

Based on the financial analysis and discussions with key stakeholders, we believe that option 3 is the best option.

6.0 Preliminary Project Requirements

The main requirements of this project include the following:

1. Based on survey results, the only current training that does not need to change is the Six Sigma training. No changes will be made in that area. The tuition reimbursement program will continue as is.

2. Training for improving supplier management and negotiating skills, especially international negotiations, has the highest priority because these areas are the most important to the business today and will continue to be so for the next few years. Internal staff will work with outside firms to develop a customized approach to this training that takes advantage of internal experts and new technologies.

3. Demand is also high for training in project management and software applications. The project team will analyze several approaches for this training, including in-house courses, courses offered by local colleges/universities, and computer-based/online courses. They will develop and implement the best combination of approaches for these courses.

4. The project will include updating the corporate intranet site to explain the new training program, to allow employees to sign up for and evaluate courses, and to track training demand and expenses.

5. The project team will develop an approach for measuring the effect of training on productivity on an annual basis.

7.0 Budget Estimate and Financial Analysis

A preliminary estimate of costs for the entire project is $1,000,000. Half of the costs are for internal labor, $250,000 is for outsourced labor, and $250,000 is for outsourced training programs. These are preliminary estimates that will be revised as more details become known. Projected benefits are estimated very conservatively. Because the average amount spent on training last year was $1000/employee, we assumed only a 10 percent or $100-per-employee reduction. This number is also very conservative, especially because much of the new training will be provided outside of work hours.

Exhibit A summarizes the projected costs and benefits, and shows the estimated net present value (NPV), return on investment (ROI), and year in which payback occurs. It also lists assumptions made in performing this preliminary

TABLE 3-4 Sample business case (continued)

financial analysis. All of the financial estimates are very encouraging. The estimated payback is in the second year after implementing the new training program. The NPV is $505,795, and the discounted ROI based on a three-year implementation is 27 percent.

8.0 Schedule Estimate

The sponsor would like to see the entire project completed within one year. Courses will be provided as soon as they are available. The impact of training on productivity will be assessed one year after training is completed and annually thereafter.

9.0 Potential Risks

There are several risks involved with this project. The foremost risk is a lack of interest in the new training program. Employee input is crucial for developing the improved training and for realizing its potential benefits on improving productivity. There are some technical risks in developing courses using advanced technologies. There are also risks related to outsourcing much of the labor and actual course materials/instruction. The main business risk is investing the time and money into this project and not realizing the projected benefits.

10.0 Exhibits

Exhibit A: Financial Analysis

		YEAR				
Discount rate	8%					
Assume the project is completed in Year 1						
	1	**2**	**3**	**4**	**TOTAL**	
Costs	1,000,000	400,000	400,000	400,000		
Discount factor	0.93	0.86	0.79	0.74		
Discounted costs	925,926	342,936	317,533	294,012	1,880,406	
Benefits	–	1,000,000	1,000,000	1,000,000		
Discount factor	0.93	0.86	0.79	0.74		
Discounted benefits	–	857,339	793,832	735,030	2,386,201	
Discounted benefits - costs	(925,926)	514,403	476,299	441,018	505,795	← NPV
Cumulative benefits - costs	(925,926)	(411,523)	64,777	505,795		
ROI ——————————→	27%					
		Payback in Year 3				
Assumptions						
Costs for the project are based on the following:						
Internal labor costs: $500,000						
Outsourced labor costs: $250,000						
Outsourced training costs: $250,000						
After implementation, maintenance costs are estimated at 40% of total development cost						
Benefits are estimated based on the following:						
$100/employee/year X 10,000 employees						
No benefits are included for increased productivity						

FIGURE 3-2 Financial analysis

CREATING A PROJECT CHARTER

After top management determines which projects to pursue, it is important to let the rest of the organization know about these projects. Management needs to create and distribute documentation to authorize project initiation. This documentation can take many different forms, but one common form is a project charter. A **project charter** is a document that formally recognizes the existence of a project and provides a summary of the project's objectives and management. It authorizes the project manager to use organizational resources to complete the project. Ideally, the project manager will play a major role in developing the project charter.

Instead of project charters, some organizations initiate projects using a simple letter of agreement, whereas others use much longer documents or formal contracts. When Global Construction initiates a building project for an outside organization, it still creates a separate charter and attaches it to the contract, which is usually a much longer, more complex document. (You will see an example of a contract for outsourced work for this project in Chapter 5.) A crucial part of the project charter is the sign-off section, where key project stakeholders sign the document to acknowledge their agreement on the need for the project.

Contents of a Project Charter

Contents of a project charter will also vary to meet individual project needs. Typical information included in a project charter includes the following:

- Project Title and Date of Authorization
- Project Start Date
- Project Finish Date
- Other Schedule Information (if available)
- Budget Information
- Project Manager (name and contact information)
- Project Objectives (brief description of what the main objectives are for the project)
- Approach (description of how the project objectives will be met, list of important assumptions, and often references to related documents)
- Roles and Responsibilities (names, roles, positions, and contact information)
- Sign-off
- Comments (allows stakeholders to document important information they want to add)

Project charters are normally short documents. Some are only one-page long, whereas others might be several pages long. The following section shows the project charter for the Just-In-Time Training project.

Sample Project Charter

Kristin drafted a project charter and had the project team members review it before showing it to Lucy. Lucy made a few minor changes, which Kristin incorporated, and then all the key stakeholders who would be working on the project signed the project charter. Table 3-5 shows the final project charter. Note that Lucy stated her concern about totally changing most training and terminating several contracts with local trainers. Also note that Tim

Nelson, director of supplier management, wanted to be heavily involved in deciding how to provide the supplier management training. Kristin knew that she would have to consider these concerns when managing the project.

TABLE 3-5 Sample project charter

Project Charter
July 16, 2007

Project Title: Just-In-Time Training Project
Project Start Date: July 1, 2007   **Projected Finish Date:** June 30, 2008

Budget Information: The firm has allocated $1,000,000 for this project. Approximately half of these costs will be for internal labor, whereas the other half will be for outsourced labor and training programs.

Project Manager: Kristin Maur, (610) 752-4896, kristin_maur@globalconstruction.com

Project Objectives: Develop a new training program that provides just-in-time training to employees on key topics, including supplier management, negotiating skills, project management, and software applications (spreadsheets and Web development). Reduce the training cost per employee by 10 percent, or $100 per employee per year. Develop an approach for measuring productivity improvements from this approach to training on an annual basis.

Approach:
- Terminate all internal training courses except the Six Sigma training after new courses are developed.
- Communicate to all employees the plans to improve internal training and let them know that tuition reimbursement will continue as is.
- Work closely with internal managers and employees to determine the best approaches for providing training in supplier management, negotiating skills, project management, and software applications.
- Research existing training, and work with outside experts to develop several alternatives for providing each training topic.
- Develop and implement new training.
- Take advantage of new training approaches and technologies, and encourage employees to take some training during nonworking hours.
- Encourage experts within the company to mentor other workers on current job duties.
- Determine a way to measure the effectiveness of the training and its impact on productivity on an annual basis.

Roles and Responsibilities:

Name and Signature	Role	Position	Contact Information
Mike Sundby	Project champion	VP of HR	mike_sundby@globalconstruction.com
Lucy Camarena	Project sponsor	Training director	lucy_camarena@globalconstruction.com
Kristin Maur	Project manager	Project manager	kristin_maur@globalconstruction.com
Julia Portman	Steering committee member	VP of IT	julia_portman@globalconstruction.com

TABLE 3-5 Sample project charter (continued)

Tim Nelson	Steering committee member	Supplier management director	tim_nelson@globalconstruction.com
Mohamed Abdul	Team member	Senior programmer/analyst	mohamed_abdul@globalconstruction.com
Kim Johnson	Team member	Curriculum designer	kim_johnson@globalconstruction.com
Etc.			

Comments: (Handwritten or typed comments from above stakeholders, if applicable)
"I am concerned about people's reactions to totally changing most training classes. I also hate to terminate some contracts with local training firms we've used for several years. We should try to get some of them involved in this project." Lucy
"I want to review all of the information related to providing the supplier management training. We need to make something available quickly." Tim

Because many projects fail because of unclear requirements and expectations, starting with a project charter makes sense. If project managers are having difficulty obtaining support from project stakeholders, for example, they can refer to what everyone agreed to in the project charter. After the charter is completed, it is good practice to hold an official kick-off meeting for the project.

MEDIA SNAPSHOT

Many people enjoy watching television shows like *Changing Rooms* or *Trading Spaces*, in which participants have two days and $1000 to update a room in their neighbor's house. Because the time and cost are set, it's the scope that has the most flexibility. Examples of some of the work completed include new flooring, light fixtures, paint, new shelves, and artwork to brighten up a dull room.

Designers on these shows often have to change initial scope goals due to budget or time constraints. For example, designers often go back to local stores to exchange such items as lights, artwork, or fabric for less-expensive items to meet budget constraints. Or they might describe a new piece of furniture they want the carpenter to build, but the carpenter changes the design or materials to meet time constraints. Occasionally, designers can buy more expensive items or have more elaborate furniture built because they underestimated costs and schedules.

continued

Another important issue related to project scope management is meeting customer expectations. Who wouldn't be happy with a professionally designed room at no cost to them? Although most homeowners are very happy with work done on the show, some are obviously disappointed. Unlike most projects in which the project team works closely with the customer, homeowners have little say in what is done and cannot inspect the work along the way. They walk into their newly decorated room with their eyes closed. Modernizing a room can mean something totally different to a homeowner than it does to an interior designer. For example, one woman was obviously shocked when she saw her bright orange kitchen with black appliances. Another couple couldn't believe there was moss on their bedroom walls. What happens when the homeowners don't like the work that's been done? The FAQ section of tlc.com says, "Everyone on our show is told upfront that there's a chance they won't like the final design of the room. Each applicant signs a release acknowledging that the show is not responsible for redecorating a room that isn't to the owner's taste." Too bad you can't get sponsors for most projects to sign a similar release form. It would make project management much easier!

HOLDING A PROJECT KICK-OFF MEETING

Experienced project managers know that it is crucial to get projects off to a great start. Holding a good kick-off meeting is an excellent way to do this. A **kick-off meeting** is a meeting held at the beginning of a project so that stakeholders can meet each other, review the goals of the project, and discuss future plans. The kick-off meeting is often held after the business case and project charter are completed, but it could be held sooner, as needed.

Purpose of the Kick-Off Meeting

Project kick-off meetings are often used to get support for a project and clarify roles and responsibilities. If there is a project champion, as there is for this project, he should speak first at the kick-off meeting and introduce the project sponsor and project manager. If anyone seems opposed to the project or unwilling to support it, the project champion—an experienced senior manager—should be able to handle the situation.

As discussed earlier in the chapter, there is normally a fair amount of work done before an official kick-off meeting for a project. At a minimum, the project manager and sponsor should have met several times, and other key stakeholders should have been involved in developing the project charter. The project manager should make sure the right people are invited to the kick-off meeting and send out an agenda in advance.

Sample Kick-Off Meeting Agenda

All project meetings with major stakeholders should include an agenda. Table 3-6 provides the agenda that Kristin provided for the Just-In-Time Training project kick-off meeting. Notice the main topics in an agenda:

- Meeting objective
- Agenda (lists in order the topics to be discussed)

- A section for documenting action items, who they are assigned to, and when each person will complete the action
- A section to document the date and time of the next meeting

TABLE 3-6 Sample kick-off meeting agenda

Kick-Off Meeting
July 16, 2007

Project Name: Just-In-Time Training Project

Meeting Objective: Get the project off to an effective start by introducing key stakeholders, reviewing project goals, and discussing future plans

Agenda:
- Introductions of attendees
- Review of the project background
- Review of project-related documents (i.e., business case, project charter)
- Discussion of project organizational structure
- Discussion of project scope, time, and cost goals
- Discussion of other important topics
- List of action items from meeting

Action Item	Assigned To	Due Date

Date and time of next meeting:

It is good practice to focus on results of meetings, and having sections for documenting action items and deciding on the next meeting date and time on the agenda helps to do so. It is also good practice to document meeting minutes, focusing on key decisions and action items, and to send them to all meeting participants and other appropriate stakeholders within a day or two of a meeting.

DEVELOPING A PRELIMINARY SCOPE STATEMENT

A **scope statement** is a document used to develop and confirm a common understanding of the project scope. It describes in detail the work to be accomplished on the project and is an important tool for preventing **scope creep**—the tendency for project scope to continually increase. It is helpful to create a *preliminary,* or initial, scope statement during project initiation so that the entire project team can start important discussions and work related to the project scope. As described in Chapter 4, a more detailed scope statement is prepared later in the project's life span as part of planning. There are usually several versions of the scope statement, and each one becomes more detailed as the project progresses and more information becomes available.

WHAT WENT WRONG?

There are many examples of poor scope management in the software industry. A highly publicized example is Nike's now infamous i2 supply-chain management problem. A software glitch from the $400 million project cost Nike more than $100 million in lost sales; depressed its stock price by 20 percent; triggered several class-action lawsuits; and caused its chairman, president, and CEO, Phil Knight, to lament, "This is what you get for $400 million...a speed bump." [3]

The Nike disaster provides a classic example of spending too much money on too much software and consulting, with too little to show for the effort. The company also moved too quickly in implementing new software without knowing how it might affect its older legacy systems. Nike has since recovered from this major software disaster and learned to be more patient in understanding and managing the scope of software projects.

Many projects fail due to poor scope management. Communications are an important part of this problem. It is often difficult for people to explain what they want and for all project stakeholders to remain on the same page when it comes to meeting scope goals. Figure 3-3 provides a version of a popular cartoon illustrating this problem. Even a project as simple as creating a tire swing can have many scope problems.

Contents of a Scope Statement

Scope statements, like project charters, also vary by project type. Complex projects have very long scope statements, whereas smaller projects have shorter scope statements. Items often described in a preliminary scope statement include, as a minimum, the product or service requirements and characteristics, a summary of all deliverables, and the project success criteria.

The scope statement should expand on information provided in the business case and project charter. Many scope statements also refer to other documents, such as specifications for particular products or relevant policies, procedures, or standards. Project managers must decide what aspects of scope are most important to define early in the project and document them in the preliminary scope statement. They should also establish a process for ensuring that everyone agrees on project scope throughout the project.

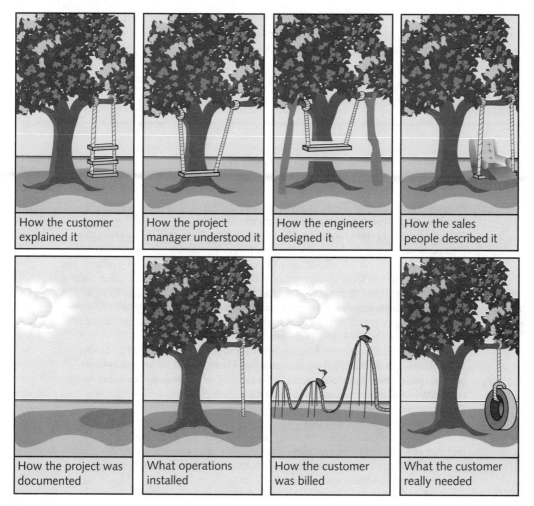

FIGURE 3-3 A swing is a swing is a swing?

For example, the project team could deliver prototypes of certain deliverables to make sure they are on track toward meeting customer needs.

Sample Sections of a Preliminary Scope Statement

Kristin and her team knew that it was crucial to provide effective training on all of the topics listed in their charter: supplier management, negotiating skills, project management, and software applications. They knew that training for improving supplier management and negotiating skills, especially international negotiations, had the highest priority. They also believed that the scope of this part of the project was the most difficult. The business case stated that internal staff would work with outside firms to develop a customized approach to this training that would take advantage of internal experts and new technologies.

Kristin had some experience working in supplier management, but she had no experience negotiating with foreign suppliers. She met with Tim Nelson, director of supplier management, to get his views on how to begin defining the scope of that part of the project. Table 3-7 provides part of the preliminary scope statement.

TABLE 3-7 Sample section of preliminary scope statement

Preliminary Scope Statement
July 23, 2007

Project Name: Just-In-Time Training Project
Product Characteristics and Requirements
1. Supplier management training: The supplier management director estimates the need to train at least 100 employees each year in supplier management. There should be three levels of courses: an executive course, an introductory course, and an advanced course. Course materials should be developed as a joint effort among internal experts, outside training firms, and key suppliers. A partnership should be developed to maximize the effectiveness of the training and minimize development costs. Different delivery methods should be explored, including instructor-led, CD-ROM, and Web-based.
2. Negotiating skills training: Employees from supplier management and other departments would benefit from this training. There should be several courses offered, including a basic course, a course tailored to negotiating contracts, and a course tailored to international negotiations.
Deliverables:
1. Supplier management training:
    1.1. Needs assessment: A study will be conducted to determine the learning objectives for the executive, introductory, and advanced courses.
    1.2 Research of existing training: A short study will identify current training courses and materials available.
    1.3. Partnerships: Partnership agreements will be made to get outside training organizations and suppliers to work on developing and providing training.
    1.4. Course design and development.
    1.5. Pilot course.
    Etc.

Project Success Criteria: Our sponsor has stated that the project will be a success if the new training courses are all available within one year, if the average course evaluations are at least 3.0 on a 1–5 scale, and if the company reduces its training costs per employee by 10 percent each year.

As you can see, substantial effort should go into initiating projects. It is crucial to get projects off to a good start.

CASE WRAP-UP

Kristin was pleased with work completed in initiating the Just-In-Time Training project, as were the project sponsor and other key stakeholders. Kristin met weekly with the project steering committee to review project progress. She found the committee to be very helpful, especially when dealing with several challenges they encountered. For example, it was difficult finding a large enough conference room for the kick-off meeting and setting up the Webcast to allow other stakeholders to participate in the meeting. She was also a bit nervous before running the meeting, but Lucy and Mike, the project sponsor and champion, helped her relax and stepped in when people questioned the need for the project. There were also indications that several key departments would not be represented at the kick-off meeting, but Mike made sure that they were. Kristin could see how important senior management support was on this project, in particular for obtaining buy-in from all parts of the organization.

Chapter Summary

The five project management process groups are initiating, planning, executing, monitoring and controlling, and closing. These processes occur at varying levels of intensity throughout each phase of a project, and specific outcomes are produced as a result of each process.

Mapping the main activities of each project management process group into the nine project management knowledge areas provides a big picture of what activities are involved in project management. Some organizations develop their own project management methodologies, often using the standards found in the *PMBOK® Guide* as a foundation. It is important to tailor project management methodologies to meet the organization's particular needs.

Global Construction's Just-In-Time Training project demonstrates the process of initiating a project. After a project is approved, senior managers often meet to perform several pre-initiating tasks, as follows:

- Determining the scope, time, and cost constraints for the project
- Assigning the project sponsor
- Selecting the project manager
- Meeting with the project manager to review the process and expectations for managing the project
- Determining if the project should be broken down into two or more smaller projects

The main tasks normally involved in project initiation are the following:

- Identifying and understanding project stakeholders
- Preparing a business case for the project
- Creating the project charter
- Holding a kick-off meeting
- Developing a preliminary scope statement

Descriptions of how each of these tasks was accomplished and samples of related outputs are described in the chapter.

Quick Quiz

1. In which of the five project management process groups is the most time and money usually spent?
   a. initiating
   b. planning
   c. executing
   d. monitoring and controlling
   e. closing

2. In which of the five project management process groups are activities performed that relate to each knowledge area?
   a. initiating
   b. planning

c. executing

d. monitoring and controlling

e. closing

3. Why are larger projects often broken down into two or more smaller projects?

a. to reduce investment costs

b. to more easily convince senior management to support them

c. so that more people can gain experience as project managers

d. because it is easier to successfully complete a small project than a large one

4. What document provides justification for investing in a project?

a. project charter

b. business case

c. preliminary scope statement

d. stakeholder analysis

5. What document formally recognizes the existence of a project and provides direction on the project's objectives and management?

a. project charter

b. business case

c. preliminary scope statement

d. stakeholder analysis

6. What is a crucial part of the project charter—a section in which key project stakeholders acknowledge their agreement on the need for the project?

a. project objectives

b. approach

c. roles and responsibilities

d. sign-off

7. Which project document should not be made available to all key project stakeholders due to its sensitive nature?

a. project charter

b. business case

c. preliminary scope statement

d. stakeholder analysis

8. All project meetings with major stakeholders should include _____ .

a. an agenda

b. food

c. name tags

d. all of the above

9. The tendency for project scope to increase is called _____ .

   a. gold-plating

   b. incremental planning

   c. scope creep

   d. analysis paralysis

10. Which of the following is not documented in a preliminary scope statement?

    a. project success criteria

    b. product characteristics and requirements

    c. deliverables

    d. roles and responsibilities

Quick Quiz Answers

1. C; 2. B; 3. D; 4. B; 5. A; 6. D; 7. D; 8. A; 9. C; 10. D

Discussion Questions

1. Briefly describe what happens in each of the five project management process groups (initiating, planning, executing, monitoring and controlling, and closing). On which process should team members spend the most time? Why?

2. What pre-initiating tasks were performed for the Just-In-Time Training project? Does it make sense to do these tasks? What are the main initiating tasks?

3. What is the main purpose of performing a stakeholder analysis? When should it be done, and who should see the results?

4. Describe the purpose of a business case and its main contents.

5. Why should projects have a project charter? What is the main information included in a project charter?

6. Discuss the process for holding a project kick-off meeting. Who should attend? What key topics should be on the agenda?

7. Why is it important to develop a preliminary project scope statement during project initiation?

Exercises

1. Find an example of a large project that took more than a year to complete, such as a major construction project. Why was the project initiated? Describe some of the pre-initiating and initiating tasks completed for the project. Write a one-page paper or prepare a short presentation summarizing your findings.

2. Review the business case for the Just-in-Time Training project. Do you think there is solid business justification for doing this project? Why or why not? What parts of the business case do you think could be stronger? How? Write a one-page paper or prepare a short presentation summarizing your findings.

3. Search the Internet for "project charter." Find at least three good references that describe project charters. Write a one-page paper or prepare a short presentation summarizing your findings.

Team Projects

1. Your organization has decided to initiate a project to raise money for an important charity. Assume that there are 1000 people in your organization. Use the pre-initiating tasks described in this chapter to develop a strategy for how to proceed. Be creative in describing your organization; the charity; the scope, time, and cost constraints for the project; and so on. Document your ideas in a one- to two-page paper or a short presentation.

2. You are part of a team in charge of a project to help people in your company (500 people) lose weight. This project is part of a competition, and the top "losers" will be featured in a popular television show. Assume that you have six months to complete the project and a budget of $10,000. Develop a project charter for this project using the sample provided in this chapter. Be creative in developing detailed information to include in the charter.

3. Using the information you developed in Team Project 1 or 2, role-play the kick-off meeting for this project. Follow the sample agenda provided in this chapter.

4. Perform the applicable pre-initiating and initiating tasks for one of the real projects your class or group developed in Chapter 1, Team Project 3. Prepare a business case, if applicable; a project charter; and key parts of a preliminary scope statement.

Companion Web Site

Visit the companion Web site for this text (*www.course.com/mis/pm/schwalbe*) to access:

- Lecture notes
- Interactive quizzes
- Template files
- Sample documents
- Guide to Using Project 2003
- VPMi enterprise project management software
- More ideas for team projects, including real projects and case studies
- Links to additional resources related to project management

Key Terms

business case — A document that provides justification for investing in a project.

champion — A senior manager who acts as a key proponent for a project.

closing processes — The actions that involve formalizing acceptance of the project or phase and bringing it to an orderly end.

deliverable — A product or service produced or provided as part of a project.

executing processes — The actions that involve coordinating people and other resources to carry out the project plans and produce the deliverables of the project.

initiating processes — The actions to begin or end projects and project phases.

kick-off meeting — A meeting held at the beginning of a project so that stakeholders can meet each other, review the goals of the project, and discuss future plans.

methodology — A plan that describes how things should be done to manage a project.

monitoring and controlling processes — The actions taken to measure progress toward achieving project goals, monitor deviation from plans, and take corrective action.

phase — A distinct stage in project development.

planning processes — The actions that involve devising and maintaining a workable scheme to ensure that the project meets its scope, time, and cost goals as well as organizational needs.

process — A series of actions directed toward a particular result.

project charter — A document that formally recognizes the existence of a project and provides a summary of the project's objectives and management.

project management office (PMO) — An organizational entity created to assist project managers in achieving project goals.

project management process groups — The progression from initiating activities to planning activities, executing activities, monitoring and controlling activities, and closing activities.

scope creep — The tendency for project scope to continually increase.

scope statement — A document used to develop and confirm a common understanding of the project scope.

stakeholder analysis — A document that provides information on key stakeholders to help manage relationships with them.

standard — A document that describes best practices for what should be done to manage a project.

template — A file with a preset format that serves as a starting point for creating various documents so that the format and structure do not have to be re-created.

End Notes

[1] William Ibbs and Justin Reginato, *Quantifying the Value of Project Management*, Project Management Institute (2002).

[2] AST Group, "Can You Quantify the Value of Enterprise Project Management in Your Organisation?" *ITWeb Tech Forum* (March 17, 2005).

[3] Christopher Koch, "Nike Rebounds: How (and Why) Nike Recovered from its Supply Chain Disaster," *CIO Magazine* (June 15, 2004).

CHAPTER 4

PLANNING PROJECTS, PART I (PROJECT INTEGRATION, SCOPE, TIME, AND COST MANAGEMENT)

LEARNING OBJECTIVES

After reading this chapter, you will be able to:

- Describe the importance of creating plans to guide project execution, and list several planning tasks and outputs for project integration, scope, time, and cost management

- Discuss project integration management planning tasks, and explain the purpose and contents of a team contract and a project management plan

- Explain the project scope management planning tasks, and create a scope management plan, scope statement, work breakdown structure (WBS), and WBS dictionary

- Describe the project time management planning tasks, and prepare a project schedule based on activity and milestone lists, activity sequencing, durations, and resources

- Discuss the project cost management planning tasks, and create a cost estimate and cost baseline

OPENING CASE

Kristin Maur continued to work with her project team and other key stakeholders on the Just-In-Time Training project. She knew that it was crucial to do a good job in planning all aspects of the project, and strongly believed that execution would be much smoother if they had good plans to follow. She also knew that it was important to involve the people who would be doing the work in actually planning the work, and that planning was an iterative process. Involving key people in the planning process and keeping the plans up to date had been her main challenges on past projects, so Kristin focused proactively on those areas.

Kristin and her team were fortunate to have many templates to use in developing several planning documents. They could also review examples of planning documents from past and current projects available on Global Construction's intranet site and use project management software to enter key planning data. Kristin also found that the project steering committee that had been set up during project initiation gave her very helpful advice. Several experienced members warned her to be thorough in planning but not to become bogged down in too much detail.

INTRODUCTION

Many people have heard the following sayings:

- If you fail to plan, you plan to fail.
- If you don't know where you're going, any road will take you there.
- What gets measured gets managed.

All of these sayings emphasize the fact that planning is crucial to achieving goals. Successful project managers know how important it is to develop, refine, and follow plans to meet project goals, and they know how easy it is to become sidetracked if they do not have good plans to follow. They also know that people are more likely to perform well if they know what they are supposed to do and when.

Project Planning Should Guide Project Execution

Planning is often the most difficult and unappreciated process in project management. Often, people do not want to take the time to plan well, but theory and practice show that good planning is crucial to good execution. *The main purpose of project planning is to guide project execution.* To guide execution, plans must be realistic and useful, so a fair amount of time and effort must go into the project planning process.

WHAT WENT WRONG?

Based on their experiences, many people have a dim view of plans. Top managers often require a plan, but then no one tracks whether the plan was followed. For example, one project manager said he would meet with each project team leader within two months to review their project plans, and he even created a detailed schedule for these reviews. He canceled the first meeting due to another business commitment; he rescheduled the next meeting for unexplained personal reasons. Two months later, the project manager had still not met with over half of the project team leaders. Why should project team members feel obligated to follow their own plans when the project manager obviously does not follow his?

Recall from Chapter 3 that project planning involves devising and maintaining a workable scheme to ensure that the project meets its scope, time, and cost goals as well as organizational needs. Also, recall that planning includes tasks related to each of the nine project management knowledge areas. This chapter describes the types of planning performed in four of the knowledge areas—project integration, scope, time, and cost management—and summarizes the planning done for Global Construction's Just-In-Time Training project. Chapter 5 focuses on planning done as part of the other five knowledge areas—quality, human resource, communications, risk, and procurement management.

Summary of Planning Tasks and Outputs

The *PMBOK® Guide* lists over 50 documents that project teams can produce as part of project planning. Other experts suggest even more potential planning documents. Every project is unique, so project managers and their teams must determine which planning outputs are needed for their projects and how they should be created.

Table 4-1 summarizes the project planning outputs for integration, scope, time, and cost management that Global Construction will use for the Just-In-Time Training project. All of these planning documents, as well as other project-related information, will be available to all team members on a project Web site. Global Construction has used project Web sites for several years, and everyone agrees that they significantly facilitate communications.

TABLE 4-1 Planning outputs for project integration, scope, time, and cost management

Knowledge area	Outputs
Project integration management	Team contract Project management plan
Project scope management	Scope management plan Scope statement Work breakdown structure (WBS) WBS dictionary

TABLE 4-1 Planning outputs for project integration, scope, time, and cost management (continued)

Knowledge area	Outputs
Project time management	Activity list and attributes
	Milestone list
	Network diagram (showing activity dependencies)
	Activity resource requirements
	Activity duration estimates
	Project schedule (in Gantt chart format)
Project cost management	Cost estimate
	Cost baseline

The following sections describe planning tasks in the first four knowledge areas and then provide examples of applying them to the Just-In-Time Training project at Global Construction. You can consider many of these planning tasks as following a chronological order, especially for the scope, time, and cost tasks. You need to plan the project scope and determine what activities need to be done before you can develop a detailed project schedule. Likewise, you need a detailed project schedule before you can develop a cost baseline. Of course, human resource planning and appointment to the project team must also be accomplished at the start of a project as part of project human resource management. As noted earlier, there are many interdependencies between various knowledge areas and process groups.

PROJECT INTEGRATION MANAGEMENT PLANNING TASKS

Project integration management involves coordinating all the project management knowledge areas throughout a project's life span. The main planning tasks performed as part of project integration management include creating a team contract and developing the project management plan.

Team Contracts

Global Construction believes in using **team contracts** to help promote teamwork and clarify team communications. After core project team members have been selected, they meet to prepare a team contract. The process normally includes reviewing a template and then working in small groups of three to four people to prepare inputs for the team contract. Creating smaller groups makes it easier for everyone to contribute ideas. Each group then shares their ideas on what the contract should contain, and then they work together to form one project team contract. Ideally, the contract should be finished in a one- to two-hour meeting. The project manager should attend the meeting and act as a coach or facilitator, observing the different personalities of team members and seeing how well they work together. It is crucial to emphasize the importance of the project team throughout the project's life cycle. The team contract should provide the groundwork for how the project team will function.

Sample Team Contract

Table 4-2 shows the team contract created for the Just-In-Time Training project. Notice that the main topics covered include the following:

- Code of conduct
- Participation
- Communication
- Problem solving
- Meeting guidelines

Everyone involved in creating the team contract should sign it. As new project team members are added, the project manager should review ground rules with them and have them read and sign the contract as well.

Project Management Plans

To coordinate and integrate information across all project management knowledge areas and across the organization, there must be a good project management plan. A **project management plan,** which is a deliverable for the project integration management knowledge area, is a document used to coordinate all project planning documents and to help guide a project's execution and control. Plans created in the other knowledge areas are subsidiary parts of the overall project management plan. Project management plans facilitate communication among stakeholders and provide a baseline for progress measurement and project control, as discussed in detail in Chapter 7. A **baseline** is a starting point, a measurement, or an observation that is documented so that it can be used for future comparison. The project management plan briefly describes the overall scope, time, and cost baselines for the project. Specific plans in each of those knowledge areas provide more detailed baseline information. For example, the project management plan might provide a high-level budget baseline for the entire project, whereas the cost baseline prepared as part of the project cost management knowledge area (explained later in this chapter) provides detailed cost projections by WBS by month.

Project management plans should be dynamic, flexible, and receptive to change when the environment or project changes. These plans should greatly assist the project manager in leading the project team and assessing project status. Just as projects are unique, so are project plans. For a small project involving a few people over a couple of months, a project charter, team contract, scope statement, and Gantt chart might be the only project planning documents needed; there would not be a need for a separate project management plan. A large project involving 100 people over three years would benefit from having a detailed project management plan and separate plans for each knowledge area. It is important to tailor all planning documentation to fit the needs of specific projects. Because all project plans should help guide the completion of the particular project, they should be only as detailed as needed for each project.

TABLE 4-2 Sample team contract

Team Contract
July 9, 2007

Project Name: Just-In-Time Training Project

Project Team Members' Names and Sign-Off:

Name	Date
Kristin Maur	July 9, 2007
Etc.	

Code of Conduct: As a project team, we will:
- Work proactively, anticipating potential problems and preventing their occurrence.
- Keep other team members informed of information related to the project.
- Focus on what is best for the entire project team.

Participation: We will:
- Be honest and open during all project activities.
- Provide the opportunity for equal participation.
- Be open to new approaches and consider new ideas.
- Let the project manager know well in advance if a team member has to miss a meeting or may have trouble meeting a deadline for a given task.

Communication: We will:
- Keep discussions on track and have one discussion at a time.
- Use the telephone, e-mail, a project Web site, instant messaging, and other technology to assist in communicating.
- Have the project manager or designated person facilitate all meetings and arrange for phone and videoconferences, as needed.
- Work together to create the project schedule and related information and enter actuals, issues, risks, and other information into our enterprise project management system by 4 p.m. every Friday.

Problem Solving: We will:
- Only use constructive criticism and focus on solving problems, not blaming people.
- Strive to build on each other's ideas.
- Bring in outside experts when necessary.

Meeting Guidelines: We will:
- Plan to have a face-to-face meeting of the entire project team every Tuesday morning.
- Arrange for telephone or videoconferencing for participants as needed.
- Hold other meetings as needed.
- Develop and follow an agenda for all meetings.
- Record meeting minutes and send them out via e-mail within 24 hours of all project meetings, focusing on decisions made and action items and issues from each meeting.

There are, however, common elements to most project management plans, as follows:

- Introduction/overview of the project
- Project organization
- Management and technical processes
- Work to be performed
- Schedule information
- Budget information
- References to other project planning documents

Sample Project Management Plan

Table 4-3 provides partial information from the initial project management plan for Global Construction's Just-In-Time Training project. Of course, the actual document would be longer because this is a one-year, $1 million project involving many different stakeholders, including outside suppliers. The document would also be updated as needed. It is important to mark the date and version number on the document to avoid confusion. Also note that project organization varies on projects, so it is helpful to provide a high-level project organizational chart in the project management plan. On some projects, the project sponsor and project champion are the same person, but not always. Projects that cross functional boundaries, as the Just-In-Time Training project does, often benefit from having a high-level project champion, such as a vice president.

TABLE 4-3 Sample project management plan

Project Management Plan Version 1.0
September 17, 2007

Project Name: Just-in-Time Training Project
Introduction/Overview of the Project
Global Construction employs 10,000 full-time employees in ten different counties and fifteen U.S. states. The company spends, on average, $1,000 per employee for training (not including tuition reimbursement), which is higher than the industry average. By redesigning training, Global Construction can reduce training costs and improve productivity. The main goal of this project is to develop a new training program that provides just-in-time training to employees on key topics, including supplier management, negotiating skills, project management, and software applications.

Project Organization
The basic organization of the project is provided in Figure 4-1. The project sponsor, Lucy Camarena, will have the final say on major decisions, with consultation from the project steering committee and the project champion, Mike Sundby. The project sponsor should have time to thoroughly review important project information and provide timely feedback to the project manager. The project manager in this case reports to the project sponsor, and the team leaders and supplier project managers report to the project manager.

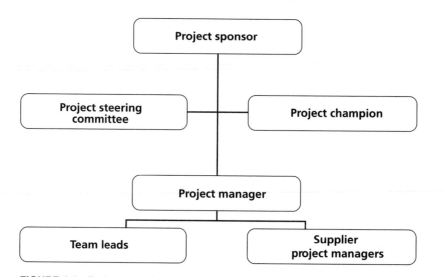

FIGURE 4-1 Project organizational chart

Management and Technical Processes
Management Processes:
1. Management Review Process: The project steering committee will meet at least monthly to provide inputs and review progress on this project.
2. Progress Measurement Process: The project steering committee will review project progress during project review meetings, and they can also review information as needed by viewing reports on the enterprise project

---

TABLE 4-3 Sample project plan (continued)

management software system. Earned value data will be provided for this project and available on a weekly basis in the system. Post-project progress will also be measured to see if the project met its goals. These goals include reducing the training cost per employee by $100/person/year and receiving positive results from survey participants on the effectiveness of the training.

3. Change Approval Process: See Attachment 1 based on corporate standards.
4. Supplier Management Process: See Attachment 2 based on corporate standards.

Technical Processes:

1. Enterprise Project Management Software: All tasks, costs, resources, issues, and risks will be tracked for this project using our enterprise project management software. Data must be entered on at least a weekly basis to provide timely information.
2. Supplier Evaluation: The project team will coordinate with the purchasing department to follow our standard procedures for selecting and working with suppliers. See Attachment 2 for corporate standards.
3. Productivity Improvement: The project team will work with the finance and quality assurance departments to develop and implement a system to measure improvements in employee productivity that result from this new training program. The finance department will report on this information annually, beginning one year after the first new training course is offered.

Work to Be Performed

Summary: Research, develop or purchase, and implement a new just-in-time training program covering the topics of supplier management, negotiating skills, project management, and software applications, and determine a way to measure the effectiveness of the training and its impact on productivity on an annual basis. See the scope statement, WBS, and other scope documents for further details.

Schedule Information

The entire project will be completed in one year, with a projected completion date of June 30, 2008. See the project schedule and other time management documents for further details.

Budget Information

The total budget for this project is $1,000,000. Approximately half of these costs will be for internal labor, whereas the other half will be for outsourced labor and training programs. See the cost estimate and cost baseline for further details.

References to Other Project Planning Documents

All current project plans created for this project are provided in Appendix A. Initial documents and revisions are available on the project Web site.

PROJECT SCOPE MANAGEMENT PLANNING TASKS

Project scope management involves defining and controlling what work is or is not included in a project. The main planning tasks performed as part of project scope management include scope planning, scope definition, and creating the WBS. The main documents produced are a scope management plan, scope statement, WBS, and WBS dictionary.

Scope Planning and the Scope Management Plan

A project's size, complexity, importance, as well as other factors affect how much effort is spent on scope planning. The main output of scope planning is a **scope management plan**, which is a document that includes descriptions of how the team will prepare the scope statement, create the WBS, verify completion of the project deliverables (described in the scope statement in Table 4-5), and control requests for changes to the project scope. Key inputs to the scope management plan include the project charter, preliminary scope statement, and project management plan, as described previously. Additional inputs include policies and procedures related to scope management and historical information about previous projects. Environmental factors, such as marketplace conditions, also affect project scope planning.

Sample Scope Management Plan

Kristin and her team had already created a project charter and a preliminary scope statement as part of project initiation. The project sponsor and other key stakeholders had reviewed and approved both of these documents. Kristin continued to work with her team to decide how they would prepare the more detailed scope statement and WBS. It was also important to document how the team would verify completion of project deliverables and manage change requests related to the project scope. (Change requests are used to formally document changes to project plans, as described more fully in Chapter 7.) Table 4-4 shows an abbreviated version of a scope statement for the Just-In-Time Training project. As with other planning documents, Krisin's team would update it as needed.

Scope Definition and the Scope Statement

Good scope definition is crucial to project success because it helps improve the accuracy of time, cost, and resource estimates; defines a baseline for performance measurement and project control; and aids in communicating clear work responsibilities. Work that is not included in the scope statement should not be done. The main techniques used in scope definition include analyzing products, identifying alternative approaches to doing the work, understanding and analyzing stakeholder needs, and using expert judgment. The main output of scope definition is the scope statement.

As described in Chapter 3, the project team develops a preliminary scope statement during project initiation. The preliminary project scope statement should provide basic scope information, and subsequent scope statements should clarify and provide information that is more specific. Although contents vary, scope statements should include, at a minimum, a description of the project, including its overall objectives and justification; detailed descriptions of all project deliverables; characteristics and requirements of products and services produced as part of the project; and project success criteria. It should also reference supporting documents, such as product specifications and corporate policies, which often affect how products or services are produced.

Sample Scope Statement

Kristin worked closely with her team to develop the first full version of the scope statement, reviewing information from the preliminary scope statement and meeting several times with key stakeholders to develop a thorough document. Part of the scope statement is shown

TABLE 4-4   Sample scope management plan

Scope Management Plan
July 17, 2007

Project Name: Just-In-Time Training Project

Introduction

The purpose of this document is to provide suggestions and guidance for preparing several important scope management documents related to the Just-In-Time Training project at Global Construction.

Preparing the Scope Statement

The preliminary scope statement will provide the basis for preparing more detailed scope statements. It is also important to review the scope statement with key stakeholders, especially the project sponsor, potential suppliers, and users of the project deliverables. The scope statement will become longer and more detailed as the project progresses. To limit the length and complexity of the scope statement, it is best to reference and include several attachments, such as product descriptions, specifications, and corporate standards. Each version of the scope statement should be clearly labeled and dated to ensure that everyone uses the most recent version. Changes and additions will be highlighted and communicated to affected personnel. The scope statement will be available on the password-protected project Web site.

Creating the Work Breakdown Structure (WBS)

The project team should work together to create the WBS. The project sponsor and project steering committee should review the WBS to ensure that it includes all of the work required to complete the project. The project team should review WBSs of similar projects, review corporate guidelines for creating WBSs, and focus on determining all of the deliverables required for the project. The tasks required to complete each deliverable should also be determined. These tasks should include product- and process-related tasks. A general guideline to follow for determining the level of detail is that the lowest level of the WBS should normally take no longer than two weeks to complete. The WBS can be revised as needed, and the sponsor and steering committee must approve these revisions.

Verifying Completion of Project Deliverables

The project manager will work with the sponsor and steering committee to develop a process for verifying successful completion of project deliverables. In general, the project sponsor will be responsible for verifying the completion of major deliverables. The contract administrator will also be involved in verifying successful completion of deliverables received from outside sources. Contracts will include clauses describing the scope verification process.

Managing Requests for Changes to Project Scope

All requests for changes to project scope that may have significant effects on meeting project requirements must follow the formal change-control procedures specified in Attachment 1. A change request form will be completed and reviewed by the appropriate group. It is crucial to follow these procedures to prevent scope creep.

in Table 4-5. Note that the scope statement documents the product characteristics and requirements, summarizes the deliverables, and describes project success criteria. Kristin knew that this document would change as they finalized more details of the project scope.

TABLE 4-5 Sample scope statement

Scope Statement, Version 1.0
August 1, 2007

Project Title: Just In-Time Training Project

Project Justification
Strategic planning initiatives identified the opportunity to improve productivity and reduce costs by changing Global Construction's approach to internal training. The project team will develop a new training program that provides just-in-time training to employees on key topics, including supplier management, negotiating skills, project management, and software applications.

Product Characteristics and Requirements
1. Supplier management training: The supplier management director estimates the need to train at least 100 employees each year in supplier management. There should be three levels of courses: an executive course, an introductory course, and an advanced course. Course materials should be developed as a joint effort among internal experts, outside training experts, if needed, and key suppliers. This training must be tailored to our business needs. A partnership might be developed to maximize the effectiveness of the training and minimize development costs. Different delivery methods should be explored, including instructor-led, CD-ROM, and Web-based. About half of employees would prefer an instructor-led approach, and about half would prefer a self-paced course they could take at their convenience.

2. Negotiating skills training: Employees from supplier management and other departments would benefit from this training. There should be several courses offered, including a basic course, a course tailored to negotiating contracts, and a course tailored to international negotiations. Different delivery methods should be explored, including instructor-led, CD-ROM, and Web-based.

Etc.

Deliverables
Project Management-Related Deliverables: Team contract, project management plan, scope management plan, scope statement, WBS, etc.
Product-Related Deliverables:
1. Supplier management training:
    1.1. Needs assessment: A survey will be conducted to determine the learning objectives for the executive, introductory, and advanced courses.
    1.2 Research of existing training: A study will be done to identify current training courses and materials available.
    1.3. Partnerships: Partnership agreements will be explored to get outside training organizations and suppliers to work on developing and providing training.
    1.4. Course development: Appropriate materials will be developed for each course. Materials could take various formats, including written, video, CD-ROM, and Web-based. Materials should include interactivity to keep learners engaged.
    1.5. Pilot course: A pilot course will be provided for the introductory supplier management course. Feedback from the pilot course will be incorporated into future courses.
2. Negotiating skills training:
    2.1. Needs assessment: A survey will be conducted to determine the learning objectives for the basic negotiations, contract negotiations, and international negotiations courses.

TABLE 4-5 Sample scope statement (continued)

> 2.2 Research of existing training: A study will be done to identify current training courses and materials available.
> Etc.
> **Project Success Criteria**
> Our sponsor has stated that the project will be a success if the new training courses are all available within one year, if the average course evaluations are at least 3.0 on a 1-5 scale, and if the company recoups the cost of the project in reduced training costs within two years after project completion.

As more information becomes available and decisions are made related to project scope—such as specific products that will be purchased or changes that have been approved—the project team should update the project scope statement. Different iterations of the scope statement should be named Version 1.0, Version 2.0, and so on. These updates might also require changes to the scope management plan. For example, if the team decides to purchase products or services for the project from a supplier with whom it has never worked, the scope management plan should include information on working with that new supplier.

An up-to-date project scope statement is an important document for developing and confirming a common understanding of the project scope. It describes in detail the work to be accomplished on the project and is an important tool for ensuring customer satisfaction and preventing scope creep.

Creating the Work Breakdown Structure

A **work breakdown structure (WBS)** is a deliverable-oriented grouping of the work involved in a project that defines the total scope of the project. In other words, the WBS is a document that breaks all the work required for the project into discrete tasks, and groups those tasks into a logical hierarchy. Because most projects involve many people and many different deliverables, it is important to organize and divide the work into logical parts based on how the work will be performed. The WBS is a foundation document in project management because it provides the basis for planning and managing project schedules, costs, resources, and changes. Because the WBS defines the total scope of the project, some project management experts believe that work should not be done on a project if it is not included in the WBS. Therefore, it is crucial to develop a good WBS.

A WBS is often depicted in a graphical format, similar to an organizational chart. The name of the entire project is the top box, called level 0, and the main groupings for the work are listed in the second tier of boxes, called level 1. Each of those boxes can be broken down into subsequent tiers of boxes to show the hierarchy of the work. Project teams often organize the WBS around project products, project phases, or other logical groupings. People often like to create a WBS in a graphical format first to help them visualize the whole project and all of its main parts. You can also show a WBS in tabular form as an indented list of tasks showing the groupings of the work. Note that the term "task" is used to describe each level of work in the WBS. For example, in Figure 4-2, the following items can be referred to as tasks: the level 1 item called Concept, the level 2 item below that called Define

Requirements, and the level 3 item below that called Define User Requirements. Tasks that are decomposed into smaller tasks are called summary tasks.

Figure 4-2 shows a sample WBS in both chart and tabular form. Notice that both of these formats show the same information. Many documents, such as contracts, use the tabular format. Project management software also uses this format. The WBS becomes the contents of the Task Name column in Microsoft Project 2003, and the hierarchy or level of tasks is shown by indenting and numbering tasks within the software.

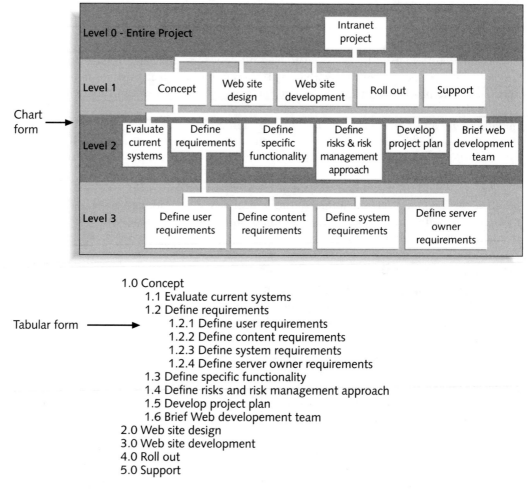

Chart form →

Tabular form →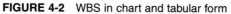

1.0 Concept
    1.1 Evaluate current systems
    1.2 Define requirements
        1.2.1 Define user requirements
        1.2.2 Define content requirements
        1.2.3 Define system requirements
        1.2.4 Define server owner requirements
    1.3 Define specific functionality
    1.4 Define risks and risk management approach
    1.5 Develop project plan
    1.6 Brief Web developement team
2.0 Web site design
3.0 Web site development
4.0 Roll out
5.0 Support

FIGURE 4-2   WBS in chart and tabular form

In Figure 4-2, the lowest level of the WBS is level 3. A **work package** is a task at the lowest level of the WBS. It also represents the level of work that the project manager monitors and controls. You can think of work packages in terms of accountability and reporting. If a project has a relatively short time frame and requires weekly progress reports, a work package might represent work completed in one week or less. On the other hand, if a project has a very long time frame and requires quarterly progress reports, a work package might represent work completed in one month or more. A work package might also be the procurement of a specific product or products, such as an item or items purchased from an outside source.

The sample WBS shown here seems somewhat easy to construct and understand. *Nevertheless, it is very difficult to create a good WBS.* To create a good WBS, you must understand both the project and its scope, and incorporate the needs and knowledge of the stakeholders. The project manager and the project team must decide as a group how to organize the work and how many levels to include in the WBS. Many project managers have found that it is better to focus on getting the top levels done well to avoid being distracted by too much detail.

Many people confuse tasks on a WBS with specifications. Tasks on a WBS represent work that needs to be done to complete the project. For example, if you are creating a WBS to redesign a kitchen, you might have level 1 categories called design, purchasing, flooring, walls, cabinets, and appliances. Under flooring, you might have work packages to remove the old flooring, install the new flooring, and install the trim. You would not have items like "12' by 14' of light oak" or "flooring must be durable" on a WBS.

Another concern when creating a WBS is how to organize it so that it provides the basis for the project schedule. You should focus on what work needs to be done and how it will be done, not when it will be done. In other words, the tasks do not have to be developed as a sequential list of steps. If you do want some time-based flow for the work, you can create a WBS using the project management process groups of initiating, planning, executing, controlling, and closing as level 1 in the WBS. By doing this, not only does the project team follow good project management practice, but the WBS tasks can be mapped more easily against time.

MEDIA SNAPSHOT

Few events get more media attention than the Olympic Games. Imagine all the work involved in planning and executing an event that involves thousands of athletes from around the world with millions of spectators. The 2002 Olympic Winter Games and Paralympics took five years to plan and cost more than $1.9 billion. PMI awarded the Salt Lake Organizing Committee (SLOC) the Project of the Year award for delivering world-class games that, according to the International Olympic Committee, "made a profound impact upon the people of the world."[1]

Four years before the Games began, the SLOC used a Primavera software-based system with a cascading color-coded WBS to integrate planning. A year before the Games, they added a Venue Integrated Planning Schedule to help the team integrate resource needs, budgets, and plans. For example, this software helped the team coordinate different areas involved in controlling access into and around a venue, such as roads, pedestrian pathways, seating and safety provisions, and hospitality areas, saving nearly $10 million.[2]

Sample WBS

The Just-In-Time Training project team decided to use the project management process groups for the level 1 tasks in its WBS. (Remember that the process groups include initiating, planning, executing, controlling, and closing.) The level 2 tasks under "Executing" (where the products and services of the project are produced) included course design and development, course administration, course evaluation, and stakeholder communications. The project team knew that they had to have strong communications to make the project a success, so they created a separate WBS level 2 category for communications under "Executing." They focused on the product deliverables they had to produce in breaking down the course design and development task by having level 3 categories based on the types of courses: supplier management, negotiating skills, project management, and software applications.

Table 4-6 shows part of the initial WBS Kristin and her team created. You will see this same information later in this chapter as the task names in the Gantt chart. Some tasks have been broken down into more detail while others have not. Recall that the scope statement should list and describe all the work required for the project. To define the scope of the project accurately, it is very important to ensure consistency between the project charter, scope statement, WBS, Gantt chart, and related documents. It is also very important to involve the entire project team and other stakeholders in creating and reviewing the WBS. *People who will do the work should help to plan the work* by creating the WBS. It is important to let workers be creative and know that they have a say in how their work is done. Having group meetings to develop a WBS helps everyone understand *what* work must be done for the entire project and *how* it should be done, given the people involved. It also helps to identify where coordination between different work packages will be required.

Creating the WBS Dictionary

Many of the tasks listed on a WBS can be rather vague. What exactly does "Administer survey" mean, for example? The person responsible for this task might think that it does not need to be broken down any further, which could be fine. However, the task should be described in more detail so that everyone has the same understanding of what it involves. What if someone else has to perform the task? What would you tell him to do? What will it cost to complete the task? How many resources are required? How long will it take to complete? Information that is more detailed is needed to answer these and other questions.

A **WBS dictionary** is a document that describes each WBS task in detail. The format of the WBS dictionary can vary based on project needs. It might be appropriate to have just a short paragraph describing each work package. For a more complex project, an entire page or more might be needed for the work-package descriptions. Some projects might require that each WBS item describe the responsible person or organization, resource requirements, estimated costs, and other information.

TABLE 4-6   Sample WBS

Work Breakdown Structure (WBS) for the Just-In-Time Training Project
August 1, 2007

1. Initiating
    1.1. Prepare stakeholder analysis
    1.2. Prepare business case
    1.3. Create project charter
    1.4. Hold project kick-off meeting
    1.5. Develop preliminary scope statement
2. Planning
    2.1. Project integration management
        2.1.1. Create team contract
        2.1.2. Develop project management plan
    2.2. Project scope management
        2.2.1. Develop scope statement
        2.2.2. Create WBS and WBS dictionary
    2.3. Project time management
    2.4. Project cost management
    2.5. Project quality management
    2.6. Project human resources management
    2.7. Project communications management
    2.8. Project risk management
    2.9. Project procurement management
3. Executing
    3.1. Course design and development
        3.1.1. Supplier management training
            3.1.1.1. Needs assessment
                3.1.1.1.1. Develop survey
                3.1.1.1.2. Administer survey
                3.1.1.1.3. Analyze survey results
            3.1.1.2. Research of existing training
            3.1.1.3. Partnerships
                3.1.1.3.1. Research potential partners for providing training
                3.1.1.3.2. Meet with potential partners
                3.1.1.3.3. Develop partnership agreements
            3.1.1.4. Course development
                3.1.1.4.1. Develop executive course
                3.1.1.4.2. Develop introductory course
                3.1.1.4.3. Develop advanced course
            3.1.1.5. Pilot course
                3.1.1.5.1. Plan pilot course
                3.1.1.5.2. Hold pilot course
                3.1.1.5.3. Prepare report on pilot course
                3.1.1.5.4. Review results of pilot course
        3.1.2. Negotiating skills training
        3.1.3. Project management training
        3.1.4. Software applications training
    3.2. Course administration
    3.3. Course evaluation

TABLE 4-6 Sample WBS (continued)

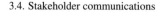

    3.4. Stakeholder communications
        3.4.1. Communications regarding project and changes to training
            3.4.1.1.   Prepare e-mails, posters, memos, and other information
            3.4.1.2.   Plan and hold meetings
            3.4.1.3.   Prepare information for the corporate intranet
        3.4.2. Communications regarding productivity improvements
    4. Monitoring and controlling
    5. Closing

Sample WBS Dictionary Entry

The project manager should work with his or her team and sponsor to determine the level of detail needed in the WBS dictionary. Project teams often review WBS dictionary entries from similar tasks to get a better idea of how to create these entries. They should also decide where this information will be entered and how it will be updated. For the Just-In-Time Training project, Kristin and her team will enter all of the WBS dictionary information into their enterprise project management system. Table 4-7 provides an example of one of the entries.

TABLE 4-7 Sample WBS dictionary entry

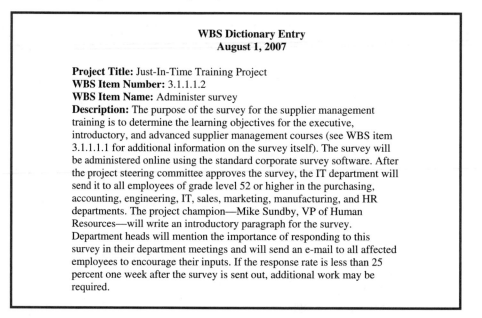

WBS Dictionary Entry
August 1, 2007

Project Title: Just-In-Time Training Project
WBS Item Number: 3.1.1.1.2
WBS Item Name: Administer survey
Description: The purpose of the survey for the supplier management training is to determine the learning objectives for the executive, introductory, and advanced supplier management courses (see WBS item 3.1.1.1.1 for additional information on the survey itself). The survey will be administered online using the standard corporate survey software. After the project steering committee approves the survey, the IT department will send it to all employees of grade level 52 or higher in the purchasing, accounting, engineering, IT, sales, marketing, manufacturing, and HR departments. The project champion—Mike Sundby, VP of Human Resources—will write an introductory paragraph for the survey. Department heads will mention the importance of responding to this survey in their department meetings and will send an e-mail to all affected employees to encourage their inputs. If the response rate is less than 25 percent one week after the survey is sent out, additional work may be required.

The approved project scope statement and its associated WBS and WBS dictionary form the **scope baseline**. Performance in meeting project scope goals is based on the scope baseline.

PROJECT TIME MANAGEMENT PLANNING TASKS

Project time management involves the processes required to ensure timely completion of a project. The main planning tasks performed as part of project time management are activity definition, activity sequencing, activity resource estimating, activity duration estimating, and schedule development. The main documents produced are an activity list and attributes, a milestone list, a network diagram, the activity resource requirements, the activity duration estimates, and a project schedule. Samples of these documents are provided later in this section.

Activity Definition

Project schedules grow out of the basic documents that initiate a project. The project charter often mentions planned project start and end dates, which serve as the starting points for a more detailed schedule. The project manager starts with the project charter and then develops a project scope statement and WBS, as discussed in the previous section. Using this information with the scope statement, WBS, WBS dictionary, project management plan, and other related information, the project team begins to develop a schedule by first clearly defining all the activities it needs to perform.

Creating the Activity List and Attributes

The **activity list** is a tabulation of activities to be included on a project schedule. The list should include the activity name, an activity identifier or number, and a brief description of the activity. The **activity attributes** provide schedule-related information about each activity, such as predecessors, successors, logical relationships, leads and lags, resource requirements, constraints, imposed dates, and assumptions related to the activity. The activity list and activity attributes should be in agreement with the WBS and WBS dictionary. Recall that a work package is the lowest level task in a WBS. Activities in the activity list are based on the detailed work required to complete each work package.

The goal of the activity definition process is to ensure that project team members have a complete understanding of all the work they must do as part of the project scope so that they can start scheduling the work. For example, one of the work packages in the WBS for the Just-In-Time Training project is "Prepare report on pilot course." The project team would have to understand what that means before it can make schedule-related decisions. How long should the report be? Does it require a survey or extensive research to produce it? What skill level does the report writer need to have? Further defining the task will help the project team determine how long it will take to do and who should do it.

The WBS is often expanded during the activity definition process as the project team members further define the activities required for performing the work. For example, the task "Prepare report on pilot course" might be broken down into several subtasks describing the steps involved in producing the report, such as developing a survey, administering the survey, analyzing the survey results, conducting interviews, writing a draft report, editing the report, and finally producing the report.

To avoid too much detail, some people prefer *not* to include these additional schedule-related activities in the WBS. They keep the lowest level of the WBS at the previously defined work package and describe detailed activities separately in the activity list and schedule. With most project management software, however, it is easy to include *all* the activity data in one place and then view information at whatever level of detail is desired. In this example, the activity list refers to the lowest level of work described for the project, be it a work package or a more detailed activity required for a work package.

The project team should review the activity list and activity attributes with project stakeholders. If they do not, they could produce an unrealistic schedule and deliver unacceptable results. For example, if a project team simply estimated that it would take one day for the "Prepare report on pilot course" task and had an intern or trainee write a two-page report to complete that task, the result could be a furious sponsor who expected extensive research, surveys, and a 50 page report. Clearly defining the work and having a realistic schedule for all activities is crucial to project success.

Sample Activity List and Attributes

Kristin and her team developed an activity to assist in developing the project schedule. Table 4-8 provides a sample entry in the activity list. Notice the detailed information provided, such as the predecessors, successors, resource requirements, and assumptions.

TABLE 4-8   Sample activity list and attributes

Activity List and Attributes
August 1, 2007

Project Name: Just-In-Time Training Project
WBS Item Number: 3.1.1.1.2
WBS Item Name: Administer survey
Predecessors: 3.1.1.1.1 Develop survey
Successors: 3.1.1.1.3 Analyze survey results
Logical Relationships: finish-to-start
Leads and Lags: None
Resource Requirements: IT personnel, corporate survey software, corporate Intranet
Constraints: None
Imposed dates: None
Assumptions: The survey for the supplier management training will be administered online using the standard corporate survey software. It should include questions measured on a Likert scale. For example, a question might be as follows: "I learned a lot from this course." Respondents would enter 1 for Strongly Agree, 2 for Agree, 3 for Undecided, 4 for Disagree, or 5 for Strongly Disagree. There should also be several open-ended questions, such as "What did you like most about the pilot course? What did you like least about the pilot course?" After the project steering committee approves the survey, the IT department will send it to all employees of grade level 52 or higher in the purchasing, accounting, engineering, IT, sales, marketing, manufacturing, and HR departments. The project champion—Mike Sundby, VP of Human Resources— will write an introductory paragraph for the survey. Department heads will mention the importance of responding to this survey in their department meetings and will send an e-mail to all affected employees to encourage their inputs. If the response rate is less than 25 percent one week after the survey is sent out, additional work may be required, such as a reminder e-mail to follow-up with people who have not responded to the survey.

Creating a Milestone List

To ensure that all major activities are accounted for, project teams often create a milestone list. A **milestone** is a significant event on a project. It often takes several activities and a lot of work to complete a milestone, but the milestone itself is like a marker to help in identifying necessary activities. There is usually no cost or duration associated with a milestone. Milestones are also useful tools for setting schedule goals and monitoring progress, and project sponsors and senior managers often focus on major milestones when reviewing projects. For example, milestones for many projects include sign-off of key documents; completion of specific products; and completion of important process-related work, such as awarding a contract to a supplier.

Sample Milestone List

Kristin and her team reviewed the draft WBS and activity list to develop an initial milestone list. They reviewed the list with their sponsor and other key stakeholders. Project teams often estimate completion dates for milestones early in the scheduling process. Table 4-9 shows part of the milestone list for the Just-In-Time Training project. This section focuses on the milestones related to the needs assessment for supplier management training (WBS item 3.1.1.1). Kristin knew her team had to complete this survey early in the project and that the results would affect many of the other tasks required for the project. Her team might need to see all the milestones provided in Table 4-9, but the steering committee might only need to see the last milestone, "Survey results reported to steering committee." The steering committee might focus on other milestones, including the project kick-off meeting, results of the pilot course, dates for each training class provided as part of the project, results of the course evaluations, and projected end date for the project.

TABLE 4-9 Sample milestone list

Milestone List
August 1, 2007

Project Name: Just-In-Time Training Project

Milestone	Estimated Completion Date*
Draft survey completed	8/3/07
Survey comments submitted	8/8/07
Survey sent out by IT	8/10/07
Percentage of survey respondents reviewed	8/17/07
Survey report completed	8/22/07
Survey results reported to steering committee	8/24/07

*Note: Dates are in U.S. format. 8/3/07 means August 3, 2007.

Activity Sequencing

After defining project activities, the next step in project time management is activity sequencing. Activity sequencing involves reviewing the activity list and attributes, project scope statement, and milestone list to determine the relationships or dependencies between activities. It also involves evaluating the reasons for dependencies and the different types of dependencies.

A **dependency** or **relationship** relates to the sequencing of project activities or tasks. For example, does a certain activity have to be finished before another one can start? Can the project team do several activities in parallel? Can some overlap? Determining these relationships or dependencies between activities has a significant impact on developing and managing a project schedule.

There are three basic reasons for creating dependencies among project activities:

- **Mandatory dependencies** are inherent in the nature of the work being performed on a project. They are sometimes referred to as hard logic because their relationships are unavoidable. For example, you cannot hold training classes until the training materials are ready, the training materials cannot be created until the objectives of the course are determined, and so on.
- **Discretionary dependencies** are defined by the project team. For example, a project team might follow good practice and not start detailed design work until key stakeholders sign off on all of the analysis work. Discretionary dependencies are sometimes referred to as soft logic and should be used with care because they might limit later scheduling options.
- **External dependencies** involve relationships between project and non-project activities. The installation of new software might depend on delivery of new hardware from an external supplier. Even though the delivery of the new hardware might not be in the scope of the project, it should have an external dependency added to it because late delivery will affect the project schedule.

As with activity definition, it is important that project stakeholders work together to define the activity dependencies that exist on their project. If you do not define the sequence of activities, you cannot use some of the most powerful schedule tools available to project managers: network diagrams and critical path analysis. The main output of activity sequencing is a network diagram.

Network Diagrams

Network diagrams are the preferred technique for showing activity sequencing. A **network diagram** is a schematic display of the logical relationships among, or sequencing of, project activities. Some people refer to network diagrams as PERT charts. PERT is described later in this section. Figure 4-3 shows a sample network diagram for Project X, which uses the arrow diagramming method (ADM), or activity-on-arrow (AOA) approach.

Note the main elements on this network diagram. The letters A through J represent activities with dependencies that are required to complete the project. These activities come from the WBS and activity definition process described earlier. The arrows represent the activity sequencing, or relationships between tasks. For example, Activity A must be done before Activity D, Activity D must be done before Activity H, and so on.

The format of this network diagram uses the **activity-on-arrow (AOA)** approach, or the **arrow diagramming method (ADM)**—a network diagramming technique in which activities are represented by arrows and connected at points called nodes to illustrate the sequence of activities. A **node** is simply the starting and ending point of an activity. The first node signifies the start of a project, and the last node represents the end of a project.

Keep in mind that the network diagram represents activities that must be done to complete the project. It is not a race to get from the first node to the last node. *Every* activity on

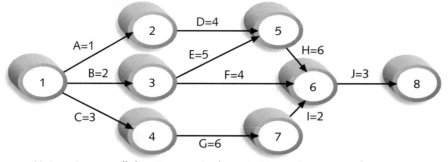

Note: Assume all durations are in days; A=1 means Activity A has a
duration of 1 day.

FIGURE 4-3 Activity-on-arrow (AOA) network diagram for Project X

the network diagram must be completed for the project to finish. It is also important to note that not every single item on the WBS needs to be on the network diagram; only activities with dependencies need to be shown on the network diagram. However, some people like to have start and end milestones and to list every activity. It is a matter of preference. For projects with hundreds of activities, it might be simpler to include only activities with dependencies on a network diagram.

Assuming you have a list of the project activities and their start and finish nodes, follow these steps to create an AOA network diagram:

1. Find all of the activities that start at Node 1. Draw their finish nodes, and draw arrows between Node 1 and each of those finish nodes. Put the activity letter or name on the associated arrow. If you have a duration estimate, write that next to the activity letter or name, as shown in Figure 4-3. For example, A = 1 means that the duration of Activity A is one day, week, or other standard unit of time. Also be sure to put arrowheads on all arrows to signify the direction of the relationships.

2. Continue drawing the network diagram, working from left to right. Look for bursts and merges. **Bursts** occur when two or more activities follow a single node. A **merge** occurs when two or more nodes precede a single node. For example, in Figure 4-3, Node 1 is a burst because it goes into Nodes 2, 3, and 4. Node 5 is a merge preceded by Nodes 2 and 3.

3. Continue drawing the AOA network diagram until all activities are included on the diagram.

4. As a rule of thumb, all arrowheads should face toward the right, and no arrows should cross on an AOA network diagram. You might need to redraw the diagram to make it look presentable.

Even though AOA network diagrams are generally easy to understand and create, a different method is more commonly used: the precedence diagramming method. The **precedence diagramming method (PDM)** is a network diagramming technique in which boxes represent activities. It is particularly useful for visualizing certain types of time relationships.

Figure 4-4 illustrates the types of dependencies that can occur among project activities. After you determine the reason for a dependency between activities (mandatory, discretionary, or external), you must determine the type of dependency. Note that the terms "activity" and "task" are used interchangeably, as are "relationship" and "dependency." The four types of dependencies, or relationships, between activities include the following:

- *Finish-to-start:* A relationship in which the "from" activity must finish before the "to" activity can start. For example, you cannot provide training until after the training materials are available. Finish-to-start is the most common type of relationship, or dependency, and AOA network diagrams use only finish-to-start dependencies.
- *Start-to-start:* A relationship in which the "from" activity cannot start until the "to" activity is started. For example, as soon as you start a project review meeting, you can start documenting attendees, serving refreshments, taking minutes, and so on.
- *Finish-to-finish:* A relationship in which the "from" activity must be finished before the "to" activity can be finished. One task cannot finish before another finishes. For example, quality control efforts cannot finish before production finishes, although the two activities can be performed at the same time.
- *Start-to-finish:* A relationship in which the "from" activity must start before the "to" activity can be finished. This type of relationship is rarely used, but it is appropriate in some cases. For example, an organization might strive to stock raw materials just in time for the manufacturing process to begin. A delay in the start of the manufacturing process should delay completion of stocking the raw materials.

Task dependencies

The nature of the relationship between two linked tasks. You link tasks by defining a dependency between their finish and start dates. For example, the "Contact caterers" task must finish before the start of the "Determine menus" task. There are four kinds of task dependencies in Microsoft Project:

Task dependency	Example	Description
Finish-to-start (FS)	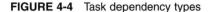	Task (B) cannot start until task (A) finishes.
Start-to-start (SS)		Task (B) cannot start until task (A) starts.
Finish-to-finish (FF)		Task (B) cannot finish until task (A) finishes.
Start-to-finish (SF)		Task (B) cannot finish until task (A) starts.

FIGURE 4-4   Task dependency types

Figure 4-5 illustrates Project X using the precedence diagramming method. Notice that the activities are placed inside boxes, which represent the nodes on this diagram. Arrows show the relationships between activities. This figure was created using Microsoft Project 2003, which automatically places additional information inside each node. Each task box includes the start and finish date, labeled "Start" and "Finish"; the task ID number, labeled "ID"; the task's duration, labeled "Dur"; and the names of resources, if any, assigned to the task, labeled "Res." The border of the boxes for tasks on the critical path (discussed later in this section) appears automatically in red in the Project 2003 network diagram view. In Figure 4-5, the boxes for critical tasks have a thicker border and are not shaded.

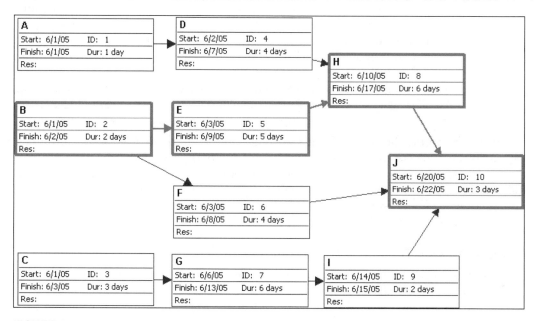

FIGURE 4-5   Precedence diagramming method (PDM) network diagram for Project X

Although the AOA diagram might seem easier to understand, the precedence diagramming method is used more often than AOA network diagrams. Its main advantage is that it allows you to show different types of dependencies among tasks, whereas AOA network diagrams use only finish-to-start dependencies and sometimes use dummy activities to define logical relationships correctly.

Kristin and her team reviewed all the project activities and determined which ones had dependencies. They also determined which tasks could be overlapped (or have "lead" time) and which needed some lag time. For example, they wanted to wait 30 days after holding the first supplier management course before holding the second one. They entered the information into Project 2003 to begin building a detailed Gantt chart for the project, as described later in this section. The Project 2003 file would be integrated with their enterprise project management system to have all information in one place.

Activity Resource Estimating

Before you can estimate the duration for each activity, you must have a good idea of the quantity and type of resources (people, equipment, and materials) that will be assigned to each activity. It is important that the people who help determine what resources are necessary include people who have experience and expertise in similar projects and with the organization performing the project.

Important questions to answer in activity resource estimating include the following:

- How difficult will it be to do specific activities on this project?
- Is there anything unique in the project's scope statement that will affect resources?
- What is the organization's history in doing similar activities? Has the organization done similar tasks before? What level of personnel did the work?
- Does the organization have appropriate people, equipment, and materials available for performing the work? Are there any organizational policies that might affect the availability of resources?
- Does the organization need to acquire more resources to accomplish the work? Would it make sense to outsource some of the work? Will outsourcing increase or decrease the amount of resources needed and when they will be available?

It is important to thoroughly brainstorm and evaluate alternatives related to resources, especially on projects that involve people from multiple disciplines and companies. Because most projects involve many human resources and the majority of costs are for salaries and benefits, it is often effective to solicit ideas from different people and to address resource-related issues early in a project. The resource estimates should also be updated as more detailed information becomes available.

Sample Activity Resource Requirements

A key output of the resource estimating process is documentation of activity resource requirements. This list can take various formats. For the Just-In-Time Training project, Kristin met with her team, her sponsor, and the project steering committee, as needed, to discuss resource requirements for the project. They also discussed which training might be best to outsource, which would be best to perform with internal resources, and which should use both internal and external resources. They entered important resource information for each task in their enterprise project management software.

Table 4-10 provides an example of one of the resource requirement entries for the activity described earlier in the WBS dictionary entry called "Administer survey."

TABLE 4-10 Sample activity resource requirements information

Activity Resource Requirements
August 1, 2007

Project Name: Just-In-Time Training Project
WBS Item Number: 3.1.1.1.2
WBS Item Name: Administer survey
Description: Internal members of our IT department will perform this task. The individuals must be knowledgeable in using our online survey software so that they can enter the actual survey into this software. They must also know how to run a query to find the e-mail addresses of employees of grade level 52 or higher in the purchasing, accounting, engineering, IT, sales, marketing, manufacturing, and HR departments.

Activity Duration Estimating

After working with key stakeholders to define activities, determine their dependencies, and estimate their resources, the next process in project time management is to estimate the duration of activities. It is important to note that **duration** includes the actual amount of time spent working on an activity *plus* elapsed time. For example, even though it might take one workweek or five workdays to do the actual work, the duration estimate might be two weeks to allow extra time needed to obtain outside information or to allow for resource availability. Do not confuse duration with **effort**, which is the number of workdays or work hours required to complete a task. A duration estimate of one day could be based on eight hours of work or eighty hours of work. Duration relates to the time estimate, not the effort estimate. Of course, the two are related, so project team members must document their assumptions when creating duration estimates and update the estimates as the project progresses.

The outputs of activity duration estimating include updates to the activity attributes, if needed, and duration estimates for each activity. Duration estimates are provided as a discrete number, such as four weeks; as a range, such as three to five weeks; or as a three-point estimate. A **three-point estimate** is an estimate that includes an optimistic, most likely, and pessimistic estimate, such as three weeks, four weeks, and five weeks, respectively. The optimistic estimate is based on a best-case scenario, whereas the pessimistic estimate is based on a worst-case scenario. The most likely estimate, as it sounds, is an estimate based on a most likely or expected scenario.

A three-point estimate is required for performing PERT estimates. **Program Evaluation and Review Technique (PERT)** is a network analysis technique used to estimate project duration when there is a high degree of uncertainty about the individual activity duration estimates. By using the PERT weighted average for each activity duration estimate, the total project duration estimate accounts for the risk or uncertainty in the individual activity estimates. To use PERT, you calculate a weighted average for the duration estimate of each project activity using the following formula:

$$\text{PERT weighted average} = \frac{\text{optimistic time} + 4 \times \text{most likely time} + \text{pessimistic time}}{6}$$

Sample Activity Duration Estimates

Many project teams use one discrete estimate—the most likely estimate—to estimate activity durations. For example, Kristin's team could enter these discrete estimates into their enterprise project management system. If Kristin's project team used PERT to determine the schedule for the Just-In-Time Training project, they would have to collect numbers for the optimistic, most likely, and pessimistic duration estimates for each project activity. For example, suppose the person assigned to administer the survey for the supplier management training estimated that it would take two workdays to do this activity. Without using PERT, the duration estimate for that activity would be two workdays. Suppose an optimistic time estimate for this activity is one workday, and a pessimistic time estimate is nine workdays. Applying the PERT formula, you get the following:

$$\text{PERT weighted average} = \frac{1 \text{ workdays} + 4 \times 2 \text{ workdays} + 9 \text{ workdays}}{6} = 3 \text{ workdays}$$

Instead of using the most likely duration estimate of two workdays, the project team would use three workdays. The main advantage of PERT is that it attempts to address the risk associated with duration estimates. Because many projects exceed schedule estimates, PERT might help in developing schedules that are more realistic.

PERT also has disadvantages: It involves more work because it requires several duration estimates, and there are better probabilistic (based on probability) methods for assessing schedule risk, such as Monte Carlo simulations. To perform a Monte Carlo simulation, in addition to the three-point estimate, you also collect probabilistic information for each activity duration estimate. For example, Kristin would ask the person assigned to administer the survey for the supplier management training what the probability was of completing that activity between the optimistic and most likely times (one and two days, in this example). If he estimated only a 10 percent probability, Kristin would know that a two-day estimate or even a three-day estimate might be unrealistic. For this project, however, Kristin and her team decided to enter realistic discrete estimates for each activity instead of using PERT or a Monte Carlo simulation. She stressed that people who would do the work should provide the estimate, and they should have 50 percent confidence in meeting each estimate. If some tasks took longer, some took less time, and some were exactly on target, they should still meet their overall schedule.

Schedule Development

Schedule development uses the results of all the preceding project time management processes to determine the start and end dates of project activities and of the entire project. There are often several iterations of all the project time management processes before a project schedule is finalized. The ultimate goal of schedule development is to create a realistic project schedule that provides a basis for monitoring project progress for the time dimension of the project. Project managers must lead their teams in creating realistic schedules and then following them during project execution.

WHAT WENT RIGHT?

Chris Higgins used the discipline he learned in the Army to transform project management into a cultural force at Bank of America. Higgins learned that taking time on the front end of a project could save significant time and money on the back end. As a quartermaster in the Army, when Higgins's people had to pack tents, he devised a contest to find the best way to fold a tent and determine the precise spots to place the pegs and equipment for the quickest possible assembly. Higgins used the same approach when he led an interstate banking initiative to integrate incompatible check processing, checking account, and savings account platforms in various states.

Law mandated that the banks solve the problem in one year or less. Higgins's project team was pushing to get to the coding phase of the project quickly, but Higgins held them back. He made the team members develop a realistic project schedule that included adequate time to analyze, plan, and document requirements for the system in detail. It turned out that they needed six months just to complete that work. However, the discipline up front enabled the software developers on the team to do all of the coding in only three months, as planned, and the project was completed on time.[3]

The main output of the schedule development process is the project schedule, which is often displayed in the form of a Gantt chart.

Gantt charts provide a standard format for displaying project schedule information by listing project activities and their corresponding start and finish dates in a calendar format. Figure 4-6 shows a simple Gantt chart for Project X, described earlier, created with Project 2003.

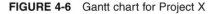

FIGURE 4-6   Gantt chart for Project X

Recall that the activities on the Gantt chart should coincide with the activities on the WBS, the activity list, and the milestone list. Before showing a Gantt chart for the Just-In-Time Training project, it is important to explain a fundamental concept that assists project teams in developing and meeting project schedules: critical path analysis.

Critical Path Analysis

Many projects fail to meet schedule expectations. **Critical path method (CPM)**—also called **critical path analysis**—is a network diagramming technique used to predict total project duration. This important tool will help you combat project schedule overruns. A **critical path** for a project is the series of activities that determine the *earliest* time by which the project can be completed. It is the *longest* path through the network diagram and has the least amount of slack or float. **Slack** or **float** is the amount of time an activity may be delayed without delaying a succeeding activity or the project finish date. There are normally several tasks done in parallel on projects, and most projects have multiple paths through a network diagram. The longest path or the path containing the critical tasks is what is driving the completion date for the project. Remember that you are not finished with the project until you have finished *all* the tasks.

Calculating the Critical Path

To find the critical path for a project, you must first develop a good network diagram as described earlier, which requires a good activity list based on the WBS. To create a network diagram, you must determine the dependencies of activities and also estimate their durations. Calculating the critical path involves adding the durations for all activities on each path through the network diagram. The longest path is the critical path.

Figure 4-7 shows the AOA network diagram for Project X again. Note that you can use either the AOA or the precedence diagramming method to determine the critical path on projects. Figure 4-7 shows all of the paths—a total of four—through the network diagram. Note that each path starts at the first node (1) and ends at the last node (8) on the AOA network diagram. This figure also shows the length or total duration of each path through the network diagram. These lengths are computed by adding the durations of each activity on the path. Because path B-E-H-J at 16 days has the longest duration, it is the critical path for the project.

What does the critical path really mean? *The critical path shows the shortest time in which a project can be completed.* If one or more of the activities on the critical path takes longer than planned, the whole project schedule will slip *unless* the project manager takes corrective action.

Project teams can be creative in managing the critical path. For example, Joan Knutson, a well-known author and speaker in the project management field, often describes how a gorilla helped Apple computer complete a project on time. Team members worked in an area with cubicles, and whoever was in charge of a task currently on the critical path had a big, stuffed gorilla on top of her cubicle. Everyone knew that that person was under the most time pressure, so they tried not to distract her. When a critical task was completed, the person in charge of the next critical task received the gorilla (see Figure 4-8).

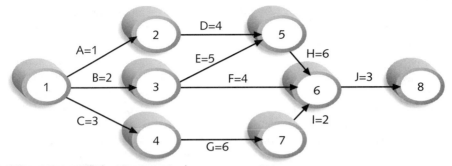

Note: Assume all durations are in days.

Path 1:	A-D-H-J	Length = 1+4+6+3 = 14 days
Path 2:	**B-E-H-J**	**Length = 2+5+6+3 = 16 days**
Path 3:	B-F-J	Length = 2+4+3 = 9 days
Path 4:	C-G-I-J	Length = 3+6+2+3 = 14 days

Because the critical path is the longest path through the network diagram, Path 2, B-E-H-J, is the critical path for Project X.

FIGURE 4-7 Critical path calculation for Project X

FIGURE 4-8 Who's stuck with the gorilla this week?

Growing Grass Can Be on the Critical Path

People are often confused about what the critical path is for a project or what it really means. Some people think the critical path includes the most critical activities. However, the critical path involves only with the time dimension of a project. The fact that its name includes the word "critical" does *not* mean that it includes all critical activities. For example, Frank Addeman, executive project director at Walt Disney Imagineering, explained in a keynote address at the May 2000 PMI-ISSIG Professional Development Seminar that growing grass was on the critical path for building Disney's Animal Kingdom theme park. This 500-acre park required special grass for its animal inhabitants, and some of the grass took years to grow. Another misconception is that the critical path is the shortest path through the network diagram. In areas such as transportation modeling, multiple network diagrams are drawn in which identifying the shortest path is the goal. For a project, however, each task or activity must be done in order to complete the project. It is not a matter of choosing the shortest path.

Other aspects of critical path analysis may cause confusion. Can there be more than one critical path on a project? Does the critical path ever change? In the Project X example, suppose that Activity A has a duration estimate of three days instead of one day. This new duration estimate would make the length of Path 1 equal to 16 days. Now the project has two paths of the longest duration, so there are two critical paths. Therefore, there *can* be more than one critical path on a project. Project managers should closely monitor performance of activities on the critical path to avoid late project completion. If there is more than one critical path, project managers must keep their eyes on all of them.

The critical path on a project can change as the project progresses. For example, suppose everything is going as planned at the beginning of the project. In this example, suppose Activities A, B, C, D, E, F, and G from Figure 4-7 all start and finish as planned. Then suppose Activity I runs into problems. If Activity I takes more than four days, it will cause path C-G-I-J to be longer than the other paths, assuming they progress as planned. This change would cause path C-G-I-J to become the new critical path. Therefore, the critical path can change on a project.

Using Critical Path Analysis to Make Schedule Trade-Offs

It is important to know what the critical path is throughout the life of a project so that the project manager can make trade-offs. If the project manager knows that one of the tasks on the critical path is behind schedule, he needs to decide what to do about it. Should the schedule be renegotiated with stakeholders? Should more resources be allocated to other items on the critical path to make up for that time? Is it okay if the project finishes behind schedule? By keeping track of the critical path, the project manager and his team take a proactive role in managing the project schedule.

It is common for stakeholders to want to shorten a project schedule estimate. Your team may have done its best to develop a project schedule by defining activities, determining sequencing, and estimating resources and durations for each activity. The results of this work may have shown that your team needs 10 months to complete the project. Your sponsor might ask if the project can be done in eight or nine months. Rarely do people ask you to take longer than you suggested. By knowing the critical path, the project manager and his team can use several duration compression techniques to shorten the project schedule. One technique is to reduce the duration of activities on the critical path. The project manager can shorten the duration of critical path activities by allocating more resources to those activities or by changing their scope.

Crashing is a technique for making cost and schedule trade-offs to obtain the greatest amount of schedule compression for the least incremental cost. For example, suppose one of the items on the critical path for the Just-In-Time Training project was to design and develop an advanced course for supplier management. If this task is yet to be done and was originally estimated to take four weeks based on key people working 25 percent of their time on this task, Kristin could suggest that people work 50 percent of their time to finish the task faster. This change might cost some additional money if people had to work paid over-time, but it could shorten the project end date by two weeks. By focusing on tasks on the critical path that could be finished more quickly for either no extra cost or a small cost, the project schedule could be shortened. The main advantage of crashing is shortening the time it takes to finish a project. The main disadvantage of crashing is that it often increases total project costs. If used too often, however, crashing can affect staff negatively by low-ering morale or causing burnout.

Another technique for shortening a project schedule is fast tracking. **Fast tracking** involves doing activities in parallel that you would normally do in sequence. For example, Kristin's project team may have planned not to start any of the work on the negotiating skills training until they finished most of the work on the supplier management training. Instead, they could consider performing several of these tasks in parallel to shorten the schedule. As with crashing, the main advantage of fast tracking is that it can shorten the time it takes to finish a project. The main disadvantage of fast tracking is that it can end up lengthening the project schedule, because starting some tasks too soon often increases project risk and results in rework.

Importance of Updating Critical Path Data

In addition to finding the critical path at the beginning of a project, it is important to update the schedule with actual data. After the project team completes activities, the project man-ager should document the actual duration of each of those activities. She should also document revised estimates for activities in progress or yet to be started. These revisions often cause a project's critical path to change, resulting in a new estimated completion date for the project. Again, proactive project managers and their teams stay on top of changes so that they can make informed decisions and keep stakeholders informed of, and involved in, major project decisions.

Sample Project Schedule

Kristin worked with her team to define project activities, determine activity sequencing, describe activity resources, estimate activity durations, and make schedule trade-offs to per-form all of the work required for the project within one year, as desired by the project sponsor.

Figure 4-9 provides part of the resulting Gantt chart the team will use to guide their project schedule. To fit the information on one page, the executing tasks have been col-lapsed, which means that you cannot see the tasks under that category but you can expand them on the computer screen. Notice that the items in the Task Name column come from the WBS, and duration estimates are entered in the "Duration" column. Some tasks have been added to help develop the schedule. Also notice the flow between the initiat-ing, planning, executing, monitoring and controlling, and closing tasks. Dependencies between activities are shown by the entries in the "Pred" (short for Predecessors) column and the arrows connecting symbols on the Gantt chart. You can download and review the entire Project 2003 file from the companion Web site for this text as well as the *Guide to Using Microsoft Project 2003*.

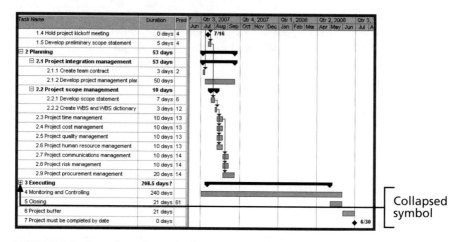

FIGURE 4-9   Sample project schedule

Figure 4-10 shows another view of the Gantt chart for the Just-In-Time Training project, showing all of the summary tasks (represented by thick black lines) and milestones (represented by black diamonds). Note that the milestones include the schedule items that the project steering committee would be most interested in seeing. By using project management software like Project 2003, you can easily see different levels of detail in the schedule information. Also note that Kristin decided to include a **project buffer**—additional time added before the project's due date to account for unexpected factors. This buffer (shown as the second to last item in the Task Name column in Figure 4-9) will help ensure that the project is completed on time. Kristin has learned from past projects that no matter how well you try to schedule everything, it can still be a challenge to finish on time without a mad rush at the end. For this reason, she decided to include a 21-day project buffer, which the project steering committee thought was an excellent idea.

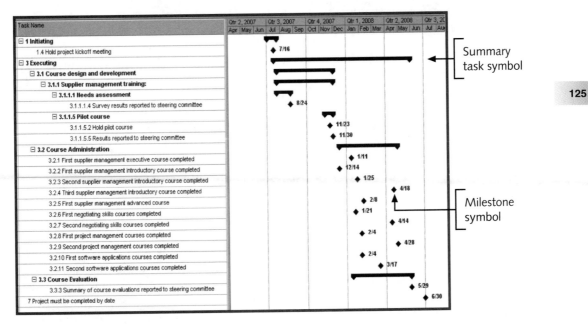

FIGURE 4-10 Sample Gantt chart showing summary tasks and milestones

PROJECT COST MANAGEMENT PLANNING TASKS

Project cost management includes the processes required to ensure that a project team completes a project within an approved budget. The main planning tasks performed as part of project cost management are cost estimating and cost budgeting. Cost estimating involves developing an approximation or estimate of the costs of the resources needed to complete a project. Cost budgeting involves allocating the overall cost estimate to individual tasks over time to establish a baseline for measuring performance. The main documents produced include a cost estimate and a cost baseline.

Cost Estimating

Project teams normally prepare cost estimates at various stages of a project, and these estimates should be fine-tuned as time progresses. Before management approves a project, someone must develop a rough estimate of what it will cost to complete the project. After the project manager and team are assigned to a project, they normally prepare a more detailed cost estimate. If this estimate is substantially different from the initial budgeted amount, the project manager should negotiate with the project sponsor to increase or decrease the budget, or to make changes to the scope or time goals to meet cost constraints. As more detailed information becomes available, the project team should update the cost estimates and continue negotiating with the sponsor to meet project goals.

   In addition to creating cost estimates, it is also important to provide supporting details for the estimates. The supporting details include the ground rules and assumptions used in creating the estimate, the description of the project (including references to the scope statement, WBS, and so on) that was used as a basis for the estimate, and details on the cost estimation tools and techniques used to create the estimate. These supporting details should make it easier to prepare an updated estimate or similar estimate as needed.

A large percentage of total project costs are often labor costs. Many organizations estimate the number of people or hours they need for major parts of a project over the life cycle of the project. They also determine the labor rate to apply based on the category of labor. It is important to work with people in the organization's finance and accounting departments to determine these labor rates and apply the appropriate amounts for benefits and overhead so that total labor costs are included in the estimate.

Cost Estimation Tools and Techniques

As you can imagine, developing a good cost estimate is difficult. Fortunately, several tools and techniques are available to assist in creating them. Three commonly used techniques for creating estimates include the following:

1. **Analogous estimates**, also called **top-down estimates**, use the actual cost of a previous, similar project as the basis for estimating the cost of the current project. This technique requires a good deal of expert judgment and is generally less costly than others are, but it can also be less accurate. Analogous estimates are most reliable when the previous projects are similar in fact, not just in appearance.

2. **Bottom-up estimates** involve estimating individual activities and summing them to get a project total. The size of the individual activities and the experience of the estimators drive the accuracy of the estimates. If a detailed WBS is available for a project, the project manager could have each person responsible for a work package develop his own cost estimate for that particular work package. The project manager would then add all of the cost estimates to create cost estimates for each higher-level WBS item and finally for the entire project. This approach can increase the accuracy of the cost estimate, but it can also be time intensive and, therefore, expensive to develop.

3. **Parametric modeling** uses project characteristics (parameters) in a mathematical model to estimate project costs. A parametric model might provide an estimate of $5 per square foot for flooring, for example, based on the type of flooring, total square feet required, and location of the job. Parametric models are most reliable when the historical information used to create the model is accurate, the parameters are readily quantifiable, and the model is flexible in terms of the size of the project.

It is good practice to use more than one approach for creating a cost estimate. For example, a project team might develop an analogous estimate and a parametric model and compare the results. If the estimates were far apart, the team would need to collect more information to develop a better estimate.

Sample Cost Estimate

Every cost estimate is unique, just as every project is unique. This section includes a step-by-step approach for developing the major parts of the cost estimate for the Just-In-Time Training project. Of course, this example is much shorter and simpler than a real cost estimate would be, but it illustrates an easy-to-follow process and uses several of the tools and techniques described earlier.

It is also important to clarify and document the ground rules and assumptions for the estimate. For the Just-In-Time Training project cost estimate, these include the following:

- This project was preceded by a project that provided valuable information, such as the training taken in the last two years by all internal employees, the cost of all training, the process for approving/assigning training, the evaluation of the training by participants, what training employees would need in the next two years, how they would like to take the training (that is, instructor-led in-house; instructor-led through a local college, university, or training company; online; and so on).
- There is a WBS for the project, as described earlier. The level 1 and some of the level 2 categories are shown as follows:

    1. Initiating
    2. Planning
    3. Executing
        3.1 Course design and development
        3.2 Course administration
        3.3 Course evaluation
        3.4 Stakeholder communications
    4. Monitoring and controlling
    5. Closing

- Costs must be estimated by WBS and by month. The project manager will report progress on the project using earned value analysis, which requires this type of estimate.
- Costs will be provided in U.S. dollars. Because the project length is one year, inflation will not be included.
- There will be a project manager who spends three-quarters of her time on the project, and a manager and three core team members assigned to the project half-time. Two of the team members will be from the training department and one will be from the supplier management department. Additional internal resources from various departments will support the project as needed and charge their time to the project.
- The project steering committee members' time is not directly charged to the project. Internal labor costs include a 40 percent overhead charge as well as a 30 percent benefits charge. For example, if the direct labor rate is $30/hour, the burdened rate, or the rate including benefits and overhead, is $30*1.3* 1.4=$55 (rounded to the nearest whole-dollar amount).
- The project cost estimate does not include any hardware, software, or facilities that will be used to develop and administer the courses.
- The project team should purchase training materials and related products and services from qualified suppliers to take advantage of their expertise and to reduce internal costs. Estimates are based on analogous projects and will be updated as contracts are awarded.

- Labor costs for employees to cover their salaries while they attend training classes are not included in this estimate.
- Because several risks are related to this project, the estimate includes 10 percent of the total estimate as reserves.
- A computer model of the project estimate will be developed to facilitate the changing of inputs, such as the number of labor hours for various activities or labor rates.

Fortunately, the project team can easily access cost estimates and actual information from similar projects. A great deal of information is available from the Phase I project, and the team can talk to supplier personnel from the past project to help them develop the estimate.

Because the estimate must be provided by WBS monthly, Kristin and her team reviewed the draft of the project schedule and made further assumptions. They decided first to estimate the cost of each WBS task and then determine when the work would be performed, even though costs might be incurred at times other than when the work was actually performed. Their budget expert had approved this approach for the estimate. Further assumptions and information for estimating the costs for each WBS category are as follows:

1. *Initiating*: The team used the actual labor costs charged to the project for project initiation activities.
2. *Planning*: The team used actual labor costs to date and added the projected hours and costs per hour to develop this part of the estimate.
3. *Executing*:
   3.1 *Course design and development:* The team used labor hour and rate estimates for internal and external staff, plus estimates for purchasing existing course materials for each course (that is, supplier management, negotiating skills, project management, and software applications). Some of the purchased costs were based on the number of students using the materials each year. The majority of project costs should be applied to this category.
   3.2 *Course administration:* Estimates were made based on the number of courses and number of people expected to take each course using various delivery methods (that is, instructor-led, CD-ROM, Web-based). The external labor cost per hour is normally higher for course delivery.
   3.3 *Course evaluation:* The team estimated labor hours and rates.
   3.4 *Stakeholder communications:* The team estimated labor hours and rates.
4. *Monitoring and controlling*: The team estimated labor hours and rates.
5. *Closing*: The team estimated labor hours and rates.
6. *Reserves*: As directed, reserved costs were estimated at 10 percent of the total estimate.

The project team developed a cost model using the preceding information. Figure 4-11 shows a spreadsheet that summarizes the costs by WBS based on that information. There are columns for entering the number of labor hours and the costs per hour. Several tasks are estimated using this approach. There are also some short comments within the estimate, such as reserves being 10 percent of the total estimate. With this computerized model, you can easily change input variables, such as number of hours or cost per hour, to revise the estimate.

WBS Categories	Internal Labor	$/hour	Internal $ Total	External Labor	$/hour	External $ Total	Total Labor	Non-labor $	Total Cost
1. Initiating	200	$ 65	$ 13,000			$ -	$ 13,000		$ 13,000
2. Planning	600	$ 60	$ 36,000			$ -	$ 36,000		$ 36,000
3. Executing			$ -			$ -	$ -		$ -
3.1 Course design and development			$ -			$ -	$ -		$ -
3.1.1 Supplier management training	600	$ 60	$ 36,000	600	$ 150	$ 90,000	$ 126,000	$ 100,000	$ 226,000
3.1.2 Negotiating skills training	300	$ 55	$ 16,500	300	$ 150	$ 45,000	$ 61,500	$ 50,000	$ 111,500
3.1.3 Project management training	400	$ 60	$ 24,000	400	$ 150	$ 60,000	$ 84,000	$ 50,000	$ 134,000
3.1.4 Software applications training	400	$ 60	$ 24,000	400	$ 150	$ 60,000	$ 84,000	$ 50,000	$ 134,000
3.2 Course administration	400	$ 55	$ 22,000	300	$ 250	$ 75,000	$ 97,000	$ 80,000	$ 177,000
3.3.Course evaluation	300	$ 55	$ 16,500			$ -	$ 16,500		$ 16,500
3.4 Stakeholder communications	300	$ 55	$ 16,500			$ -	$ 16,500		$ 16,500
4. Monitoring and Controlling	500	$ 55	$ 27,500			$ -	$ 27,500		$ 27,500
5. Closing	200	$ 55	$ 11,000			$ -	$ 11,000		$ 11,000
Subtotal									$ 903,000
Reserves			$ -			$ -	$ -		90,300.0
Total	4,200		243,000	2,000	850	330,000	573,000	330,000	$ 993,300

Assumptions

Internal labor rates include benefits and overhead. Average hourly rates are based on skill levels and departments of stakeholders.

External labor rates are based on historical averages; may change as contracts are awarded.

Non-labor costs include purchasing licenses for using training materials, books, CD/ROMs, travel expenses, etc.

Non-labor costs may change as contracts are awarded.

Reserves are calculated by taking 10% of the total estimate.

FIGURE 4-11 Sample cost estimate

It is very important to have several people review the project cost estimate, including the ground rules and assumptions. It is also helpful to analyze the total dollar value as well as the percentage of the total amount for each major WBS category. For example, a senior executive could quickly look at the Just-In-Time Training project cost estimate and decide whether the costs are reasonable and whether the assumptions are well documented. In this case, Global Construction had budgeted $1 million for the project, so the estimate was right in line with that amount. The WBS level 1 and 2 tasks also seem to be at appropriate percentages of the total cost based on similar past projects. In some cases, a project team might also be asked to provide a range estimate for each task instead of one discrete amount.

After the total cost estimate is approved, Kristin's team can then allocate costs for each month based on the project schedule and when costs will be incurred. Many organizations also require that the estimated costs be allocated into certain budget categories, such as compensation or travel.

Cost Budgeting

Project cost budgeting involves allocating the project cost estimate to tasks over time. These tasks are based on the work breakdown structure for the project. The WBS, therefore, is a required input to the cost budgeting process. Likewise, the project scope statement, WBS dictionary, activity cost estimates and supporting detail, project schedule, and other plans provide useful information for cost budgeting.

The main goal of the cost budgeting process is to produce a cost baseline. A **cost baseline** is a time-phased budget that project managers use to measure and monitor cost performance. Estimating costs for each major project activity over time provides project managers and top management with a foundation for project cost control using earned value management, as described in Chapter 7. See the *Guide to Using Microsoft Project 2003* on the companion Web site for information on using Project 2003 for cost control.

Sample Cost Baseline

The Just-In-Time Training project team used the cost estimate from Figure 4-11 along with the project schedule and other information to allocate costs for each month. Figure 4-12 provides an example of a cost baseline for this project. Again, it is important for the team to document the assumptions they made when developing the cost baseline and have several experts review it. The cost baseline should also be updated as more information becomes available.

WBS Categories	1	2	3	4	5	6	7	8	9	10	11	12	Total Cost
1. Initiating	13,000												$ 13,000
2. Planning	6,000	16,000	8,000	1,000	1,000	1,000	1,000	1,000	1,000				$ 36,000
3. Executing			-			-	-						$ -
3.1 Course design and development			-			-	-						$ -
3.1.1 Supplier management training			5,000	73,667	73,667	73,667							$ 226,000
3.1.2 Negotiating skills training			5,000	35,500	35,500	35,500							$ 111,500
3.1.3 Project management training			5,000	43,000	43,000	43,000							$ 134,000
3.1.4 Software applications training			5,000	43,000	43,000	43,000							$ 134,000
3.2 Course administration						17,000	53,333	53,333	53,333				$ 177,000
3.3 Course evaluation							3,000	3,000	3,000	7,500			$ 16,500
3.4 Stakeholder communications		1,500	1,500	1,500	1,500	1,500	1,500	1,500	1,500	1,500	1,500	1,500	$ 16,500
4. Monitoring and Controlling	1,000	2,000	2,000	2,000	3,000	3,500	3,000	3,000	2,000	3,000	2,000	1,000	$ 27,500
5. Closing											8,000	3,000	$ 11,000
Subtotal													$ 903,000
Reserves*		-				-	-					90,300	$ 90,300
Total	20,000	19,500	31,500	199,667	200,667	218,167	61,833	61,833	60,833	12,000	11,500	95,800	993,300

*Reserves are all entered in month 12

FIGURE 4-12   Sample cost baseline

CASE WRAP-UP

Kristin learned a lot by leading her team during the planning phase of the Just-In-Time Training project. She did her best to get key stakeholders involved, including those who had little experience in planning. She could see that some people jumped to the planning details right away while others wanted to do as little planning as possible. She continued to consult members of the project steering committee for their advice, especially in helping everyone see how crucial it was to understand and document the scope, time, and cost of the project to provide a good baseline for measuring progress.

Chapter Summary

Successful project managers know how important it is to develop, refine, and follow plans to meet project goals. It is important to remember that the main purpose of project plans is to guide project execution. Planning is done in all nine project management knowledge areas. This chapter summarizes the planning tasks and outputs for integration, scope, time, and cost management.

Planning tasks for integration management include developing a team contract and a project management plan. Samples of these documents are provided for the Just-In-Time Training project.

Planning tasks for scope management include creating a scope management plan, a scope statement, a WBS, and a WBS dictionary. Samples of these documents are provided for the Just-In-Time Training project.

Planning tasks for time management include developing a project schedule by creating an activity list, a milestone list, network diagrams, activity resource requirements, and activity duration estimates. Samples of these documents are provided for the Just-In-Time Training project. It is also important to understand critical path analysis to make schedule trade-off decisions.

Planning tasks for cost management include developing a project cost estimate and a cost baseline. Samples of these documents are provided for the Just-In-Time Training project.

Quick Quiz

1. What can project teams create to help promote teamwork and clarify team communications?

    a. a project Web site

    b. a team-building plan

    c. a team roster

    d. a team contract

2. The main purpose of project planning is to:

    a. obtain funding for the project

    b. guide project execution

    c. clarify roles and responsibilities

    d. keep senior managers informed

3. Project teams develop a _____ to coordinate all other project plans.

    a. strategic plan

    b. project management plan

    c. master plan

    d. project Web site

4. A _____ is a deliverable-oriented grouping of the work involved in a project that defines the total scope of the project.

   a. contract

   b. Gantt chart

   c. WBS

   d. network diagram

5. A _____ is a task at the lowest level of the WBS that represents the level of work that the project manager uses to monitor and control the project.

   a. WBS dictionary

   b. budget item

   c. line item

   d. work package

6. What is the first step in planning a project schedule?

   a. developing a budget

   b. developing an activity list

   c. assigning resources to the project

   d. determining activity sequencing

7. What is the most common type of dependency between activities?

   a. finish-to-start

   b. start-to-finish

   c. start-to-start

   d. finish-to-finish

8. The _____ method is a network diagramming technique used to predict total project duration.

   a. PERT

   b. Gantt chart

   c. critical path

   d. crashing

9. What cost estimating technique uses project characteristics in a mathematical model to estimate project costs?

   a. parametric modeling

   b. fast-track estimating

   c. analogous estimating

   d. bottom-up estimating

10. A _____ is a time-phased budget that project managers use to measure and monitor cost performance.

   a. cost baseline

   b. cost estimate

   c. life-cycle budget

   d. cash flow analysis

Quick Quiz Answers

1. D; 2. B; 3. B; 4. C; 5. D; 6. B; 7. A; 8. C; 9. A; 10. A

Discussion Questions

1. Why does having good plans help project teams during project execution? Why is it difficult to develop good plans?

2. What are the main planning tasks performed as part of project integration management? What are the main documents created, and what are some of their main contents?

3. What are the main planning tasks performed as part of project scope management? What are some approaches for creating a WBS? Why is it important to develop a good WBS? What do you think about the scope planning documents prepared by the Just-In-Time Training project team? Do they seem too broad or too detailed in certain areas?

4. What are the main planning tasks performed as part of project time management? What is the critical path for a project, and why is it important to know which tasks are on the critical path?

5. What are the main planning tasks performed as part of project cost management? What is the difference between a cost estimate and a cost baseline? Why is it important to have clear ground rules and assumptions for a cost estimate?

Exercises

1. Find an example of a large project that took more than a year to complete, such as a major construction project. Describe some of the tasks done in planning the integration, scope, time, and cost aspects of the project. Write a one-page paper or prepare a short presentation summarizing your findings.

2. Review the sample scope statement in Table 4-5. Assume you are responsible for planning and then managing the course development for the introductory supplier management course. What additional information would you want to know to develop a good schedule and cost estimate, and why? Write a one-page paper or prepare a short presentation summarizing your response.

3. Consider Table 4-11. All duration estimates are in days, and the network proceeds from Node 1 to Node 9.

TABLE 4-11 Network diagram data for a small project

Activity	Initial node	Final node	Duration estimate
A	1	2	2
B	2	3	2
C	2	4	3
D	2	5	4
E	3	6	2
F	4	6	3
G	5	7	6
H	6	8	2
I	6	7	5
J	7	8	1
K	8	9	2

a. Draw an AOA network diagram representing the project. Put the node numbers in circles and draw arrows from node to node, labeling each arrow with the activity letter and estimated duration.

b. Identify all the paths on the network diagram and note how long they are, using Figure 4-7 as a guide for how to represent each path.

c. What is the critical path for this project, and how long is it?

d. What is the shortest possible time it will take to complete this project?

e. Enter the information into Project 2003. See the *Guide to Using Microsoft Project 2003* on the companion Web site for detailed instructions on using this software. View the network diagram and task schedule table to see the critical path and float or slack for each activity. Print the Gantt chart and network diagram views and the task schedule table. Write a short paper that interprets this information for someone unfamiliar with project time management.

4. Create a cost estimate/model for redecorating a room using spreadsheet software. Assume you have one month and $5,000 to spend. Develop a WBS for the project and create a cost model based on your WBS. Document the assumptions you made in preparing the estimate and provide explanations for key numbers.

Team Projects

1. Your organization initiated a project to raise money for an important charity. Assume that there are 1,000 people in your organization. Also assume that you have six months to raise as much money as possible, with a goal of $100,000. Develop a scope statement, WBS, and Gantt chart for the project. Be creative in deciding how you will raise the money and the major work packages required to complete the project. Assume that the only costs are volunteer labor, so you do not need to prepare a cost estimate.

2. You are part of a team in charge of a project to help people in your company (500 people) lose weight. This project is part of a competition, and the top "losers" will be featured in a popular television show. Assume that you have six months to complete the project and a budget of $10,000. Develop a scope statement, WBS, Gantt chart, and cost estimate for the project.

3. Using the information you developed in Project 1 or 2, role-play a meeting to review one of these planning documents with key stakeholders. Determine who will play what role (project manager, team member from a certain department, senior managers, and so on). Be creative in displaying different personalities (a senior manager who questions the importance of the project to the organization, a team member who is very shy or obnoxious).

4. Perform the applicable integration, scope, time, and cost planning tasks for one of the real projects your class or group developed in Chapter 1. At a minimum, prepare a team contract, a project management plan, a scope statement, a WBS, a Gantt chart, and a cost estimate. Remember to be thorough in your planning so that your execution goes smoothly.

Companion Web Site

Visit the companion Web site for this text (*www.course.com/mis/pm/schwalbe*) to access:

- Lecture notes
- Interactive quizzes
- Template files
- Sample documents
- Guide to Using Microsoft Project 2003
- VPMi enterprise project management software
- More ideas for team projects, including real projects and case studies
- Links to additional resources related to project management

Key Terms

activity attributes — Information that provides schedule-related information about each activity, such as predecessors, successors, logical relationships, leads and lags, resource requirements, constraints, imposed dates, and assumptions related to the activity.

activity list — A tabulation of activities to be included on a project schedule.

activity-on-arrow (AOA) approach, or the **arrow diagramming method (ADM)** — A network diagramming technique in which activities are represented by arrows and connected at points called nodes to illustrate the sequence of activities.

analogous estimates, or **top-down estimates** — The estimates that use the actual cost of a previous, similar project as the basis for estimating the cost of the current project.

baseline — A starting point, a measurement, or an observation that is documented so that it can be used for future comparison; also defined as the original project plans plus approved changes.

bottom-up estimates — Cost estimates created by estimating individual activities and summing them to get a project total.

burst — An occurence when two or more activities follow a single node on a network diagram.

cost baseline — A time-phased budget that project managers use to measure and monitor cost performance.

crashing — A technique for making cost and schedule trade-offs to obtain the greatest amount of schedule compression for the least incremental cost.

critical path — The series of activities that determine the *earliest* time by which the project can be completed; it is the *longest* path through the network diagram and has the least amount of slack or float.

critical path method (CPM), or **critical path analysis** — A network diagramming technique used to predict total project duration.

dependency, or **relationship** — The sequencing of project activities or tasks.

discretionary dependencies — The dependencies that are defined by the project team.

duration — The actual amount of time spent working on an activity *plus* elapsed time.

effort — The number of workdays or work hours required to complete a task.

external dependencies — The dependencies that involve relationships between project and non-project activities.

fast tracking — A schedule compression technique where you do activities in parallel that you would normally do in sequence.

Gantt charts — A standard format for displaying project schedule information by listing project activities and their corresponding start and finish dates in a calendar format.

mandatory dependencies — The dependencies that are inherent in the nature of the work being performed on a project.

merge — A situation when two or more nodes precede a single node on a network diagram.

milestone — A significant event on a project.

network diagram — A schematic display of the logical relationships among, or sequencing of, project activities.

node — The starting and ending point of an activity on an activity-on-arrow network diagram.

parametric modeling — A technique that uses project characteristics (parameters) in a mathematical model to estimate project costs.

precedence diagramming method (PDM) — A network diagramming technique in which boxes represent activities.

Program Evaluation and Review Technique (PERT) — A network analysis technique used to estimate project duration when there is a high degree of uncertainty about the individual activity duration estimates.

project buffer — The additional time added before a project's due date to account for unexpected factors.

project cost management — The processes required to ensure that a project team completes a project within an approved budget.

project integration management — The process of coordinating all the project management knowledge areas throughout a project's life cycle.

project management plan — A document, which is a deliverable for the project integration management knowledge area, used to coordinate all project planning documents and to help guide a project's execution and control.

project scope management — The process of defining and controlling what work is or is not included in a project.

project time management — The process required to ensure timely completion of a project.

scope baseline — The approved project scope statement and its associated WBS and WBS dictionary.

scope management plan — A document that includes descriptions of how the team will prepare the project scope statement, create the WBS, verify completion of the project deliverables, and control requests for changes to the project scope.

slack or **float** — The amount of time an activity may be delayed without delaying a succeeding activity or the project finish date.

team contract — A document created to help promote teamwork and clarify team communications.

three-point estimate — An estimate that includes an optimistic, most likely, and pessimistic estimate.

work breakdown structure (WBS) — A deliverable-oriented grouping of the work involved in a project that defines the total scope of the project.

work breakdown structure (WBS) dictionary — A document that describes detailed information about each WBS task.

work package — A task at the lowest level of the WBS.

End Notes

[1] Ross Foti, "The Best Winter Olympics, Period," *PM Network* (January 2004) p. 23.

[2] Ibid, p. 23.

[3] Kathleen Melymuke, "Spit and Polish," *ComputerWorld* (February 16, 1998).

CHAPTER 5

PLANNING PROJECTS, PART 2 (PROJECT QUALITY, HUMAN RESOURCE, COMMUNI- CATIONS, RISK, AND PROCUREMENT MANAGEMENT)

LEARNING OBJECTIVES

After reading this chapter, you will be able to:

- List several planning tasks and outputs for project quality, human resource, communications, risk, and procurement management

- Discuss the project quality management planning tasks, and explain the purpose and contents of a quality management plan, quality metrics, and quality checklists

- Explain the project human resource management planning tasks, and create a project organizational chart, responsibility assignment matrix, resource histogram, and staffing management plan

- Describe the project communications management planning tasks, and describe the importance of using a project communications manage- ment plan and project Web site

- Discuss the project risk management planning tasks, and explain how a risk management plan, a probability/impact matrix, a risk register, and risk-related contractual agreements are used in risk management planning

- Discuss the project procurement management planning tasks, and explain a make-or-buy analysis, procurement management plans, requests for proposal/quote, contract statements of work, and supplier evaluation matrices

INTRODUCTION

Everyone knows that it is important to effectively plan the scope, time, and cost dimensions of a project and to develop the overall project management plan as part of integration management. However, some project managers neglect planning in the other knowledge areas—quality, human resource, communications, risk, and procurement management. It is important to skillfully plan *all* of these areas because they are all crucial to project success. This chapter summarizes key information on planning in these knowledge areas and specific actions that Kristin and her team took. The next chapter, which covers executing projects, shows how plans provide the basis for executing tasks.

SUMMARY OF PLANNING TASKS AND OUTPUTS

Table 5-1 shows the project planning outputs for quality, human resource, communications, risk, and procurement management that Global Construction will use on the Just-In-Time Training project. As mentioned in Chapter 4, these planning documents, as well as other project-related information, will be available to all team members on a project Web site.

TABLE 5-1 Planning outputs for project quality, human resource, communications, risk, and procurement management

Knowledge area	Outputs
Project quality management	Quality management plan Quality metrics Quality checklist
Project human resource management	Project organizational chart Responsibility assignment matrix Resource histogram Staffing management plan
Project communications management	Communications management plan Project Web site
Project risk management	Risk management plan Probability/impact matrix Risk register Risk-related contractual agreements
Project procurement management	Make-or-buy analysis Procurement management plan Requests for proposal/quote Contract statement of work Supplier evaluation matrix

The following sections describe planning tasks in the quality, human resource, communications, risk, and procurement management knowledge areas, and then provide examples of applying them to the Just-In-Time Training project at Global Construction. You can download templates for creating these planning documents and access the sample Web site and the documents provided in this chapter from the companion Web site for this text.

PROJECT QUALITY MANAGEMENT PLANNING TASKS

Project quality management ensures that the project will satisfy the stated or implied needs for which it was undertaken. Key outputs produced as part of project quality management include a quality management plan, quality metrics, and quality checklists. Before describing these outputs, it is important to understand what quality is and why it is an important part of project management.

The International Organization for Standardization (ISO) defines **quality** as "the degree to which a set of inherent characteristics fulfill requirements" (ISO9000:2000). Other experts define quality based on conformance to requirements and fitness for use. **Conformance to requirements** means that the project's processes and products meet written specifications. For example, Kristin's project team might write specifications stating that a course must cover certain topics and be written in English, Chinese, and Japanese. As part of quality management, Kristin's team would verify that the training vendors meet those written requirements. **Fitness for use,** on the other hand, means that a product can be used as it was intended. For example, a training vendor might develop a course in English and then translate it into Chinese and Japanese, but the translations might be faulty, causing confusion to learners. These translated courses, then, would not be fit for use, even though they might have met the written specifications.

Recall that project management involves meeting or exceeding stakeholder needs and expectations. To understand what quality means to the stakeholders, the project team must develop good relationships with them—especially the main customer for the project. *After all, the customer ultimately decides that the quality level is acceptable.* Many projects fail because the project team focuses only on meeting the written requirements for the main products being produced and ignores other stakeholder needs and expectations for the project.

Quality, therefore, must be considered on an equal level of importance with project scope, time, and cost. If a project's stakeholders are not satisfied with the quality of the project management or the resulting products, the project team will need to adjust scope, time, and cost to satisfy stakeholder needs and expectations. Meeting only written requirements for scope, time, and cost is not sufficient.

Quality Planning and the Quality Management Plan

Quality planning includes identifying which quality standards are relevant to the project and how best to satisfy those standards. It also involves designing quality into the products of the project as well as the processes involved in managing the project. It is important to describe important factors that directly contribute to meeting customer requirements. Organizational policies related to quality, the scope statement and product descriptions, and related standards and regulations are all important inputs to the quality planning process.

The quality management plan describes how the project management team will implement quality policies. Like other project plans, its format and contents vary based on the particular project and organizational needs. It can be a long, formal document or short and informal.

Sample Quality Management Plan

Kristin and her team worked together to create a quality management plan for the Just-In-Time Training project (see Table 5-2). The primary purpose of the plan was to ensure that all the products and services produced as part of the project are of known quality and sufficient quantity to meet customer expectations.

TABLE 5-2 Sample quality management plan

> ### Quality Management Plan
> ### August 20, 2007
>
> **Project Name:** Just-In-Time Training Project
>
> **Introduction**
>
> The main goal of this project is to develop a new training program that provides just-in-time training to employees on key topics, including supplier management, negotiating skills, project management, and software applications.
>
> **Quality Standards**
>
> The standards that apply to this project are summarized as follows:
>
> 1. Survey standards: See Attachment 1 for corporate standards for developing and administering surveys to employees. Quantitative and qualitative information will be collected. Quantitative data will use a 5-point Likert scale as much as possible. A corporate expert on surveys will review the survey before it is administered.
>
> 2. Supplier selection standards: See Attachment 2 for corporate standards regarding supplier selection. Past performance and developing partnerships will be key issues for this project.
>
> 3. Training standards: See Attachment 3 for corporate standards regarding training. The training provided as part of this project will be available in several formats, including instructor-led, CD-ROM, and Web-based. Employees will have access to CD-ROM and Web-based training at any time to meet individual and business needs on a just-in-time manner.
>
> Etc.
>
> **Metrics**
>
> Metrics measure quality performance. Several metrics apply to this project, and more may be developed as the project progresses. The project team will use a few key metrics, as follows:
>
> 1. Survey response rate: For the survey to be successful, a response rate of at least 25 percent must be achieved.
>
> 2. Course evaluations: All course participants must complete a course evaluation, In addition to evaluations on more detailed topics, there will be an overall course rating. The average course rating should be 3.0 or better on a 5.0 scale.
>
> Etc.
>
> **Problem Reporting and Corrective Action Processes**
>
> Project plans will include clear roles and responsibilities for all stakeholders. The person responsible for an individual task should report problems to appropriate managers (see the project organizational chart) and work with them to determine and implement corrective actions. Major problems should be brought to the attention of the project manager, who should elevate problems that might affect project success—including meeting scope, time, cost, and quality goals—to the project steering committee and then the project sponsor. It is crucial to address problems as early as possible and develop several alternative solutions
>
> **Supplier Quality and Control**
>
> The project manager will closely monitor work performed by suppliers, with assistance from our supplier management department. The contract must clearly state quality standards, metrics, etc.
>
> Etc.

Quality Metrics

A **metric** is a standard of measurement. Metrics allow organizations to measure their performance in certain areas and to compare them over time or with other organizations. Examples of common metrics used by organizations include failure rates of products produced, availability of goods and services, and customer satisfaction ratings.

Sample Quality Metrics

As mentioned in the sample quality management plan, two important metrics related to the Just-In-Time Training project include the survey response rate and course evaluation ratings. Table 5-3 provides more information on these metrics.

TABLE 5-3 Sample quality metrics

Quality Metrics
August 20, 2007

Project Name: Just-In-Time Training Project

The following quality metrics apply to this project:

1. Survey response rate: In order for the survey to be successful, a response rate of at least 25 percent must be achieved. Most surveys will be administered online using the standard corporate survey software, which can track the response rate automatically. If the response rate is less than 25 percent one week after the survey is sent out, the project manager will alert the project steering committee to determine corrective action.

2. Course evaluations: All course participants must complete a course evaluation so that their training can be tracked in our corporate professional development system. In addition to evaluations on more detailed topics, there will be an overall course rating. The average course rating should be at least 3.0, with 5.0 being the highest score. Surveys should include questions measured on a Likert scale. For example, a question might be as follows: "My overall evaluation of this course is _____." Respondents would select 1 for Poor, 2 for Fair, 3 for Average, 4 for Good, or 5 for Excellent.

Etc.

Quality Checklists

A **checklist** is a list of items to be noted or consulted. Checklists help project teams verify that a set of required topics or steps has been covered or performed. A single project can have many different checklists. For example, there can be checklists related to interviewing project team members, selecting suppliers, reviewing important documents, ensuring a room is ready for training, and so on.

Sample Quality Checklist

Kristin and her team developed several checklists for their project and used others that were available on the corporate intranet. Table 5-4 is a sample checklist that the company uses for ensuring that training rooms are in proper order.

TABLE 5-4 Sample quality checklist

> **Quality Checklist**
> **August 20, 2007**
>
> **Project Name:** Just-In-Time Training Project
> **Checklist Purpose:** Ensure the training classroom is in proper order.
> - ☐ Tables and chairs are arranged in a U-shape and properly aligned.
> - ☐ Room has been cleaned and is free of trash.
> - ☐ Whiteboards are clean.
> - ☐ Projection system is in working order.
> - ☐ Overhead, flip chart, or other ordered equipment is available.
> - ☐ Supplies are readily available (i.e., markers, sticky notes, name plates)
> - ☐ Food and beverages have been ordered.

PROJECT HUMAN RESOURCE MANAGEMENT PLANNING TASKS

Many corporate executives have said, "People are our most important asset." People determine the success and failure of organizations and projects. **Project human resource management** is concerned with making effective use of the people involved with a project. Key outputs produced as part of project human resource management planning include developing a project organizational chart, a responsibility assignment matrix, a resource histogram, and a staffing management plan. Chapter 6, which covers project execution, includes much more information on project human resource management, as Kristin faces many challenges related to this topic. Planning human resources effectively will help her face these challenges.

Project Organizational Charts

After identifying the important skills and types of people needed to staff a project, the project manager should work with top management and project team members to create an organizational chart for the project. Similar to a company's organizational chart, a **project organizational chart** is a graphic representation of how authority and responsibility is distributed within the project. The size and complexity of the project determines how simple or complex the organizational chart is.

Sample Project Organizational Chart

Figure 5-1 shows a project organizational chart that Kristin put together. After supplier project managers and other personnel were assigned, Kristin would fill in more of the chart. Notice that Kristin has a direct reporting line to the project sponsor. Also note that the project steering committee and project sponsor have a strong role on the project. Sometimes, dotted lines are used to represent indirect reporting relationships.

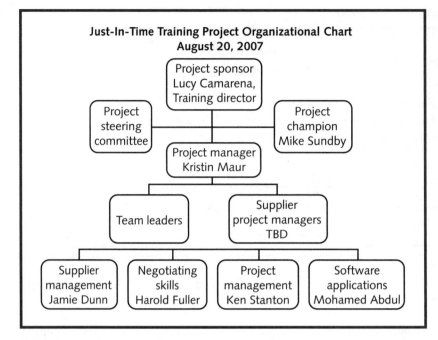

FIGURE 5-1   Sample project organizational chart

Responsibility Assignment Matrices

A **responsibility assignment matrix (RAM)** is a matrix that maps the work of the project as described in the work breakdown structure (WBS) to the people responsible for performing the work. A RAM allocates work to responsible and performing organizations, teams, or individuals, depending on the desired level of detail. For smaller projects, it is best to assign WBS activities to individuals. For larger projects, it is more effective to assign the work to organizational units or teams. In addition to using a RAM to assign detailed work activities, you can use a RAM to define general roles and responsibilities on projects. This type of RAM can include the stakeholders in the project. The project team should decide what to use as categories in the RAM and include a key to explain those categories. For example, a RAM can show whether stakeholders are accountable for (A) or just participants (P) in part of a project, and whether they are required to provide input (I), review (R), or sign off (S) on parts of a project. This simple tool enables the project manager to efficiently communicate the roles of project team members and expectations of important project stakeholders.

Sample Responsibility Assignment Matrix

Some organizations, including Global Construction, use **RACI charts**—a type of responsibility assignment matrix that shows **R**esponsibility, **A**ccountability, **C**onsultation, and **I**nformed roles for project stakeholders. Table 5-5 shows a RACI chart that Kristin developed for the supplier management training part of the project. Jamie and Mohamed were early members of the project team, and Supplier A represents the supplier who would be selected to provide the supplier management training courses. Notice that the RACI chart lists tasks vertically and individuals or groups horizontally, and that each intersecting cell contains at least one of the letters R, A, C, or I. Each task may have multiple A, C, or I entries, but there can only be one R entry to clarify which particular individual or group has responsibility for each task. One person can also have multiple roles for each task, such as being responsible and accountable.

TABLE 5-5 Sample RACI chart

Just-In-Time Training Project RACI Chart
August 20, 2007

Tasks	Kristin	Jamie	Mohamed	Supplier A
Needs assessment	R	A	C	I
Research of existing training	I	R, A	C	I
Partnerships	R, A	I	I	C
Course development	R	C	C	A
Pilot course	R	C	I	A
Course administration	I	R	A	I
Course evaluation	I	R	A	I
Stakeholder communications	R, A	A	C	C

R: Responsible
A: Accountable
C: Consulted
I: Informed

Resource Histograms

A **resource histogram** is a column chart that shows the number of resources required for or assigned to a project over time. In planning project staffing needs, senior managers often create a resource histogram in which columns represent the number of people needed in each skill category, such as managers, IT specialists, and HR specialists. By stacking the columns, you can see the total number of people needed each month. After resources are assigned to a project, you can view a resource histogram for each person to see how his time has been allocated. You can create resource histograms using spreadsheets or project management software. See the companion Web site for information on using Project 2003 to view resource allocations.

Sample Resource Histogram

Kristin worked with other managers to estimate how many internal resources they would need for the Just-In-Time Training project over time. They decided that in addition to herself (the project manager [PM]), they would require people from human resources (HR), supplier management (SM), information technology (IT), the project management office

(PMO), and the contracting department. After contracts were written, Kristin could request a similar resource histogram from each supplier to review overall staffing for the project. Figure 5-2 is the resulting resource histogram for internal resources, showing the total number of people, or head count, by month. If needed, Kristin could also develop a similar chart showing the estimated number of hours.

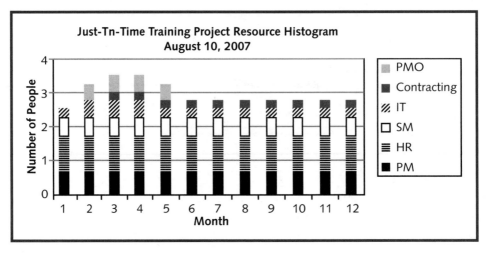

FIGURE 5-2   Sample resource histogram

Staffing Management Plans

A **staffing management plan** describes when and how people will be added to and removed from a project. The level of detail can vary based on the type of project. The staffing management plan describes the types of people needed to work on the project, and the numbers needed for each type of person each month. It also describes how these resources will be acquired, trained, rewarded, and reassigned after the project, and so on. All these issues are important to meeting the needs of the project, the employees, and the organization.

Sample Staffing Management Plan

Table 5-6 provides part of a staffing management plan that Kristin created for the Just-In-Time Training project.

TABLE 5-6 Sample staffing management plan

Staffing Management Plan
August 20, 2007

Project Name: Just-in-time training project

Introduction

The main goal of this project is to develop a new training program that provides just-in-time training to employees on key topics, including supplier management, negotiating skills, project management, and software applications.

Staffing Requirements

This project will require the following internal staff:

- Project manager (PM) (assigned 3/4 time)

- Project team members from the training department (two people assigned half-time) to help with all project training

- Project team member from the supplier management (SM) department (assigned half-time) to assist with supplier management training

- Information technology (IT) department staff to help with technical support and software applications training

- Project management (PM) staff to help with project management training

- Contracting department staff to assist in administering project contracts

See the resource histogram in Atch A for projected staffing needs over time.

Staff Assignments

The project manager will work through functional managers to assign individuals to the project. The project manager will interview potential candidates to determine suitability. If particular expertise is required for part of the project, the functional managers will plan to make experts available. Employees will be paid overtime if needed.

Training, Rewards, and Reassignment

Ideally, people assigned to this project will have appropriate experience or be willing to learn quickly on the job. The project manager will do his or her best to provide a challenging and enjoyable work environment. Assignment to the project will not affect an individual's salary, but the project manager will write a performance evaluation and recommend appropriate rewards. If an individual is not performing as expected, the project manager will work with him or her and the appropriate functional manager to determine reassignment.

Atch A: Resource histogram

PROJECT COMMUNICATIONS MANAGEMENT PLANNING TASKS

Many experts agree that the greatest threat to the success of any project is a failure to communicate. Many project managers say that 90 percent of their job is communicating. Yet many project managers fail to take the time to plan for project communications. Even though having a plan does not guarantee that all communications will flow smoothly, it certainly helps.

WHAT WENT WRONG?

An amusing example of miscommunication comes from a director of communications at a large firm:

I was asked to prepare a memo reviewing our company's training programs and materials. In the body of the memo in one of the sentences, I mentioned the *"pedagogical approach"* used by one of the training manuals. The day after I routed the memo to the executive committee, I was called into the HR director's office, and told that the executive vice president wanted me out of the building by lunch. When I asked why, I was told that she wouldn't stand for perverts (pedophiles?) working in her company. Finally, he showed me her copy of the memo, with her demand that I be fired—and the word *"pedagogical"*—circled in red. The HR manager was fairly reasonable, and once he looked the word up in his dictionary and made a copy of the definition to send back to her, he told me not to worry. He would take care of it. Two days later, a memo to the entire staff came out directing us that no words that could not be found in the local Sunday newspaper could be used in company memos. A month later, I resigned. In accordance with company policy, I created my resignation memo by pasting words together from the Sunday paper.[1]

Project communications management involves generating, collecting, disseminating, and storing project information. Key outputs produced for the Just-In-Time Training project include a communications management plan and a project Web site.

Communications Management Plans

Because project communication is so important, every project should include a **communications management plan**—a document that guides project communications. The communications management plan will vary with the needs of the project, but some type of written plan should always be prepared. The communications management plan should address the following items:

- Stakeholder communications requirements
- Information to be communicated, including format, content, and level of detail
- Identification of who will receive the information and who will produce it
- Suggested methods or guidelines for conveying the information
- Description of the frequency of communication
- Escalation procedures for resolving issues
- Revision procedures for updating the communications management plan
- A glossary of common terminology used on the project

Sample Communications Management Plan

Kristin and her team drafted a communications management plan (Table 5-7) for the Just-In-Time Training project. The project steering committee reviewed it and provided suggestions on how to keep communication lines open. They advised Kristin to stress the importance of communications with *all* project stakeholders. They also mentioned the fact that people communicate in different ways, and so recommended that her team not be afraid of overcommunicating by providing the same information in multiple formats. The steering committee noted that it is not enough to provide formal documents; Kristin and her team should use face-to-face communications, e-mails, phone calls, and other communications media to ensure optimal communications. Recall that the WBS for this project included an item called stakeholder communications to ensure good project communications.

TABLE 5-7 Sample communications management plan

Communications Management Plan Version 1.0
August 28, 2007

Project Name: Just-In-Time Training Project

1. Stakeholder communications requirements:

Because this project involves many people from all over the company as well as outside suppliers, the project team will use surveys, interviews, checklists, and other tools and techniques to determine the communications requirements for various stakeholders. Employees will have specific communications needs in that several training programs are being totally changed, and they will likely be uncomfortable with that change. Suppliers will have communications needs to ensure that they are developing courses that will meet our organization's needs. Internal experts providing content will have communications needs related to providing useful information, and so on.

2. Communications summary:

The following table summarizes various stakeholders; communications required; the delivery method or format of the communications; who will produce the communications; and when they will be distributed, or the frequency of distribution. All communications produced will be archived and available on the project Web site. As more communications items are defined, they will be added to this list. The project team will use various templates and checklists to enhance communications. The team will also be careful to use the appropriate medium (that is, face-to-face meeting, phone, e-mail, hard copy, Web site, and so on) and follow corporate guidelines for effective communications.

Stakeholders	Communications Name	Delivery Method/Format	Producer	Due/Frequency
Project steering committee	Weekly status report	Hard copy and short meeting	Kristin Maur	Wednesdays at 9 a.m.
Sponsor and champion	Monthly status report	Hard copy and short meeting	Kristin Maur	First Thursday of month at 10 a.m.
Affected employees	Project announcement	Memo, e-mail, intranet site, and announcement at department meetings	Lucy Camarena and Mike Sundby	July 1, 2007
Project team	Weekly status report	Short meeting	All team members	Tuesdays at 2 p.m.

TABLE 5-7 Sample communications management plan (continued)

3. **Guidelines:**
   - Make sure people understand your communications. Use commonsense techniques to check comprehension, such as having them explain what you mean in their own words. Don't overuse/misuse e-mail or other technologies. Short meetings or phone calls can be very effective.
   - Use templates as much as possible for written project communications. The project Web site includes a link to all project-related templates.
   - Use the titles and dates of documents in e-mail headings, and have recipients acknowledge receipt.
   - Prepare and post meeting minutes within 24 hours of a meeting.
   - Use checklists for reviewing product requirements, conducting interviews, and so on.
   - Use corporate facilitators for important meetings, such as kick-off meetings and supplier negotiations.

4. **Escalation procedures for resolving issues:**

   Issues should be resolved at the lowest level possible. When they cannot be resolved, affected parties should alert their immediate supervisors of the issues. If it is critical to the project or extremely time sensitive, the issue should be brought directly to the project manager. If the project manager cannot resolve an issue, he or she should bring it to the project steering committee or appropriate senior management, as required.

5. **Revision procedures for this document:**

   Revisions to this plan will be approved by the project manager. The revision number and date will be clearly marked at the top of the document.

6. **Glossary of common terminology:**

   actual cost—The total direct and indirect costs incurred in accomplishing work on an activity during a given period.

   baseline—The original project plan plus approved changes.

   bid—A document prepared by sellers providing pricing for standard items that have been clearly defined by the buyer.
   Etc.

Project Web Sites

In the past few years, more and more project teams have started posting all or part of their project information to project Web sites. Project Web sites provide a centralized way of delivering project documents and other communications. Some project teams also create **blogs**—easy-to-use journals on the Web that allow users to write entries, create links, and upload pictures, while allowing readers to post comments to particular journal entries. Project teams can develop project Web sites using Web-authoring tools, such as Microsoft FrontPage or Macromedia Dreamweaver; enterprise project management software, if available; or a combination of the two approaches. Part of the Web site might be open to outside users, whereas other parts might be accessible only by certain stakeholders. It is important to decide if and how to use a project Web site to help meet project communications requirements.

Sample Project Web Site

Kristin and her team entered detailed project information into the company's enterprise project management software. From within that system, Kristin could control who could and could not see various types of information. In addition, she worked with her team and the IT department to create a simple project Web site using a project Web site template of Microsoft FrontPage. This site would be available on the corporate intranet. Kristin's team felt it was important to let all employees access basic information about the project. Figure 5-3 shows the home page of the Web site for the Just-In-Time Training project. It includes summary information, such as project objectives, new information, and key milestones. It also includes links to information on team members, the project schedule, the project archive, a search feature, a discussions feature, and contact information.

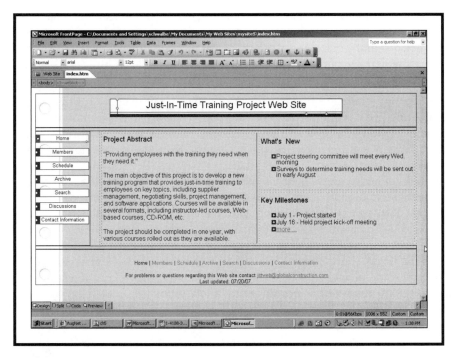

FIGURE 5-3   Sample project web site

PROJECT RISK MANAGEMENT PLANNING TASKS

As a frequently overlooked aspect of project management, risk management can often result in significant improvements in the chance of a project succeeding. What is risk as it relates to a project? PMI defines a project **risk** as an uncertainty that can have a *negative or positive* effect on meeting project objectives. Key outputs of project risk management planning include a risk management plan, a probability/impact matrix, a risk register, and risk-related contractual agreements.

Risk Management Plans

A risk management plan documents the procedures for managing risk *throughout the life of a project*. Project teams should hold several planning meetings early in the project's life cycle to help develop the risk management plan. The project team should review project documents as well as corporate risk management policies, risk categories, lessons learned from past projects, and templates for creating a risk management plan. It is also important to review the risk tolerances of various stakeholders. For example, if the project sponsor is risk-averse, the project might require a different approach to risk management than if the project sponsor were a risk seeker.

A risk management plan summarizes how risk management will be performed on a particular project. Like other specific knowledge area plans, it becomes a subset of the project management plan. The general topics that a risk management plan should address include the methodology for risk management, roles and responsibilities, budget and schedule estimates for risk-related activities, risk categories, probability and impact matrices, and risk documentation. The level of detail included in the risk management plan will vary with the needs of the project.

In addition to a risk management plan, many projects also include contingency plans, fallback plans, and contingency reserves.

- **Contingency plans** are predefined actions that the project team will take if an identified risk event occurs. For example, if the project team knows that the new version of a product they need might not be available in time, they might have a contingency plan to use the existing, older version of the product.
- **Fallback plans** are developed for risks that have a high impact on meeting project objectives, and are put into effect if attempts to reduce the risk are not effective. For example, a new college graduate might have a main plan and several contingency plans on where to live after graduation, but if none of those plans work out, a fallback plan might be to live at home for a while. Sometimes the terms *contingency plan* and *fallback plan* are used interchangeably, and some people view fallback plans as contingency plans of last resort.
- **Contingency reserves** or **contingency allowances** are funds held by the project sponsor that can be used to mitigate cost or schedule overruns if unknown risks occur. For example, if a project appears to be off course because the staff is not experienced with a new technology and the team had not identified that as a risk, the project sponsor might provide additional funds from contingency reserves to hire an outside consultant to train and advise the project staff in using the new technology. All of these contingency plans, fallback plans, and contingency reserves show the importance of taking a proactive approach to managing project risks by purchasing extra wide computer monitors to display the long schedules.

Figure 5-4 provides a humorous example of preparing for risks that might cause schedule delays by purchasing extra wide computer monitors to display the long schedules.

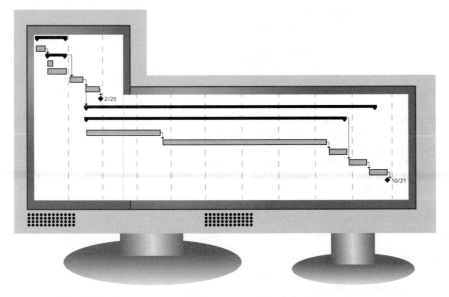

FIGURE 5-4 Special monitor to help manage schedule delays

Sample Risk Management Plan

Kristin knew that it was important to plan efficiently for the risk management of the Just-In-Time Training project. There were several negative and positive risks associated with this project. Kristin asked Ron Ryan, the project manager of the Phase I project, to assist her in drafting the first version of the risk management plan. She also received input from the project steering committee, and as her team and suppliers were identified, they would work together to update the plan as needed. Table 5-8 shows the initial risk management plan.

TABLE 5-8 Sample risk management plan

Risk Management Plan
September 3, 2007

Project Name: Just-In-Time Training Project

1. Methodology

The project team will review data available from the Phase I project and past training programs within Global Construction to assist in risk management planning. They will also review information related to external projects similar to this one. The team will use several tools and techniques, including brainstorming, surveys, and risk-related checklists to assist in risk management.

2. Roles and Responsibilities

The project manager will be responsible for leading the team and other stakeholders in performing risk-related activities. As detailed tasks and deliverables are determined, the project manager will delegate those tasks as appropriate.

3. Budget and Schedule Estimates

As specific risk-related tasks and deliverables are determined, budget and schedule information will be provided.

4. Risk Categories

General categories and subcategories for risk on this project include business risks (suppliers and cash flow), technical risks (course content, hardware, software, and network), organizational risks (executive support, user/employee support, supplier support, and team support), and project management risks (estimates, communication, and resources).

5. Risk Probability and Impact

Risk probability and impact will initially be estimated as high, medium, or low based on expert advice. If more advanced scoring is needed, the project team will determine an appropriate approach.

6. Risk Documentation

All risk-related information will be summarized in a risk register. Detailed documentation will be available in a secure area on the project Web site.

Probability/Impact Matrices

It is important to evaluate risks to determine which ones need the most attention. **Risk events** refer to specific, uncertain events that may occur to the detriment or enhancement of the project. For example, negative risk events might include the performance failure of a product produced as part of a project, delays in completing work as scheduled, increases in estimated costs, supply shortages, litigation against the company, and strikes. Examples of positive risk events include completing work sooner than planned or at an unexpectedly reduced cost, collaborating with suppliers to produce better products, and obtaining good publicity from the project.

There are two important dimensions of risk events: probability of the risk event occurring and the impact or consequence if the risk does occur. People often describe a risk event probability or impact as being high, medium, or low. For example, a meteorologist might predict that there is a high probability of severe rain showers on a certain day. If that happens to be your wedding day and you are planning a large outdoor wedding, the impact or consequences of severe showers would also be high.

A project manager can chart the probability and impact of risk events on a probability/impact matrix or chart. One side (axis) of a probability/impact matrix or chart lists the relative *probability* of a risk event occurring, and the other side (axis) of the chart shows the relative *impact* of the risk event occurring. To use this approach, project stakeholders identify and list the risk events related to their projects. They then label each risk event as being high, medium, or low in terms of its probability of occurrence and level of impact. The project manager then summarizes the results in a probability/impact matrix. Project teams should initially focus on risk events that fall in the high sections of the probability/impact matrix and develop strategies for minimizing negative risk events and maximizing positive ones.

Sample Probability/Impact Matrix

Kristin Maur worked with several project stakeholders early in the project to begin identifying several negative and positive risk events related to the Just-In-Time Training project. She held a brainstorming session in which over 100 risk events were identified. To differentiate between the two, she asked participants to identify negative risk events and then positive ones. After people identified a risk event and wrote it down on a sticky note, Kristin asked them to mark each one as having a high, medium, or low probability of occurrence and impact. Kristin had posted on the whiteboard large probability/impact matrices—one for negative risk events and another for positive risk events. Everyone put their sticky notes in the appropriate sections of the appropriate matrix. They then examined the results to combine and reword risk events to improve collaboration and avoid duplicates.

Figure 5-5 shows part of the resulting probability/impact matrix. For example, risks 1 and 4 are listed as high in both categories of probability and impact. Risk 6 is high in the probability category but low in the impact category. Risk 9 is high in the probability category and medium in the impact category. Risk 12 is low in the probability category but high in the impact category. The team then discussed how they planned to respond to risks in the medium and high categories, and documented the results in the risk register, as described in the following section.

Risk Registers

A **risk register** is a document that contains results of various risk management processes, often displayed in a table or spreadsheet format. It is a tool for documenting potential risk events and related information. The risk register often includes the following main headings:

- *An identification number for each risk event:* The project team might want to sort or quickly search for specific risk events, so they need to identify each risk with some type of unique descriptor, such as an identification number.
- *A rank for each risk event:* The rank can be indicated as high, medium, or low, or it can be a number, with 1 being the highest-ranked risk. The project team would have to determine these rankings.
- *The name of the risk event:* For example, defective product, poor survey results, reduced consulting costs, or good publicity.

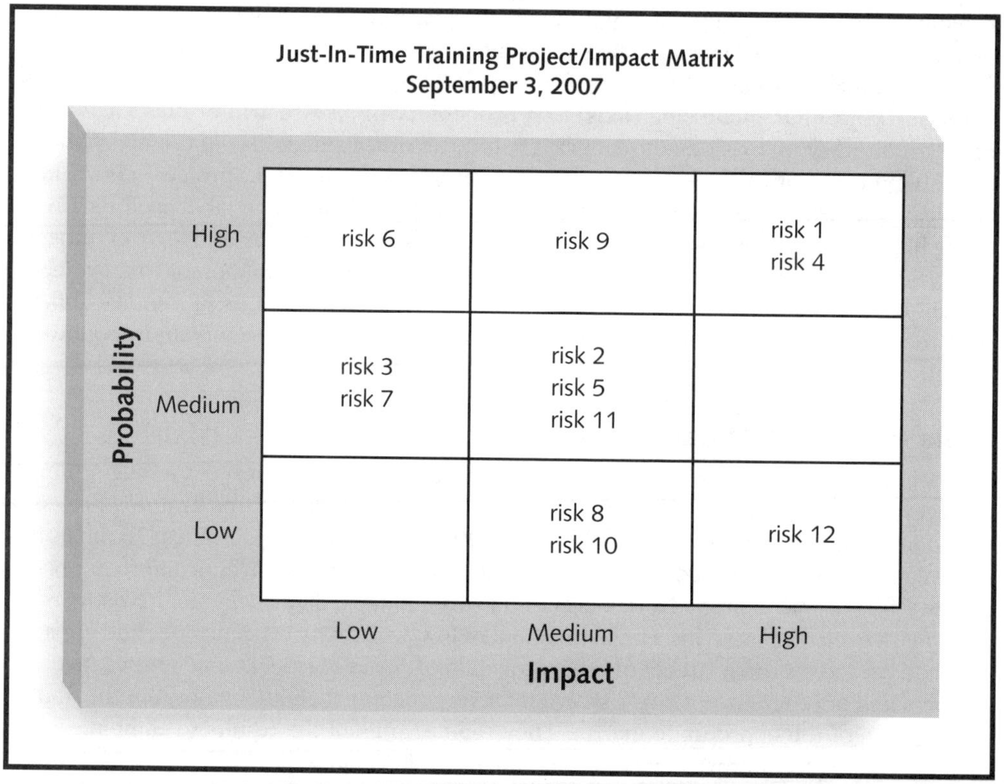

Just-In-Time Training Project/Impact Matrix
September 3, 2007

Probability	Low	Medium	High
High	risk 6	risk 9	risk 1 risk 4
Medium	risk 3 risk 7	risk 2 risk 5 risk 11	
Low		risk 8 risk 10	risk 12
	Low	Medium	High

Impact

FIGURE 5-5   Sample probability/impact matrix

- *A description of the risk event:* Because the name of a risk event is often abbreviated, it helps to provide a detailed description in the risk register. For example, reduced consulting costs might be expanded in the description to say that the organization might be able to negotiate lower-than-average costs for a particular consultant because the consultant enjoys working for the company in that particular location.
- *The category under which the risk event falls:* For example, a defective product might fall under the broader category of technology.
- *The root cause of the risk event:* It is important to find the **root cause** of a problem—the real or underlying reason a problem occurs. By finding the root cause, you can deal with it directly rather than dealing with the symptoms of the problem. You can help identify the root cause of problems by creating a cause-and-effect or fishbone diagram (see Chapter 7), or continually asking why until you find a root cause. For example, the root cause of a defective product, like a defective computer, might be a defective hard drive. Instead of purchasing a brand-new computer or wasting time on other potential causes of the defect, knowing that you need to replace the hard drive provides valuable information that you can act on to fix the problem.

- *Triggers for each risk event:* **Triggers** are indicators or symptoms of actual risk events. For example, cost overruns on early activities might be symptoms of poor cost estimates. The root cause of those poor cost estimates might be inexperienced estimators who received little guidance in preparing the estimates. Documenting potential risk symptoms for projects also helps the project team identify more potential risk events.
- *Potential responses to each risk event:* There can be one or more potential responses to each risk event.
- *The risk owner, or person who will own or take responsibility for the risk event:* One person should be responsible for monitoring each risk event.
- *The probability of the risk event occurring:* The chance of the risk event becoming a reality is rated as high, medium, or low.
- *The impact to the project if the risk event occurs:* The impact to project success if the risk event actually occurs can be rated as high, medium, or low.
- *The status of the risk event:* Did the risk event occur? Was the response strategy completed? Is the risk event no longer relevant to the project? For example, a clause may have been written into a contract to address the risk event of a defective product so that the supplier would have to replace the item at no additional cost.

Sample Risk Register

Kristin began developing a risk register after she and the other stakeholders had prepared the probability/impact matrix. Table 5-9 shows the format of the risk register and one of the entries. Note that the risk event identification (ID) number is shown in the first column, followed by the rank of the risk event. The risk events are sorted by rank order. As information is added, deleted, or changed, the risk register will be updated on the project Web site.

Risk-Related Contractual Agreements

Many projects, including the Just-In-Time Training project, involve outside suppliers. Work done by outside suppliers or sellers should be well documented in **contracts,** which are mutually binding agreements that obligate the seller to provide the specified products or services, and obligate the buyer to pay for them. Project managers should include clauses in contracts to help manage project risks. For example, sellers can agree to be responsible for certain negative risks and incur the costs themselves if they occur. Or there can be incentive or penalty clauses in contracts based on seller performance to encourage positive risks and discourage negative risks. Project teams can also use certain types of contracts, such as fixed-price contracts, to reduce their risk of incurring higher costs than expected. Competition for supplying goods and services can also help reduce negative risks and enhance positive risks on projects.

TABLE 5-9 Sample risk register

Risk Register
September 3, 2007

Project Name: Just-In-Time Training Project

ID No.	Rank	Risk	Description	Category	Root Cause	Triggers	Potential Responses	Risk Owner	Probability	Impact	Status
R15	1										
R21	2										
R7	3										

To understand the risk register more fully, imagine that the following data is entered for the first risk in the register.

- ID No.: R15
- Rank: 1
- Risk: Poor survey response.
- Description: Many people dislike surveys and avoid filling them out, or if they do, they don't offer good or honest feedback.
- Category: Organizational/user support risk
- Root cause: People don't want to take the time and think their inputs aren't important.
- Triggers: Low survey response rate the first few days; incomplete surveys.
- Potential Responses: Make sure senior management emphasizes the importance of this project and the survey for designing good courses. Have the functional managers personally mention the survey to their people and stress its importance. Offer a reward to the department with the most responses. Ensure that the survey instructions say it will take ten minutes or less to complete. Extend the deadline for survey responses.
- Risk owner: Mike Sundby, project champion
- Probability: Medium
- Impact: High
- Status: PM will set up a meeting within a week with a project steering committee to decide which response strategies to implement if the survey response is low.

Sample Risk-Related Contractual Agreements

Kristin's team had not yet prepared any contractual documents for the Just-In-Time Training project, but they did have access to several other contracts that Global Construction had used in the past. Kristin had come from the supplier management area of the company, so she had personal experience working with suppliers and contracts. She also knew several people who could advise her on writing risk-related contractual agreements. Table 5-10 provides a list of a few risk-related contractual agreements that Kristin's team would consider for this project. Kristin received these guidelines from the project team's representative from the contracting department. These agreements can take the form of contracts or clauses within contracts that can help prevent negative risk events and promote positive ones related to the project. Kristin also knew that the company's legal professionals would have to review all contracts because they were legally binding.

TABLE 5-10 Sample guidelines for risk-related contractual agreements

---

Guidelines for Risk-Related Contractual Agreements
January 10, 2007

The following guidelines are provided for your consideration as you develop contracts between Global Construction (the buyer) and its suppliers (the seller). Be sure to work with a member of the contracting department to write your specific contracts. All contracts must be reviewed and signed by the legal department, as well.

- Contract termination clauses: These clauses list circumstances under which the buyer and/or seller can terminate a contract and how final payment will be settled. All the contracts must include a termination clause.

- Incentive clauses: These clauses provide incentives for the seller to provide goods or services at certain times, of certain quality, and so on. Incentive clauses can include extra payments or profit sharing, if appropriate.

- Penalty clauses: These clauses specify penalties that will be applied when the seller does not provide goods or services as specified in the contract. For example, if a product is delivered late, the seller might be required to pay a certain dollar amount for each day the product is late.

- Fixed-price contracts: To minimize the negative risk of paying more than planned for specific goods or services, Global Construction issues fixed-priced contracts, which specify that the seller agrees to a fixed price and bears the risk if it costs more to provide the goods or services than originally assumed.

- Competitive contracts: In many situations, Global Construction can use competition to help reduce risks. In addition to reviewing bids from several sellers, a good strategy may be to award two small contracts and then award the following larger contract to the seller that does the best job on the first job.

The example in the following What Went Right? passage shows another contractual approach for managing positive risk on a large project. By having suppliers visibly compete against each other, the buyers reduced their risks and benefited from competition.

WHAT WENT RIGHT?

The Petronis Twin Towers in Malaysia are famous landmarks in Kuala Lumpur. They were the tallest buildings constructed at the time, and the first large construction project to use GPS (Global Positioning System). Over 7000 people were working on the site during the peak of construction. The project management team decided to use competition to help keep the project on time and on budget. The Japanese firm Hazama Corporation led the construction of Tower 1, and the Korean firm Samsung Engineering Co. led the construction of Tower 2. Because the towers were constructed simultaneously, everyone could see the progress of the two competitors as the 88-story towers rose into the sky. "Construction of the towers was fast paced, thanks in part to the decision to grant two contracts, one for each tower, to two separate contractors. This naturally created a competitive environment, to the benefit of the building." [2]

As you can see, risk management planning addresses procurement-related topics, such as preparing risk-related contractual agreements. The following section addresses planning tasks directly related to project procurement management.

PROJECT PROCUREMENT MANAGEMENT PLANNING TASKS

Project procurement management includes acquiring or procuring goods and services for a project from outside the organization. As the business world continues to become more competitive and global, more and more projects include procurement, often referred to as outsourcing. Many project managers realize the advantages of buying goods and services required for their projects, especially as sellers with better goods and services continue to become increasingly available. They also realize that they can find qualified sellers throughout the world. Remember that project managers strive to do what is best for the project and the organization, and that often means acquiring goods and services from the outside. Good procurement management often provides a win-win situation for both buyers and sellers.

MEDIA SNAPSHOT

Several companies, including those owned by famous celebrities, work closely with outside sources to help both parties come out ahead. For example, Oprah Winfrey celebrated the premiere of her show's nineteenth season by giving each of her 276 audience members a new car.

"We're calling this our wildest dream season, because this year on the Oprah show, no dream is too wild, no surprise too impossible to pull off," said Winfrey. Everyone in the audience was there because their friends or family had written about their need for a new

continued

car. Winfrey's organization did an excellent job of planning the event and keeping it a secret. They also worked closely with suppliers, including Pontiac, which donated all of the cars, which retailed for $28,000 each. The audience members were obviously overjoyed, and Winfrey's organization was happy they did not have to pay for the cars. Many marketing experts say Pontiac's generosity was also outstanding for their business.

In other segments on the same show, Winfrey surprised a 20-year-old woman who had spent years in foster care and homeless shelters with a four-year college scholarship, sponsored by the telecommunications company SBC. The young woman also received a makeover and $10,000 in clothes, provided by several other companies. Winfrey also showed how her organization worked with many suppliers to provide a needy family with $130,000 and several new products to buy and repair their home. The Web site for the show includes a detailed list of sponsoring organizations and links to their Web sites. By collaborating with outside companies, everyone can come out ahead.[3]

Key outputs produced by project procurement management planning include make-or-buy analyses, procurement management plans, requests for proposal or quote, contract statements of work, and supplier evaluation matrices.

Make-or-Buy Analyses

With a make-or-buy decision, an organization decides if it would benefit more by making a product or performing a service itself, or by buying the product or service from a supplier. If there is no need to buy products or services from outside the organization, the organization can avoid the costs involved in managing procurement management processes. **Make-or-buy analysis** involves estimating the internal costs of providing a product or service, and comparing that estimate to the cost of outsourcing.

Many organizations also use make-or-buy analysis, often called a lease-or-buy analysis, to decide if they should purchase or lease items for a particular project. For example, suppose you need a piece of equipment for a project that has a purchase price of $12,000. Assume it also has a daily operational cost of $400. Suppose you can lease the same piece of equipment for $800 per day, including the operational costs. You can set up an equation that shows the amount of time it will take for the purchase cost to equal the lease cost. In this way, you can determine when it makes sense financially to buy rather than lease the equipment. In the equation that follows, d = the number of days you need the piece of equipment.

$$\$12,000 + \$400d = \$800d$$

Subtracting $400d from both sides, you get:

$$\$12,000 = \$400d$$

Dividing both sides by $400, you get:

$$d = 30,$$

which means that the purchase cost equals the lease cost in 30 days. Therefore, if you need the equipment for less than 30 days, it would be more economical to lease it. If you need the equipment for more than 30 days, you should purchase it. Note that this simple example assumes there is no disposal value for the purchased item.

Figure 5-6 graphically shows the costs each day to lease or buy the equipment in the preceding example. Notice that the lines cross at Day 30, showing that the costs are the same to lease or buy the equipment that day.

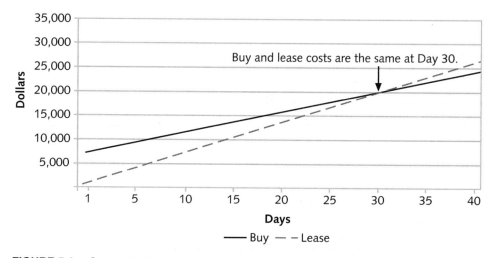

FIGURE 5-6   Comparing the cost of leasing versus buying

Sample Make-or-Buy Analysis

Kristin and her team needed to make several make-or-buy decisions for the Just-In-Time Training project. They knew that they wanted to outsource most of the development and delivery for much of the new training, but because internal expertise existed, it might make sense to do some of the work in-house.

For example, based on information collected in the Phase I project, it was suggested that Global Construction could probably identify internal people to conduct some of the face-to-face training or provide online advice for several courses. Internal resources would be much less expensive than external contractors. In particular, one of the requirements for the Just-In-Time Training project was to provide instructor-led basic project management training and facilitation for online materials. There would be 10 two-day instructor-led classes with 20 participants in each class. There would also be 500 hours of online facilitation.

One specific suggestion was to have current employees conduct the basic project management training—the "make" option—instead of having an outside firm provide the training—the "buy" option. There were a couple of project management professionals (PMPs) in the training department with experience in teaching face-to-face and online courses. They had taken college courses in basic project management and knew of excellent books with online materials. They also knew of several companies that conducted their own in-house courses for basic project management training and then brought in an outside expert, often a qualified college professor, who would conduct advanced courses. They found that college professors or other independent consultants provided high-quality training for much less than most training firms.

Table 5-11 summarizes the make-or-buy analysis for the basic project management training. In this case, Kristin's team recommended doing the training in-house; for much of the other training, however, they did not have internal experts or training materials available.

TABLE 5-11   Sample make-or-buy analysis

Make-or-Buy Analysis
September 1, 2007

Project Name: Just-In-Time Training Project
Decision Being Analyzed: Project management training
Option 1: Make: Use in-house instructors for the instructor-led basic project management training and facilitation for online materials (includes purchasing course materials)
Estimated cost per hour for in-house trainer (excludes employee time): $60
Estimated training hours: 80 (10 total days of training x 8 hours per day)
Subtotal: $4,800
Materials cost: $7,500 ($75/participant/course, 100 participants total)
Estimated cost per hour for online facilitation (excludes employee time): $60
Estimated hours: 500
Subtotal: $30,000
Materials cost: $7,500
    Total: $49,800 ($4,800 + 7,500 + 30,000 + 7,500)
Option 2: Buy: Outsource instructor-led basic project management training and facilitation for online materials (includes purchasing course materials)
Estimated cost per person per day of training (excludes employee time): $500
Estimated hours: 200 (assumes 20 participants/class, 10 total days of training, 2 days average course length)
Subtotal: $100,000
Estimated cost per hour for online facilitation (excludes employee time): $100
Estimated hours: 500
Subtotal: $50,000
    Total: $150,000
Cost Difference: $150,000 - $49,800 = $100,200
Recommendation: Because we have qualified internal staff and can purchase suitable materials, we recommend Option 1, in which we conduct the basic project management training in-house. Global Construction could save even more money by having employees take the courses after hours or on weekends. Employee time is not included in these estimates.

Procurement Management Plans

A procurement management plan is a document that describes how the procurement processes will be managed, from developing documentation for making outside purchases or acquisitions to contract closure. Like other project plans, the contents of the procurement management plan varies with project needs. Topics that can be included in a procurement management plan are as follows:

- Guidelines on types of contracts to be used in different situations
- Standard procurement documents or templates to be used, if applicable
- Guidelines for creating contract work breakdown structures, statements of work, and other procurement documents
- Roles and responsibilities of the project team and related departments, such as the purchasing or legal department
- Guidelines on using independent estimates for evaluating sellers' cost proposals
- Suggestions on managing multiple providers
- Processes for coordinating procurement decisions, such as make-or-buy decisions, with other project areas
- Constraints and assumptions related to purchases and acquisitions
- Lead times for purchases and acquisitions
- Risk-mitigation strategies for purchases and acquisitions, such as insurance contracts and bonds
- Guidelines for identifying prequalified sellers and organizational lists of preferred sellers
- Procurement metrics to assist in evaluating sellers and managing contracts

Types of Contracts

Contract type is a key consideration in a procurement management plan. Different types of contracts can be used in different situations. Three broad categories of contracts are fixed price, or lump sum; cost reimbursable; and time and material. A single contract can actually include all three of these categories, if it makes sense for that particular procurement. For example, you could have a contract with a seller that includes purchasing specific products for a fixed price or lump sum, some services that are provided on a cost-reimbursable basis, and other services that are provided on a time-and-material basis. It is important to understand and decide which approaches to use to meet particular project needs.

- **Fixed-price** or **lump-sum contracts** involve a fixed total price for a well-defined product or service. The buyer incurs little risk or uncertainty in this situation because the price is predetermined. Sellers often pad their estimates somewhat to reduce their risk, while keeping in mind that their price must still be competitive. For example, using a two-week, fixed-price contract, Global Construction could hire a consultant to develop a survey to determine requirements for its new supplier management training courses under the Just-In-Time Training project. Fixed-price contracts generally have well-defined deliverables and deadlines, and may include incentives for meeting or exceeding selected project objectives. For example, the contract could include an incentive fee that would be paid for early delivery of the survey. A firm-fixed price (FFP) contract has the least amount of risk for the buyer, followed by a fixed-price incentive (FPI) contract.

- **Cost-reimbursable contracts** involve payment to the seller for direct and indirect actual costs. For example, the salaries for people working directly on a project and materials purchased for a specific project are direct costs, whereas the cost of providing a work space for those workers, office furniture, electricity, a cafeteria, and so on, are indirect costs. Indirect costs are often calculated as a percentage of direct costs. Cost-reimbursable contracts often include fees such as a profit percentage, or incentives for meeting or exceeding selected project objectives. For example, many contracts to build homes are cost-reimbursable contracts. The buyer might expect the home to cost a certain amount, but the total cost could vary if any of the costs of individual goods or services increase or decrease. The buyer reimburses the contractor for costs incurred, and pays a fee or profit percentage as well. Buyers absorb more of the risk with cost-reimbursable contracts than they do with fixed-price contracts. For example, if the cost of wood doubles, the buyer would have to absorb the additional cost.

- **Time-and-material contracts** are a hybrid of both fixed-price and cost-reimbursable contracts. For example, an independent consultant might have a contract with a company based on a fee of $100 per hour for her services plus a fixed price of $10,000 for providing specific materials for the project. The materials fee might also be based on approved receipts for purchasing items, with a ceiling of $10,000. The consultant would send an invoice to the company each week or month, listing the materials fee, the number of hours worked, and a description of the work produced. This type of contract is often used for services that are needed when the work cannot be clearly specified and total costs cannot be estimated in a contract. Many consultants prefer time-and-material contracts.

Unit pricing can also be used in various types of contracts to require the buyer to pay the supplier a predetermined amount per unit of service. The total value of the contract is a function of the quantities needed to complete the work. For example, many companies use unit price contracts for purchasing computer hardware. If the company purchases only one unit, the cost is $1000. If it purchases 10 units, the cost is $10,000 if there were no volume discounts involved, but this type of pricing often does involve volume discounts. For example, if the company purchases between 10 and 50 units, the contracted cost is $900 per unit. If it purchases over 50 units, the cost reduces to $800 per unit. This flexible pricing strategy is often advantageous to both the buyer and the seller.

Sample Procurement Management Plan

Table 5-12 displays a section of a procurement management plan for the Just-In-Time Training project.

TABLE 5-12 Sample procurement management plan

Procurement Management Plan
September 17, 2007

Project Name: Just-In-Time Training Project

Guidelines on types of contracts: To reduce Global Construction's risk, contracts for the Just-In-Time Training project should be fixed price as often as possible. When goods or services cannot be well defined, cost-reimbursable or time-and-material contracts may be used. The representative from the contracting department assigned to this project will work with the project manager to determine the appropriate contract type for each contract developed.

Standard procurement documents or templates: Global Construction's intranet site includes many sample documents and templates for project procurement. The project team will review these documents and templates and use them as often as possible.

Guidelines for creating procurement documents: Global Construction's intranet site provides guidelines for creating many procurement documents. The Just-In-Time Training project team should review our current work breakdown structure and scope statement to provide the basis for contract work breakdown structures and statements of work.

Roles and responsibilities: The project manager is the main contact for all procurement matters directly related to the Just-In-Time Training project. The representative from the contracting department assigned to this project will coordinate with other staff in the contracting and legal departments, as needed. Etc.

Requests for Proposal or Quote

When organizations decide to procure goods or services, they often create documents to describe what they plan to procure and how potential sellers should respond. Two common examples of procurement documents include a Request for Proposal (RFP) and a Request for Quote (RFQ).

- A **Request for Proposal (RFP)** is a document used to solicit proposals from prospective suppliers. A **proposal** is a document in which sellers describe what they will do to meet the requirements of a buyer. For example, there are several different ways to meet many of Global Construction's training needs. Kristin and her team can write and issue an RFP that outlines training needs so that suppliers can respond with their unique proposals describing how they would meet those needs.

- A **Request for Quote (RFQ)** is a document used to solicit quotes or bids from prospective suppliers. A **bid** (also called a quote) is a document prepared by sellers providing pricing for standard items that have been clearly defined by the buyer. For example, if Kristin's team decided to use a specific book for training courses, they could ask for bids from different sellers for those books. Creating and responding to RFQs is usually much quicker than the same process for RFPs. Selections are often made based on the lowest bid.

RFPs and RFQs can be issued in several ways. The organization might contact one or several preferred sellers directly and send the RFP or RFQ only to them. To reach more sellers, the organization might post the information on its Web site, or advertise on other sites or in newspapers. Project managers must carefully consider which approaches are most appropriate in various situations.

Topics addressed in an RFP usually include the following:

- Purpose of the RFP
- Background information, describing the organization issuing the RFP and the project itself
- Basic requirements for the products and/or services being proposed
- Hardware and software environment (for technology-related proposals)
- RFP process, describing how sellers should prepare and submit their proposals
- Statement of work and schedule information
- Appendices providing more detailed information, as appropriate

A simple RFP might be three- to five-pages long, whereas an RFP for a larger, more complicated procurement might be hundreds of pages long.

Sample Requests for Proposal or Quote

Kristin knew that the project would require several RFPs and RFQs, but it was still very early in the project. Because procurement was not her area of expertise, Kristin asked the project steering committee for advice. They suggested that Kristin's team work with the contracting department to issue an RFP for expert advise to help make major procurement decisions related to the project. The RFP would be for a fixed-price contract to hire an expert to help develop a list of qualified sellers for developing the courses for the Just-In-Time Training project. Table 5-13 shows the RFP. Lucy, the project sponsor and training director for Global Construction, suggested that they send the RFP to several preferred vendors. They estimated that the work required to develop this qualified-sellers list should take no more than a couple weeks and cost no more than $5000.

TABLE 5-13 Sample RFP

Request for Proposal
August 1, 2007

Project Name: Just-In-Time Training Project
RFP Name: Qualified-Sellers List for Just-In-Time Training Project
Purpose of RFP

Global Construction wants to improve training in supplier management, negotiating skills, project management, and software for its employees. In the fast-paced, ever-changing construction market, effectively training employees across a globally dispersed company with different populations is a challenge. By redesigning our current training, Global Construction can reduce training costs and improve productivity. In addition to providing traditional instructor-led courses on-site, we want to allow our employees to learn about specific topics on a just-in-time basis by having quick access to materials and expert advice. The purpose of this RFP is to hire experts to help us find qualified sellers to develop and deliver these new training courses.

Background Information

Global Construction employs 10,000 full-time employees in ten different countries and fifteen U.S. states. We want to increase the productivity of our employees, especially in the sales, purchasing, engineering, and information technology departments. The Just-In-Time Training project, a one-year project, began on July 2, 2007. A key part of this project is working with outside firms to develop and provide just-in-time training in supplier management, negotiating skills, project management, and software applications. See Appendix A for detailed information on the project and specific training needs.

Basic Requirements

The basic requirements for this work include the following:

1. Develop a list of qualified sellers to develop and provide the training as described in Appendix A.
2. Provide a summary description and detailed evaluation of each seller. Provide company brochures, Web sites, annual reports, and other appropriate information.
3. Work with Global Construction to develop an evaluation system to assess each seller.
4. Provide an objective assessment of each seller using this evaluation system.
5. Develop a list of the top five sellers for each course.
6. Provide recommendations for developing partnerships/relationships with each of the top five sellers.
7. Complete the above work no later than September 9, 2007.

RFP Process

Prospective sellers will send written proposals to Global Construction no later than August 10, 2007. To prepare your proposal, use the outline in Appendix B, and examine Appendix C for our evaluation criteria. We expect to award the contract no later than August 20, 2007.

TABLE 5-13 Sample RFP (continued)

Statement of Work and Schedule Information
See Appendix C for a statement of work. The work must be completed no later than September 9, 2007.
Appendices
Appendix A: Just-In-Time Training Project Documents
Appendix B: Proposal Outline
Appendic C: Evaluation Criteria
Appendix D: Statement of Work

Contract Statements of Work

A **contract statement of work (SOW)** is a description of the work that is to be purchased. The contract SOW is a type of scope statement that describes the work in sufficient detail to allow prospective suppliers to both determine if they are capable of providing the goods and services required, and determine an appropriate price. A contract SOW should be clear, concise, and as complete as possible. It should describe all services required and include performance information, such as the location and timing of the work. It is important to use appropriate words in a contract SOW—for example, *must* instead of *may*. *Must* implies that something has to be done; *may* implies that there is a choice involved. The contract SOW should specify the products and services required for the project, use industry terms, and refer to industry standards.

Sample Contract Statement of Work

Table 5-14 shows the contract statement of work for the qualified-sellers list described in the RFP.

Supplier Evaluation Matrices

It is highly recommend that buyers use formal supplier evaluation procedures to help select sellers. In addition to reviewing their proposals or quotes, buyers should also review sellers' past performance, talk to recent customers, interview their management team, and request sample products or demos, if applicable. After doing a thorough evaluation, many organizations summarize evaluations using a supplier evaluation matrix—a type of weighted scoring model. Recall from Chapter 2 that a weighted scoring model provides a systematic process for selection based on numerous criteria. For example, suppliers are often evaluated on criteria related to cost, quality, technology, past performance, and management.

TABLE 5-14 Sample contract statement of work

Contract Statement of Work
August 1, 2007

Project Name: Just-in-Time Training Project
Contract Name: Qualified-Sellers List
Scope of Work:
1. Develop a list of qualified sellers to develop and provide the training as described in Appendix A.
2. Provide a summary description and detailed evaluation of each seller. Provide company brochures, Web sites, annual reports, and other appropriate information.
3. Work with Global Construction to develop an evaluation system to assess each seller.
4. Provide an objective assessment of each seller using this evaluation system.
5. Develop a list of the top five sellers for each course.
6. Provide recommendations for developing partnerships/relationships with each of the top five sellers.
7. Complete the above work no later than September 9, 2007.
Location of Work:
The seller can perform the work at any location. The seller must physically meet with representatives from Global Construction in our corporate office at least twice during the term of the contract.
Period of Performance:
Work is expected to start on or around August 20, 2007, and end no later than September 9, 2007. The seller will prepare a detailed schedule for all work required, including dates for deliverables and meetings. After meeting with representatives from Global Construction to review and update the schedule, the seller will agree to the schedule for this work.
Deliverables Schedule:
The seller will prepare a detailed schedule for all of the work required, including dates for all deliverables and meetings. After meeting with representatives from Global Construction to review and update the schedule, the seller will agree to the schedule for this work.
Applicable Standards:
The seller will use standard software to produce the required documentation for this project. Draft and final documents will be sent via e-mail.
Acceptance Criteria:
The seller will work closely with the project manager, Kristin Maur, to clarify expectations and avoid problems in providing acceptable work. Kristin will provide written acceptance/non-acceptance of all deliverables.
Special Requirements:
The seller's staff assigned to work on this contract must have appropriate education and experience. Résumés of proposed staff will be provided as part of the RFP. The seller will work with Global Construction to make all travel arrangements and minimize travel costs.

Sample Supplier Evaluation Matrix

Kristin knew her team would have to evaluate suppliers for various goods and services as part of the Just-In-Time Training project. Kristin and her team reviewed Global Construction's previously used supplier evaluation matrices, and then prepared a simple matrix to evaluate the supplier for the qualified-sellers list. Recall that part of the work of that contract included having the supplier work with Kristin's team to develop an evaluation system for the potential suppliers of the training courses. Because those suppliers would receive much larger contracts, Global Construction needed a more sophisticated supplier evaluation system. In addition to the supplier evaluation matrix, they would also determine a process for collecting information, developing evaluation criteria, determining weights, deciding on scores, and so on. Kristin knew that they would want to review each supplier's training materials for both instructor-led and online (CD-ROM) materials as well as contact several recent customers to evaluate past performance. Because there would be some customized training development, they would also need to evaluate samples of the supplier's customized training. Figure 5-7 shows the resulting supplier evaluation matrix.

Just-In-Time Training Project Supplier Evaluation Matrix September 9, 2007		Proposal 1		Proposal 2, etc.	
Criteria	Weight	Rating	Score	Rating	Score
Quality of instructor-led c	15%				
Quality of online/CD-ROM training	15%				
Cost	20%				
Past performance	20%				
Customization experience	10%				
Management approach	20%				
Total	100%				

FIGURE 5-7   Sample supplier evaluation matrix

CASE WRAP-UP

Kristin was pleased with the progress on planning tasks for the Just-In-Time Training project. Several members of her project team and the project steering committee had complimented Kristin on her ability to get key stakeholders involved. They also liked the way she admitted her own areas of weakness and sought out expert advice. Kristin was grateful for the steering committee's suggestion to hire an outside firm early in the project to help find qualified suppliers for the training courses. Everyone felt confident that the project team had a handle on risk management. Kristin felt ready to tackle the challenges she would face in leading her team during project execution.

Chapter Summary

Successful project managers know how important it is to develop, refine, and follow plans to meet project goals. This chapter summarizes the planning tasks and outputs for quality, human resource, communications, risk, and procurement management.

Planning outputs related to quality management include a quality management plan, quality metrics, and a quality checklist. Samples of these documents are provided for the Just-In-Time Training project.

Planning outputs related to human resource management include creating a project organizational chart, responsibility assignment matrix, resource histogram, and staffing management plan. Samples of these documents are provided for the Just-In-Time Training project.

Planning outputs related to communications management include developing a communications management plan and project Web site. Samples of these documents are provided for the Just-In-Time Training project.

Planning outputs related to risk management include developing a risk management plan, a probability/impact matrix, a risk register, and risk-related contractual agreements. Samples of these documents are provided for the Just-In-Time Training project.

Planning outputs related to procurement management include performing a make-or-buy analysis and preparing a procurement management plan, requests for proposal/quote, a contract statement of work, and a supplier evaluation matrix. Samples of these documents are provided for the Just-In-Time Training project.

Quick Quiz

1. _____ is defined as the degree to which a set of inherent characteristics fulfill requirements.

    a. Fitness for use

    b. Conformance to requirements

    c. Metrics

    d. Quality

2. _____ allow organizations to measure their performance in certain areas—such as failure rates, availability, and reliability—and compare them over time or with other organizations.

    a. Ratings

    b. Metrics

    c. Quality-control charts

    d. Checklists

3. A RACI chart is a type of _____ .

   a. project organizational chart

   b. resource histogram

   c. responsibility assignment matrix

   d. staffing management plan

4. A _____ describes when and how people will be added to and taken off of a project.

   a. project organizational chart

   b. resource histogram

   c. responsibility assignment matrix

   d. staffing management plan

5. Topics such as who will receive project information and who will produce it, suggested methods or guidelines for conveying the information, frequency of communication, and escalation procedures for resolving issues should be described in a _____ .

   a. communications management plan

   b. staffing management plan

   c. team contract

   d. scope statement

6. Suppose you are a member of Kristin's team and you are having difficulties communicating with one of the supplier management experts who is providing important content for a class you are developing. What strategy might you use to help improve communications?

   a. put all communications in writing

   b. put all communications on your project Web site

   c. use several different methods to communicate with this person

   d. ask Kristin to find a better person to provide the technical content

7. What two dimensions should you use when evaluating project risks?

   a. probability and impact

   b. cost and schedule

   c. negative and positive

   d. source and responsibility

8. A _____ is a document that contains results of various risk management processes, often displayed in a table or spreadsheet format.

   a. risk event

   b. trigger

   c. risk register

   d. risk management plan

9. You can purchase an item you need for a project for $10,000 and it has daily operating costs of $500, or you can lease the item for $700 per day. On which day will the purchase cost be the same as the lease cost?

   a. day 5

   b. day 10

   c. day 50

   d. day 100

10. You want to have the least risk possible in setting up a contract to purchase goods and services from an outside firm. As the buyer, what type of contract should you use?

   a. fixed price

   b. unit price

   c. cost reimbursable

   d. time and materials

Quick Quiz Answers

1. D; 2. B; 3. C; 4. D; 5. A; 6. C; 7. A; 8. C; 9. C; 10. A

Discussion Questions

1. What is the main purpose of a quality management plan? What are two metrics besides those provided in this chapter that Kristin and her team could use on the Just-In-Time Training project? Besides ensuring that classrooms are ready for training, where else might they use a checklist on the project?

2. What is the main purpose of a staffing management plan? What tool should you use to graphically show total staffing needs for a project? What tool should you use to clarify roles and responsibilities for tasks?

3. Why is it so difficult to ensure good communication on projects? What strategies can any project team use to improve communications?

4. Why is risk management often neglected on projects? Why is it important to take the time to identify and rank risks throughout the project's life?

5. What is the difference between an RFP and an RFQ? Give an example of the appropriate use of each.

Exercises

1. Find an example of a large project that took more than a year to complete, such as a major construction project. Describe some of the tasks performed in planning the quality, human resource, communications, risk, and procurement aspects of the project. Write a one-page paper or prepare a short presentation summarizing your findings.

2. Your company is planning to launch an important project starting January 1, which will last one year. You estimate that you will need one half-time project manager; two full-time business analysts for the first six months; two full-time marketing analysts for the whole year; four full-time business interns for the months of June, July, and August; and one full-time

salesperson for the last three months. Use spreadsheet software such as Microsoft Excel to create a stacked-column chart showing a resource histogram for this project, similar to the one shown in Figure 5-2. Be sure to include a legend to label the types of resources needed, and use appropriate titles and axis labels. You can use the resource histogram template on the companion Web site to make this exercise easier.

3. List three negative risk events and three positive risk events for the Just-In-Time Training project. Briefly describe each risk, and then rate each one as high, medium, or low in terms of probability and impact. Plot the results on a probability/impact matrix. Also, prepare an entry for one of the risks for the risk register.

4. Assume the source selection criteria for evaluating proposals for a project is as follows:
   - Management approach 15 percent
   - Technical approach 15 percent
   - Past performance 20 percent
   - Price 20 percent
   - Interview results and samples 30 percent

   Using Figure 5-7 as a guide and the weighted scoring model template, if desired, create a spreadsheet that could be used to calculate the total weighted scores for three proposals. Enter scores for Proposal 1 as 80, 90, 70, 90, and 80, respectively. Enter scores for Proposal 2 as 90, 50, 95, 80, and 95. Enter scores for Proposal 3 as 60, 90, 90, 80, and 65. Add a paragraph summarizing the results and your recommendation on the spreadsheet. Print your results on one page.

Team Projects

1. Your organization initiated a project to raise money for an important charity. Assume that there are 1000 people in your organization. Also, assume that you have six months to raise as much money as possible, with a goal of $100,000. Create a checklist to use in soliciting sponsors for the fundraiser, a responsibility assignment matrix for various stakeholders, a project Web site (just the home page), a probability/impact matrix with six potential negative risks, and a request for quote for obtaining items your team will need. Be creative in your responses. Remember that this project is entirely run by volunteers.

2. You are part of a team in charge of a project to help people in your company (500 people) lose weight. This project is part of a competition, and the top "losers" will be featured in a popular television show. Assume that you have six months to complete the project and a budget of $10,000. Develop metrics for the project, a project organizational chart, a communications management plan, and a risk register with at least three entries for the project.

3. Using the information you developed in Team Project 1 or 2, role-play a meeting to review one of these planning documents with key stakeholders. Determine who will play what role (project manager, team member from a certain department, senior managers, and so on). Be creative in displaying different personalities (a senior manager who questions the importance of the project to the organization, a team member who is very shy or obnoxious).

4. Perform the applicable quality, human resource, communications, risk, and procurement planning tasks for one of the real projects your class or group developed in Chapter 1. Remember to be thorough in your planning so that your execution goes smoothly. Be sure to have your sponsor and other stakeholders provide inputs on your plans.

Companion Web Site

Visit the companion Web site for this text (*www.course.com/mis/pm/schwalbe*) to access:

- Lecture notes
- Interactive quizzes
- Template files
- Sample documents
- Guide to Using Microsoft Project 2003
- VPMi enterprise project management software
- More ideas for team projects, including real projects and case studies
- Links to additional resources related to project management

Key Terms

bid — A document prepared by sellers providing pricing for standard items that have been clearly defined by the buyer.

blogs — The easy-to-use journals on the Web that allow users to write entries, create links, and upload pictures, while allowing readers to post comments to particular journal entries.

checklist — A list of items to be noted or consulted.

communications management plan — A document that guides project communications.

conformance to requirements — The process of ensuring that the project's processes and products meet written specifications.

contingency plans — The predefined actions that the project team will take if an identified risk event occurs.

contingency reserves or **contingency allowances** — The funds held by the project sponsor that can be used to mitigate cost or schedule overruns if unknown risks occur.

contracts — The mutually binding agreements that obligate the seller to provide the specified products or services, and obligate the buyer to pay for them.

contract statement of work (SOW) — A description of the work that is to be purchased.

cost-reimbursable contract — A contract that involves payment to the seller for direct and indirect actual costs.

fallback plans — The plans that are developed for risks that have a high impact on meeting project objectives, and are put into effect if attempts to reduce the risk are not effective.

fitness for use — The ability of a product to be used as it was intended.

fixed-price or **lump-sum contract** — A type of contract that involves a fixed price for a well-defined product or service.

make-or-buy analysis — The process of estimating the internal costs of providing a product or service and comparing that estimate to the cost of outsourcing.

metric — A standard of measurement.

project human resource management — Making effective use of the people involved with a project.

project organizational chart — A graphic representation of how authority and responsibility is distributed within the project.

project quality management — Processes done to ensure that the project will satisfy the stated or implied needs for which it was undertaken.

proposal — A document in which sellers describe what they will do to meet the requirements of a buyer.

quality — The degree to which a set of inherent characteristics fulfill requirements.

RACI charts — A type of resource histogram that shows Responsibility, Accountability, Consultation, and Informed roles for project stakeholders.

Request for Proposal (RFP) — A document used to solicit proposals from prospective suppliers.

Request for Quote (RFQ) — A document used to solicit quotes or bids from prospective suppliers.

resource histogram — A column chart that shows the number of resources required for or assigned to a project over time.

responsibility assignment matrix (RAM) — A matrix that maps the work of the project as described in the WBS to the people responsible for performing the work.

risk — An uncertainty that can have a negative or positive effect on meeting project objectives.

risk events — The specific, uncertain events that may occur to the detriment or enhancement of the project.

risk register — A document that contains results of various risk management processes, often displayed in a table or spreadsheet format.

root cause — The real or underlying reason a problem occurs.

staffing management plan — A plan that describes when and how people will be added to and taken off of a project.

time-and-materials contract — A type of contract that is a hybrid of both a fixed-price and cost-reimbursable contract.

triggers — The indicators or symptoms of actual risk events.

Endnotes

[1] Projectzone, "Humor" (*http://corporatedump.com/dilbertmanagers.html*) (2004).

[2] Cesar Pelli and Michael J. Crosbie, "Building Petronas Towers," *Architecture Week* (February 19, 2003).

[3] "Oprah Gives Audience 276 Cars," CBSNEWS.com (September 13, 2004).

CHAPTER 6

EXECUTING PROJECTS

LEARNING OBJECTIVES

After reading this chapter, you will be able to:

- List several tasks and outputs of project execution

- Discuss what is involved in directing and managing project execution as part of project integration management, including the importance of producing promised deliverables, implementing solutions to problems, evaluating work performance information, and requesting changes to a project

- Explain the importance of recommending corrective actions and updating project plans as part of quality assurance

- Describe the executing tasks performed as part of human resource management, summarize important concepts related to managing people, and explain what is involved in creative staffing updates and team performance assessments

- Discuss important communications concepts, and describe the executing tasks performed as part of communications management to ensure good communications

- Explain the executing tasks performed as part of procurement management, and describe how to prepare procurement document packages and contracts

Kristin reviewed initial project plans with the steering committee for the Just-In-Time Training project. Committee members felt that everything was going well so far and that it was time to commit more resources to the project. At later steering committee meetings, Kristin brought up several challenges she was facing in executing the project plans. For example, Jamie, the supplier management expert assigned to her team half-time, was not working out. In addition, there were several conflicts between various stakeholders on how to perform certain tasks, and several people complained about a lack of communication about the project. The IT people supporting the project were overallocated, yet some of their tasks were on the critical path for the project. The prototype for the supplier management basics course was not as well received as the team had hoped, and Kristin was afraid that the seller might demand more money to make major changes to the course. Kristin would need to use her experience—especially her soft (interpersonal) skills—as well as advice from the project steering committee to deal with these and other challenges.

INTRODUCTION

Whereas project planning is considered to be the most unappreciated project management process group, project execution is the most noticed. Of course, good plans are important, but it is even more important to execute them well. In fact, the June 21, 1999, issue of *Fortune* summarized research showing that without a doubt, the main reason chief executive officers (CEOs) failed was poor execution. Failed CEOs simply did not get things done, were indecisive, and did not deliver on commitments. The same is true for project managers and all leaders. Stakeholders expect to see results from their projects through effective execution.

WHAT WENT WRONG?

"The results are not acceptable," stated President Bush four days after Hurricane Katrina caused major damage to New Orleans and surrounding areas. After Federal Emergency Management Agency (FEMA) officials returned in January 2005 from a tour of the tsunami devastation in Asia, New Orleans was the number one disaster they discussed. Officials had drawn up dozens of plans and conducted preparedness drills for years, but despite all the warnings, Hurricane Katrina overwhelmed government agencies, and many people suffered from slow response to their needs for emergency aid. The mayor of New Orleans, C. Ray Nagin, blasted the government for its lack of an immediate response. "I've talked directly with the president, I've talked to the head of the Homeland Security, I've talked to everybody under the sun, I've been out there."[1] People were disappointed with the poor execution of disaster relief efforts during the first few days, and officials took corrective actions to address the challenges caused by the hurricane.

On a lighter note, Figure 6-1 shows a cartoon related to poor execution by a sports team and a play on the word *execution.*

FIGURE 6-1   All for the team's execution?

Recall that, in general, the majority of a project's time and budget is spent on project execution. Many of the tasks and outputs created in the other process groups are fairly similar from project to project, but no two projects are ever executed in the exact same way. Why? Because projects involve uncertainty. No one can ever predict the challenges that project teams will face in trying to meet project goals. This chapter summarizes the main tasks involved in executing projects and discusses some challenges that Kristin faced in managing the execution of the Just-In-Time Training project.

Summary of Executing Tasks and Outputs

Table 6-1 summarizes key outputs of project execution by knowledge area, based on the *PMBOK® Guide.* Notice that not every knowledge area is included, and requested changes are listed only under project integration management, although they are outputs of other knowledge areas as well. Although there are many planning tasks related to scope, time, cost, and risk management, these knowledge areas do not have tasks directly related to project execution. Changes to the triple constraint and risk management are addressed in the next chapter on project monitoring and control. This chapter focuses on tasks and outputs that project teams perform to execute projects, and provides specific examples for Global Construction's Just-In-Time Training project.

TABLE 6-1   Executing process summary

Knowledge area	Outputs
Project integration management	Deliverables, implemented solutions to problems, work performance information, requested changes
Project quality management	Recommended corrective actions, project plan updates
Project human resource management	Staffing updates, team performance assessment
Project communications management	Business process updates
Project procurement management	Procurement document packages and contracts

EXECUTING TASKS FOR PROJECT INTEGRATION MANAGEMENT

As part of project integration management, the project manager must perform the task of directing and managing stakeholders to complete the project. Project managers can follow several important practices to help accomplish this challenging job:

- *Coordinate planning and execution:* As mentioned earlier, the main purpose of project planning is to guide execution. If the project manager and team did a good job planning, the plans will be easier to execute. As things change, team members need to update the plans to keep everyone working on the same page.
- *Develop and use soft skills:* Several studies of project managers suggest that soft skills (for example, strong leadership, effective team building, strong communication, motivation, negotiation, conflict management, and problem solving) are crucial to the success of project managers, especially during project execution. Project managers must lead by example in demonstrating the importance of creating good project plans and then following them in project execution. Project managers often create plans for things they need to do themselves. If project managers follow through on their own plans, their team members are more likely to do the same.
- *Provide a supportive organizational culture:* Good project execution requires a supportive organizational culture. For example, organizational procedures can help or hinder project execution. If an organization has useful guidelines and templates for project management that everyone in the organization follows, it will be easier for project managers and their teams to plan and do their work. If the organization uses the project plans as the basis for performing and monitoring progress during execution, the culture will promote the relationship between good planning and execution. Even if the organizational culture is not supportive, project managers can create a supportive culture within their own project and work on improving the culture in other parts of the organization.
- *Break the rules when needed:* Even with a supportive organizational culture, project managers might sometimes find it necessary to break the rules to

produce project results in a timely manner. When project managers break the rules, politics will play a role in the results. For example, if a particular project requires use of nonstandard software, the project manager must use his political skills to convince concerned stakeholders of the need to break the rules.

- *Capitalize on product, business, and application area knowledge:* The application area of the project directly affects project execution because the products of the project are produced during project execution. For example, if a project involves constructing a new building, the project manager and other stakeholders would need to use their expertise in architecture, engineering, and construction to produce the product successfully. Project managers should use their expertise to guide their team and make important decisions.

- *Use project execution tools and techniques:* For example, following a project management methodology and using a project management information system can help project execution go more smoothly. The project management methodology should include guidelines on how to communicate project status, handle conflicts, work with suppliers and other stakeholders, and perform other important tasks.

Deliverables

Most project sponsors would say that the most important output of any project is its deliverables. Recall that deliverables are products or services produced or provided as part of a project. For the Just-In-Time Training project at Global Construction, key deliverables include the training materials and courses (instructor-led, Web-based, and CD-ROM) as well as other important deliverables related to developing and delivering those training materials and courses, such as surveys, design documents, prototypes, and meetings.

Sample Deliverables

Because the Just-In-Time Training project is fictitious, it is impossible to show the actual training materials, courses, and other deliverables produced during execution. Because you are probably reading this book as part of a course and have taken other courses in both an instructor-led or online fashion, you have some feel for what training materials and courses are like. Recall that several of the training courses for this project must be available on a just-in-time basis (that is, they must be available whenever the employee wants to learn), so deliverables must be created to provide effective Web-based and/or CD-ROM instruction. Note the word *effective*. The main objective of this training is to provide employees with the knowledge and skills they need to do their jobs when they need it. Just because training is available around the clock does not mean that it is effective. The section on quality later in this chapter describes the importance of ensuring quality during project execution.

Implemented Solutions to Problems

Of course, all project teams face numerous problems. Some surface early during project initiation or planning, but some do not occur until project execution, when many things are happening at once. Some problems can be avoided by doing a good job of initiating, planning, or monitoring and controlling the project, but other problems cannot be avoided. Some common problems encountered during project execution include the following:

1. The project sponsor and/or other senior managers are not very supportive of the project.
2. Project stakeholders, such as people who would use the products and services the project is attempting to create, are not sufficiently involved in project decision-making.
3. The project manager is inexperienced in managing people, working in a particular organization, or understanding the application area of the project.
4. The project objectives/scope are unclear.
5. Estimates for time and cost goals are unreliable or unrealistic.
6. Business needs/technology changes have impacted the project.
7. People working on the project are incompetent or unmotivated.
8. There are poor conflict-management procedures.
9. Communications are poor.
10. Suppliers are not delivering as promised.

The first five problems should have been addressed during project initiation or planning (and were addressed in previous chapters), but they can also cause difficulties during execution. Addressing business and technology changes are discussed in the next chapter on monitoring and controlling. The last four problems are discussed in this chapter and presented in the context of the Just-In-Time Training project.

Sample Implemented Solutions to Problems

Kristin Maur had been working hard to direct and manage project execution, but she encountered several problems. The following sections discuss the problems of incompetent or unmotivated people working on the project and poor conflict-management procedures. Later sections discuss strategies for improving communications and supplier delivery.

Issues with Competence and Motivation

Jamie, the project team member assigned to work half-time from the supplier management department, was not contributing much to the project. Jamie's main role was to provide expertise in developing the supplier management courses. She was well qualified for this assignment, having over 10 years' experience with Global Construction managing major accounts with suppliers. (Recall that supplier management was the most important training topic for the project.) Kristin knew that Jamie was very good at negotiating with and managing suppliers, but Jamie felt that she was assigned to the project primarily because she was available, having recently finished another large project. Although Jamie was assigned to work on this project from its start, she was on vacation for most of the first month and seemed uninterested in the project when she was around. Kristin tried her best to motivate her, but she could see that Jamie was simply not the right person for the project. (See a later section in this chapter on motivation.) Kristin talked to Jamie directly, and she admitted that she would much rather deal directly with suppliers than work on this training project. Just two months into the project, Kristin used her experience and contacts within the company to find a suitable replacement. She worked through the project steering committee and other managers to quickly approve the personnel change.

Poor Conflict Management

Most large projects are high-stake endeavors that are highly visible within organizations. They require tremendous effort from team members, are expensive, require significant resources, and can have an extensive impact on the way work is done in an organization. When the stakes are high, conflict is never far away, and even small projects with low budgets have conflicts—it is a natural part of work and life in general. Project managers should lead their teams in developing norms for dealing with various types of conflicts that might arise. For example, team members should know that disrespectful behavior toward any project stakeholder is inappropriate, and that team members are expected to try to work out small conflicts themselves before elevating them to higher levels.

Blake and Mouton (1964) delineated five basic modes for handling conflicts. Each strategy can be considered as being high, medium, or low on two dimensions: importance of the task or goal, and importance of the relationship between the people having the conflict.

1. *Confrontation*: When using the **confrontation mode**, project managers directly face a conflict using a problem-solving approach that allows affected parties to work through their disagreements. This approach is also called the problem-solving mode. It is best used when *both the task and the relationship are of high importance.* For example, Kristin confronted Jamie when she was not working well on the project. They discussed the problem and decided it was best for both parties for Jamie to leave the project team.

2. *Compromise*: With the **compromise mode**, project managers use a give-and-take approach to resolve conflicts, bargaining and searching for solutions that will bring some degree of satisfaction to all the parties in a dispute. This give-and-take approach works best when both the task and the relationship are of medium importance. For example, the IT person responsible for creating and sending out the surveys for Kristin's project might be swamped with work. Kristin might either agree to pay several hundred dollars for overtime to get the task completed on time or provide a few days extension for the task at no additional cost.

3. *Smoothing*: When using the **smoothing mode**, the project manager de-emphasizes or avoids areas of differences and emphasizes areas of agreement. This method is best used when the *relationship is of high importance and the task is of low importance.* For example, two members of the project steering committee might totally disagree on whether they should provide incentive bonuses to suppliers for achieving outstanding ratings on courses. Kristin could use the smoothing mode to ensure that the relationship between the steering committee members remains harmonious by discussing with these team members the areas in which they agree and by downplaying the topic of bonuses during meetings.

4. *Forcing*: The **forcing mode** can be viewed as the win-lose approach to conflict resolution. People exert their viewpoints even though they contradict the viewpoints of others. This approach is appropriate when *the task is of high importance and the relationship is of low importance*. For example, if you are competing against another firm for a contract, it may be appropriate to use the forcing mode.

5. *Withdrawal*: When using the **withdrawal mode**, project managers retreat or withdraw from an actual or potential disagreement. This approach is the least desirable conflict-handling mode. It may be appropriate when *both the task and the relationship are of low importance*.

Effective project managers often use confrontation for conflict resolution instead of the other four modes. However, it is important to keep in mind that the term *confrontation* may be misleading. This mode focuses on a win-win problem-solving approach, in which all parties work together to find the best way to solve the conflict.

Project managers must also realize that not all conflict is bad. In fact, conflict can often be good. Conflict often produces important results, such as new ideas, better alternatives, and motivation to work harder and more collaboratively. Project team members might become stagnant or develop **groupthink**—conformance to the values or ethical standards of a group—if there are no conflicting viewpoints on various aspects of a project. Research suggests that task-related conflict, which is derived from differences over team objectives and how to achieve them, often improves team performance. Emotional conflict, however, which stems from personality clashes and misunderstandings, often depresses team performance. Project managers should create an environment that encourages and maintains the positive and productive aspects of conflict.

Work Performance Information

One of Kristin's main jobs during project execution was collecting, assessing, and communicating work performance information. Kristin used the "management by wandering around" (MBWA) approach, meaning she informally observed and talked to her project team members, suppliers, and other stakeholders as much as possible. She wanted to know first-hand how project activities were progressing, and she wanted to offer suggestions as often as possible. Of course, she also used more formal communications, such as status reports, survey results, and course evaluations, to address work performance on the project.

Sample Work Performance Information

A common way to summarize work performance information is by using a milestone report. Recall that a milestone is a significant event on a project, such as completing a major deliverable or awarding a major contract. Table 6-2 provides part of a milestone report for the Just-In-Time Training project. Notice that in addition to listing the milestones, the report lists the planned date for completion (in month/day format), the status, the person responsible for the milestone, and issues/comments.

TABLE 6-2 Sample milestone report for reporting work performance information

Just-In-Time Training Project Milestone Report

September 1, 2007

Milestone	Date	Status	Responsible	Issues/Comments
Researched existing training	8/13	Completed	Jamie (replaced by Abner)	Many basic courses available, but not much advanced/tailored training (Note: Replaced Jamie with better candidate for project after Jamie completed this task)
Supplier management training survey results reported to steering committee	8/24	Completed	Kristin	Great feedback; many people stressed the need to have instructor-led training and mentors for soft skills development
Meetings with potential partners	9/21	In progress	Kristin/Contracting	May need more time for meetings
Partnership agreements completed	9/28	Not started yet	Kristin/Contracting	May need more times to set up agreements
Developed executive course	11/9	Not started yet	TBD Supplier	
Developed introductory course	11/9	Not started yet	TBD Supplier	
Developed advanced course	11/23	Not started yet	TBD Supplier	
Held pilot course	11/23	Not started yet	TBD Supplier	
Pilot course results reported to steering committee	11/30	Not started yet	Kristin	

Requested Changes

Often, a number of requests for changes emerge during project execution. Recall that a process for handling changes should be defined during project planning as part of the project management plan. Chapter 7, which covers monitoring and controlling projects, provides detailed information on handling changes. It is important during project execution to formally and informally request appropriate changes. Project managers, team members, suppliers, and other stakeholders can make change requests, so it is important to have a good process in place for handling them.

Sample Requested Changes

Successful project teams use well-defined processes and standard forms for requesting project changes. Some changes are requested using other established change processes. For example, when Kristin requested that Jamie be replaced with Abner as the project team member from the supplier management department, she used Global Construction's personnel transfer process. Jamie's department head and the human resources department handled necessary paperwork for the reassignment. For other change requests—especially those that may impact achieving scope, time, or cost goals of the project—a formal change request form should be submitted through the appropriate channels. Table 6-3 provides a sample of a completed change request form for the Just-In-Time Training project.

TABLE 6-3 Sample change request

Change Request

September 22, 2007

Project Name: Just-In-Time Training Project
Date Request Submitted: September 22, 2007
Title of Change Request: Additional funds for supplier management course survey
Change Order Number: A200-17
Submitted by: Kristin Maur

Change Category: __Scope __Schedule _X_Cost __Technology __Other
Description of change requested:
To avoid a schedule slip and have appropriate internal resources available, we are requesting the approval of paid overtime for creating and distributing the survey for the supplier management course.
Events that made this change necessary or desirable:
The IT person assigned to our project has several other important projects on hand. If these survey tasks are delayed, the entire project will be delayed.
Justification for the change/why it is needed/desired to continue/complete the project:
We must send out and analyze the survey in a timely manner because we need the information to develop the first supplier management course and select an appropriate supplier.
Impact of the proposed change on:
Scope: None
Schedule: None
Cost: $550
Staffing: One IT person will work 10 hours of paid overtime over a period of several weeks.
Risk: Low. This person suggested the paid overtime and has successfully worked overtime in the past.
Other: None
Suggested implementation if the change request is approved: Include the overtime pay in the normal paycheck.
Required approvals:

Name/Title	Date	Approve/Reject
Evan George/Affected Employee		
Stella Jacobs/Employee s Supervisor		
Julia Portman, VP of IT		

EXECUTING TASKS FOR PROJECT QUALITY MANAGEMENT

It is one thing to develop a plan for ensuring quality on a project; it is another to ensure delivery of quality products and services. The main quality management task required during execution is quality assurance. **Quality assurance** includes all the activities related to satisfying the relevant quality standards for a project. Another goal of quality assurance is continual quality improvement. Many companies understand the importance of quality assurance and have entire departments dedicated to this discipline. These companies have detailed processes in place to make sure that their products and services conform to various quality requirements. They also know they must produce products and services at competitive prices. To be successful in today's competitive business environment, successful companies develop their own best practices and evaluate other organizations' best practices to continuously improve the way they do business. See Chapter 8 for more information on and examples of best practices in project management.

Top management and project managers can impact the quality of projects most significantly by implementing quality assurance. Key outputs of quality assurance include recommended corrective actions and project plan updates.

Recommended Corrective Actions

Before learning about recommended corrective actions, it is important to understand how you know they are needed. The previous section addressed resolving problems. Obviously, corrective actions are developed to resolve problems. It is also important, however, for organizations to use other techniques to identify areas in which they would benefit from taking actions to improve quality. Several quality improvement techniques include benchmarking, quality audits, and cause-and-effect diagrams.

- **Benchmarking** generates ideas for quality improvements by comparing specific project practices or product characteristics to those of other projects or products within or outside of the organization itself. For example, one reason that Global Construction initiated the Just-In-Time Training project was because it discovered that its cost of training per employee was higher than that of similar firms. The amount of money that organizations spend on training is a benchmark. As another example, many organizations have overall course ratings using a Likert scale, with 1 being the lowest rating and 5 being the highest. A benchmark for a good rating might be an average rating of 3.5 or higher. If training participants rated the prototype supplier management course lower than 3.5 on average, then Kristin's team would need to take corrective actions to improve the quality of the course.

- A **quality audit** is a structured review of specific quality management activities that helps identify lessons learned, which could improve performance on current or future projects. In-house auditors or third parties with expertise in specific areas can perform quality audits, which can be either scheduled or random. Recall that several of the main goals of the Just-In-Time Training project were to reduce training costs at Global Construction, provide training when it was needed, and improve employee productivity. By establishing measurement techniques for monitoring these goals and performing an audit to see how well they are being met, Kristin's team can see how well they are doing in meeting specific goals. For example, they could send out a monthly survey asking employees if they are getting training when they need it and if it is helping improve their productivity. A quality audit could be done periodically to review the survey results. If there is a sudden decrease in ratings, Kristin's team would need to take corrective actions.

- **Cause-and-effect diagrams**—also called fishbone diagrams (because their structure resembles a fishbone) or Ishikawa diagrams (named after their founder)—can assist in ensuring and improving quality by finding the root causes of quality problems. Recall from Chapter 5 that a root cause is the real or underlying reason a problem occurs. Kristin and her team created several of these diagrams to find the root causes of quality problems, as described in the next section.

Sample Recommended Corrective Actions

After training participants rated the prototype supplier management course less than 3.5 on average, Kristin's team knew they had to recommend corrective actions. They first decided to analyze what the root cause of the problem really was. The prototype course was available in three formats: instructor-led, Web-based, and CD-ROM. The Web-based and CD-ROM courses were virtually identical, except participants in the Web-based course could also access interactive discussion boards and chat rooms as they accessed the course via the Internet. The evaluations for the instructor-led course were actually above average; however, the Web-based and CD-ROM courses were rated below average.

The student evaluation forms provided some open-ended feedback, so Kristin and her team decided to use that information plus other possible causes of the low ratings to prepare a cause-and-effect diagram, as shown in Figure 6-2. The main effect is the low course ratings, and potential causes are grouped into several main categories: content, interactivity, speed, and graphics/fonts. Potential subcategories are listed in each area, such as "too simple" and "not enough examples" under content. Kristin and her team contacted the participants in the prototype courses to get more specific information to help identify the root cause(s) of the low ratings. When they discovered that the majority of respondents rated the CD-ROM course poorly because it lacked interactivity, they discussed the option of supplementing the course with the Web-based interactivity features, such as the discussion board and chat room. Respondents were generally enthusiastic about the Web-based course, except for those who accessed it with a slow Internet connection. A simple solution would be to have them use the CD-ROM for most of the course and use the Internet for the discussion board and chat room. Because the other potential causes were not the main reasons for the low ratings, they were not addressed.

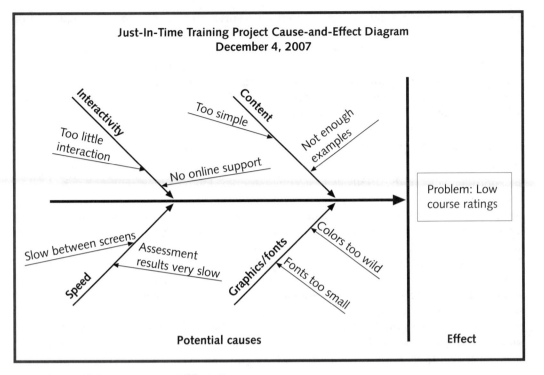

FIGURE 6-2   Sample cause-and-effect diagram

Kristin and her team recommended that the discussion board and chat room features of the Web-based course be integrated into the CD-ROM course. The supplier who developed both courses said it would be a very simple change and would not affect time or cost estimates.

EXECUTING TASKS FOR PROJECT HUMAN RESOURCE MANAGEMENT

Effective project human resource management is crucial to project execution. The two main tasks project managers perform include acquiring the project team and developing the project team. Key outputs include staffing updates and team performance assessment.

Before discussing these tasks and outputs, it is important to understand basic concepts related to dealing with people in a work setting. Key concepts include motivation, influence, and effectiveness.

Motivation

Psychologists, managers, coworkers, teachers, parents, and most people in general still struggle to understand what motivates people, or why they do what they do. **Intrinsic motivation** causes people to participate in an activity for their own enjoyment. For example, some people love to read, write, or play an instrument because it makes them feel good. **Extrinsic motivation** causes people to do something for a reward or to avoid a penalty. For example, some young children would prefer *not* to play an instrument, but do so to receive a reward or avoid a punishment. Why do some people require no external motivation whatsoever to produce high-quality work while others require significant external motivation to perform routine tasks? Why can't you get someone who is extremely productive at work to do simple tasks at home? Mankind will continue to try to answer these overarching questions, but a basic understanding of motivational theory will help anyone who has to work or live with other people.

Maslow's Hierarchy of Needs

Abraham Maslow, a highly respected psychologist who rejected the dehumanizing negativism of psychology in the 1950s, is best known for developing a hierarchy of needs. In the 1950s, proponents of Sigmund Freud's psychoanalytic theory were promoting the idea that human beings were not the masters of their destiny and that their actions were governed by unconscious processes dominated by primitive sexual urges. During the same period, behavioral psychologists saw human beings as controlled by the environment. Maslow argued that both schools of thought failed to recognize unique qualities of human behavior: love, self-esteem, belonging, self-expression, and creativity. He argued that these unique qualities enable people to make independent choices, which give them full control over their destiny.

Figure 6-3 shows the basic pyramid structure of **Maslow's hierarchy of needs**, which states that people's behaviors are guided or motivated by a sequence of needs. At the bottom of the hierarchy are physiological needs, such as air, water, and food. After physiological needs are satisfied, safety needs—such as shelter from bad weather, lack of physical or mental abuse, and a low-crime environment—guide behavior. After safety needs are satisfied, social needs—such as having friends, belonging to groups, and having a sense of community—come to the forefront, and so on up the hierarchy. Examples of esteem needs include personal achievement, recognition, and respect, whereas self-actualization needs include a sense of fulfillment and belief that one is working to his or her potential. The order of these needs in the pyramid is significant. Maslow suggests that each level of the hierarchy is a prerequisite for the level above. For example, it is not possible for a person to consider self-actualization if he has not addressed basic needs concerning security and safety. People in an emergency situation, such as a flood or hurricane, cannot be concerned with personal growth but will be motivated solely by the requirements of personal survival. After a particular need is satisfied, however, it no longer serves as a potent motivator of behavior.

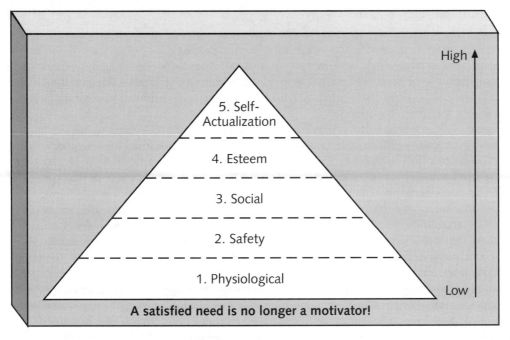

FIGURE 6-3 Maslow's hierarchy of needs

The bottom four needs in Maslow's hierarchy—physiological, safety, social, and esteem needs—are referred to as deficiency needs, and the highest level, self-actualization, is considered a growth need. Only after meeting deficiency needs can individuals act on growth needs. Self-actualized people are problem-focused, have an appreciation for life, are concerned about personal growth, and can have peak experiences.

Most people working on corporate projects probably have their basic physiological and safety needs met. If someone has a sudden medical emergency or is laid off from work, however, physiological and safety needs move to the forefront. To motivate project team members, the project manager needs to understand each person's motivation, especially with regard to social, esteem, and self-actualization needs. Team members new to a company and city might be motivated by social needs. To address social needs, some companies organize gatherings and social events for new workers. Other project members might find these events to be an invasion of their personal time, which they would rather spend with friends and family or working on an advanced degree.

Maslow's hierarchy conveys a message of hope and growth. People can work to control their own destinies and naturally strive to achieve higher and higher needs. Some cultures disagree with Maslow's philosophy and have other beliefs on motivation. Recent brain research also suggests that there are physiological reasons for certain behaviors. In any case, successful project managers know that to provide appropriate motivation and maximize team performance, they must both meet project goals and understand team members' personal goals and needs.

Herzberg's Motivation-Hygiene Theory

Frederick Herzberg is best known for distinguishing between motivational factors and hygiene factors when considering motivation in work settings. He called factors that cause job satisfaction motivators, and factors that cause dissatisfaction hygiene factors. A hygiene factor is a basic necessity, such as air-conditioning during hot weather. Air-conditioning does not in itself provide team satisfaction, but without it you would have disgruntled staff on hot workdays.

Head of Case Western University's psychology department, Herzberg wrote the book *Work and the Nature of Man* in 1966 and the famous *Harvard Business Review* article "One More Time: How Do You Motivate Employees?" in 1968. Herzberg analyzed the factors that affected productivity among a sample of 1685 employees. Popular beliefs at that time were that work output was most improved through larger salaries, more supervision, or a more attractive work environment. According to Herzberg, these hygiene factors would cause dissatisfaction if not present but would not motivate workers to do more if present. Herzberg found that people were motivated to work mainly by feelings of personal achievement and recognition. Motivators, Herzberg concluded, included achievement, recognition, the work itself, responsibility, advancement, and growth.

In his books and articles, Herzberg explained why attempts to use positive factors such as reducing time spent at work, implementing upward-spiraling wages, offering fringe benefits, providing human relations and sensitivity training, and so on did not instill motivation. He argued that people want to actualize themselves; they need stimuli for their growth and advancement needs in accordance with Maslow's hierarchy of needs. Factors such as achievement, recognition, responsibility, advancement, and growth produce job satisfaction and are work motivators.

McClelland's Acquired-Needs Theory

David McClelland proposed that an individual's specific needs are acquired or learned over time and shaped by life experiences. The main categories of acquired needs include achievement, affiliation, and power. Normally, one or two of these needs is dominant in individuals.

- *Achievement*: People with a high need for achievement (nAch) seek to excel and tend to avoid both low-risk and high-risk situations to improve their chances of achieving something worthwhile. Achievers need regular feedback and often prefer to work alone or with other high achievers. Managers should give high achievers challenging projects with achievable goals. Achievers should receive frequent performance feedback, and although money is not an important motivator to them, it is an effective form of feedback.
- *Affiliation*: People with a high need for affiliation (nAff) desire harmonious relationships with other people and need to feel accepted by others. They tend to conform to the norms of their work group and prefer work that involves significant personal interaction. Managers should try to create a cooperative work environment to meet the needs of people with a high need for affiliation.
- *Power*: People with a need for power (nPow) desire either personal power or institutional power. People who need personal power want to direct others and can be seen as bossy. People who need institutional, or social, power want to

organize others to further the goals of the organization. Management should provide those seeking institutional power with the opportunity to manage others, emphasizing the importance of meeting organizational goals.

The Thematic Apperception Test (TAT) is a tool to measure the individual needs of different people using McClelland's categories. The TAT presents subjects with a series of ambiguous pictures and asks them to develop a spontaneous story for each picture, assuming they will project their own needs into the story. Consult books or Web sites on this test for further information.

McGregor's Theory X and Theory Y

Douglas McGregor was one of the great popularizers of a human relations approach to management, and he is best known for developing Theory X and Theory Y. In his research, documented in his 1960 book *The Human Side of Enterprise,* McGregor found that although many managers spouted the right ideas, they actually followed a set of assumptions about worker motivation that he called Theory X (sometimes referred to as classical systems theory). People who believe in Theory X assume that workers dislike and avoid work if possible, so managers must use coercion, threats, and various control schemes to get workers to make adequate efforts to meet objectives. Theory X managers assume that the average worker wants to be directed and prefers to avoid responsibility, has little ambition, and wants security above all else. When research seemed to demonstrate that these assumptions were not valid, McGregor suggested a different series of assumptions about human behavior that he called Theory Y (sometimes referred to as human relations theory). Managers who believe in Theory Y assume that individuals do not inherently dislike work but consider it as natural as play or rest. The most significant rewards are the satisfaction of esteem and self-actualization needs, as described by Maslow. McGregor urged managers to motivate people based on these more valid Theory Y notions.

Influence

Many people working on a project do not report directly to project managers, and project managers often do not have control over project staff that report to them. For example, people are free to change jobs. If they are given work assignments they do not like, many workers will simply quit or transfer to other departments or projects. H. J. Thamhain and D. L. Wilemon investigated the approaches project managers use to deal with workers and how those approaches relate to project success. They identified nine influence bases available to project managers:

1. *Authority:* The legitimate hierarchical right to issue orders
2. *Assignment:* The project manager's perceived ability to influence a worker's assignment to future projects
3. *Budget:* The project manager's perceived ability to authorize the use of discretionary funds
4. *Promotion:* The ability to improve a worker's position
5. *Money:* The ability to increase a worker's pay and benefits
6. *Penalty:* The project manager's perceived ability to dispense or cause punishment

7. *Work challenge:* The ability to assign work that capitalizes on a worker's enjoyment of doing a particular task, which taps an intrinsic motivational factor

8. *Expertise:* The project manager's perceived specialized knowledge that others deem important

9. *Friendship:* The ability to establish friendly personal relationships between the project manager and others

Top management grants authority to the project manager, but not necessarily the power to control personnel assignments, budgets, promotions, and penalties. Team members, however, may misperceive their project manager's sphere of influence and expect him to have the power, for example, to grant promotions and transfers. If project managers' power is limited, they can still influence workers by providing challenging work, and they can increase the power of their influence by using expertise and friendship.

Thamhain and Wilemon found that projects were more likely to fail when project managers relied too heavily on using *authority, money, or penalty* to influence people. When project managers used *work challenge and expertise* to influence people, projects were more likely to succeed. The effectiveness of work challenge in influencing people is consistent with Maslow's and Herzberg's research on motivation. The importance of expertise as a means of influencing people makes sense on projects that involve special knowledge. For example, people working on a project to build a spaceship would expect the project manager to have appropriate education and experience in that area. They would also be impressed if she had actually worked on other space projects or traveled into space.

Effectiveness

Stephen Covey, author of *The 7 Habits of Highly Effective People* and several other books, expanded on the work done by Maslow, Herzberg, and others to develop an approach for helping people and teams become more effective. Covey's first three habits of effective people—be proactive, begin with the end in mind, and put first things first—help people achieve a private victory by becoming independent. After achieving independence, people can then strive for interdependence by developing the next three habits—think win/win; seek first to understand, then to be understood; and synergize. (**Synergy** is the concept that the whole is equal to more than the sum of its parts.) Finally, everyone can work on Covey's seventh habit—sharpen the saw—to develop and renew their physical, spiritual, mental, and social/emotional selves.

Project managers can apply Covey's seven habits to improve effectiveness on projects, as follows:

1. *Be proactive:* Covey, like Maslow, believes that people have the ability to be proactive and choose their responses to different situations. Project managers must be proactive, anticipate, and plan for problems and inevitable changes on projects. They can also encourage team members to be proactive in their work.

2. *Begin with the end in mind:* Covey suggests that people focus on their values, what they really want to accomplish, and how they really want to be remembered in their lives. He suggests writing a mission statement to help achieve this habit. Many organizations and projects have mission statements that help them focus on their main purpose.

3. *Put first things first:* Covey developed a time-management system and matrix to help people prioritize their time. He suggests that most people need to spend more time doing things that are important but not urgent. Important but not

urgent activities include planning, reading, and exercising. Project managers should focus on important and not urgent activities, such as developing various project plans, building relationships with major project stakeholders, and mentoring project team members. They also need to avoid focusing only on important and urgent activities—that is, putting out fires.

4. *Think win/win:* Covey presents several paradigms of interdependence, with "think win/win" being the best choice in most situations. When you use a win/win paradigm, parties in potential conflict work together to develop new solutions that make them all winners. Project managers should strive to use a win/win approach in making decisions, but sometimes, especially in competitive situations, they must use a win/lose paradigm.

5. *Seek first to understand, then to be understood:* **Empathic listening** is listening with the intent to understand by putting yourself in the shoes of the other person. You forget your personal interests and focus on truly understanding the other person and feeling what he or she is feeling. To really understand other people, you must learn to focus on others first. When you practice empathic listening, you can begin two-way communication. Making empathic listening a habit enables project managers to fully understand their stakeholders' needs and expectations.

6. *Synergize:* In projects, a project team can synergize by creating collaborative products that are much better than a collection of individual efforts. For example, engineers helped the crew of the *Apollo 13* return to Earth safely by working together to develop a solution to their potentially deadly technical problems. One person came up with an idea, which prompted another person to have an idea, and so on. The team devised a solution that no one person could have discovered. Covey also emphasizes the importance of valuing differences in others to achieve synergy. Synergy is essential to many complex projects; in fact, several major breakthroughs in technology, such as manned flight, drug development, and various computer technologies, occurred because of synergy.

7. *Sharpen the saw:* When you practice sharpening the saw, you take time to renew yourself physically, spiritually, mentally, and socially. The practice of self-renewal helps people avoid burnout. Project managers must make sure that they themselves and their project team have time to retrain, reenergize, and occasionally even relax to avoid burnout.

Several experts suggest that empathic listening is a powerful skill for project managers and their teams to possess. Understanding what motivates key stakeholders and customers can mean the difference between project success and project failure. After project managers and team members begin to practice empathic listening, they can communicate and work together to tackle problems more effectively.

Before you can practice empathic listening, you first have to get people to talk to you. In many cases, you must work on developing a rapport with other people before they will really open up to you. **Rapport** is a relationship of harmony, conformity, accord, or affinity. Without rapport, people cannot begin to communicate, or the strong person might dominate the weaker one. For example, if you meet someone for the first time and find that you cannot communicate, you need to focus on developing rapport.

One technique for establishing rapport is using a process called mirroring. **Mirroring** is the matching of certain behaviors of the other person. Although establishing rapport involves a number of complex human interactions, the simple technique of mirroring can sometimes help. You can mirror someone's voice tone and/or tempo, breathing, movements, or body postures. For example, when Kristin was negotiating with suppliers, she found that some of them were very abrupt, while she was fairly laid back. Kristin would use mirroring by matching the supplier's posture or voice tone to develop rapport and a strong negotiating position. In fact, mirroring was one of the skills emphasized in the negotiations course the Just-In-Time Training project team was developing.

WHAT WENT RIGHT?

A young business consultant who worked in the IT department of a major aerospace firm met with a senior project manager and his core team. The project involved providing updated electronic kits for a major aircraft program. The company was losing money on the project because the upgrade kits were not being delivered on time. Most buyers had written severe late-penalty fees into their contracts, and other customers were threatening to take their business elsewhere. The project manager blamed it all on the IT department for not letting his staff access the information system directly to track the status of kit development and delivery. The tracking system was old and difficult to use. The business consultant was warned that this project manager was very difficult to work with. When the project manager entered the meeting room with three of his staff, all older men, he threw his books on the table and started yelling at the young consultant and her even younger assistant. Instead of backing down, the consultant mirrored the project manager's behavior and started yelling right back at him. He stood back, paused, and said, "You're the first person who's had the guts to stand up to me. I like that!" After that brief introduction, rapport was established, and everyone began communicating and working together as a team to solve the problem at hand.

You should, of course, take the message of the What Went Right? episode with a grain of salt. Few circumstances merit or benefit from yelling matches, but once in a while they cut through the tangle of human complexities. (The story is completely true; the author of this book, who very rarely yells at anyone, was the business consultant and had just completed a weeklong course on communications skills.)

You can see from the material covered in this chapter so far that many important topics related to motivation, influence, and effectiveness are relevant to project management. Projects are done by and for people, so it is important for project managers and team members to understand and practice key concepts related to these topics. Kristin must keep these topics in mind and use her knowledge and skills to successfully execute the project.

Acquiring the Project Team and Making Staffing Updates

There's a saying that the project manager who is the smartest person on the team has done a poor job of recruiting. After developing a staffing management plan during project planning, project managers must work with other managers in their organizations to assign personnel to their project or to acquire additional human resources needed to staff their project. Project managers with strong influencing and negotiating skills are often good at getting internal people to work on their project. However, the organization must ensure that people assigned to the project best fit the organization's requirements, and that these people are motivated to remain on the project.

Several organizations, publications, and Web sites address the need for good staff acquisition and retention. William C. Taylor, cofounder of *Fast Company* magazine and a public speaker, also believes that people today are more demanding and have higher expectations of their jobs than just earning a paycheck. His company's research has found that the top three reasons people leave their jobs (by choice) are because:

1. They feel they do not make a difference.
2. They do not get proper recognition.
3. They are not learning anything new or growing as a person.

Sample Staffing Updates

Kristin worked with managers in the human resource department and other managers to staff the internal project team members for the Just-In-Time Training project. She also made staffing changes, such as replacing Jamie, the supplier management expert assigned to the team. Although Jamie had great qualifications, she was not a good fit for the project. Jamie needed a break after coming off of a big project, and she did not feel that she would personally enjoy working on the Just-In-Time Training project. Kristin updated the project staff by replacing Jamie with Abner. Kristin was also involved with other staffing updates as people joined and left the project team.

To keep everyone up to date on current project staffing assignments, Kristin provided a current team roster on the project Web site, including team member names, roles, and contact information. As suppliers were added to the project, she included supplier staff information as well. Table 6-4 provides a sample of part of the team roster for the Just-In-Time Training project.

TABLE 6-4 Sample team roster

<table>
<tr><td colspan="6" align="center">**Team Roster**

September 1, 2007</td></tr>
<tr><td>**Name**</td><td>**Role on Project**</td><td>**Position**</td><td>**E-Mail**</td><td>**Phone**</td><td>**Location**</td></tr>
<tr><td>Mike Sundby</td><td>Project Champion</td><td>VP of HR</td><td>mike_sundby@ globalconstruction.com</td><td></td><td></td></tr>
<tr><td>Lucy Camarena</td><td>Project Sponsor</td><td>Training Director</td><td>lucy_camarena@ globalconstruction.com</td><td></td><td></td></tr>
<tr><td>Kristin Maur</td><td>Project Manager</td><td>Project Manager</td><td>kristin_maur@ globalconstruction.com</td><td></td><td></td></tr>
<tr><td>Mohamed Abdul</td><td>Team Member</td><td>Senior Programmer/Analyst</td><td>mohamed_abdul@ globalconstruction.com</td><td></td><td></td></tr>
<tr><td>Kim Johnson</td><td>Team Member</td><td>Curriculum Designer</td><td>kim_johnson@ globalconstruction.com</td><td></td><td></td></tr>
<tr><td>Abner Tomass</td><td>Team Member</td><td>Supply Management Expert</td><td>abner_tomass@ globalconstruction.com</td><td></td><td></td></tr>
</table>

Developing the Project Team and Assessing Team Performance

Even if a project manager has successfully recruited enough skilled people to work on a project, he must ensure that people can work together as a team to achieve project goals. Many failed projects have been staffed by highly talented individuals; however, it takes teamwork to complete projects successfully. The main goal of team development is to help people work together more effectively to improve project performance.

Dr. Bruce Tuckman published his four-stage model of team development in 1965 and modified it to include an additional stage in the 1970s. The **Tuckman model** describes five stages of team development:

1. *Forming* involves the introduction of team members, either at the initiation of the team or as new members are introduced. This stage is necessary, but little work is actually achieved.
2. *Storming* occurs as team members have different opinions as to how the team should operate. People test each other, and there is often conflict within the team.
3. *Norming* is achieved when team members have developed a common working method, and cooperation and collaboration replace the conflict and mistrust of the previous phase.

4. *Performing* occurs when the emphasis shifts to reaching the team goals rather than working on team process. Relationships are settled, and team members are likely to build loyalty toward each other. At this stage, the team is able to manage tasks that are more complex and cope with greater change. Note that not all teams are able to progress through the team development stages to reach the performance level.

5. *Adjourning* involves the breakup of the team after they successfully reach their goals and complete the work. Teams might also adjourn due to poor performance or project cancellation.

There is an extensive body of literature on team development. This section highlights a few important tools and techniques for team development, including training, team-building activities, and reward and recognition systems. Keep in mind that having teams focus on completing specific tasks is often the most effective way to help teams be productive.

Training

Project managers often recommend that people take specific training courses to improve individual and team development. For example, Kristin recommended that Mohamed, the IT member of her project team, take training courses in designing e-learning courses so that he could contribute even more to this project. Early in the project, she also organized a special team-building session for her internal project team. In addition to traditional, instructor-led training, many organizations provide e-learning opportunities for their employees so that they can learn specific skills at any time and any place, similar to several of the courses being developed for the Just-In-Time Training project. It is important to make sure that the timing and delivery methods for the training are appropriate for specific situations and individuals.

Team-Building Activities

Many organizations provide in-house team-building training activities, and many also use specialized services provided by external companies that specialize in this area. Two common approaches to team-building activities include using physical challenges and psychological preference indicator tools.

Sometimes, organizations have teams of people go through certain physically challenging activities to help them develop as a team. Military basic training or boot camps provide one example. Men and women who want to join the military must first make it through basic training, which often involves several strenuous physical activities such as rappelling off towers, running and marching in full military gear, going through obstacle courses, passing marksmanship training, and mastering survival training. Many organizations use a similar approach by sending teams of people to special locations, where they work as a team to navigate white-water rapids, climb mountains or rocks, participate in ropes courses, and so on.

More often, organizations have teams participate in mental team-building activities in which they learn about themselves, about each other, and how to work as a group most effectively. It is important for people to understand and value each other's differences to work effectively as a team. Two common tools used in mental team building include the Myers-Briggs Type Indicator and the Wilson Learning Social Styles Profile.

The **Myers-Briggs Type Indicator (MBTI)** is a popular tool for determining personality preferences. During World War II, Isabel B. Myers and Katherine C. Briggs developed the first version of the MBTI based on psychologist Carl Jung's theory of psychological type. The four dimensions of psychological type in the MBTI are as follows:

1. *Extrovert/Introvert (E/I):* This first dimension determines if you are generally extroverted or introverted. The dimension also signifies whether people draw their energy from other people (extroverts) or from inside themselves (introverts). About 75 percent of people in the general population are extroverts.

2. *Sensation/Intuition (S/N):* This second dimension relates to the manner in which you gather information. Sensation (or Sensing) type people take in facts, details, and reality and describe themselves as practical. Intuitive type people are imaginative, ingenious, and attentive to hunches or intuition. They describe themselves as innovative and conceptual. About 75 percent of people in the general population have a preference for sensation.

3. *Thinking/Feeling (T/F):* This third dimension represents thinking judgment and feeling judgment. Thinking judgment is objective and logical, and feeling judgment is subjective and personal. The general population is generally split evenly between these two preferences.

4. *Judgment/Perception (J/P):* This fourth dimension concerns people's attitude toward structure. Judgment type people like closure and task completion. They tend to establish deadlines and take them seriously, expecting others to do the same. Perceiving types prefer to keep things open and flexible. They regard deadlines more as a signal to start rather than complete a project and do not feel that work must be done before play or rest begins. People are generally split evenly between these two preferences.

There are 16 MBTI categories based on combinations of the four dimensions. For example, one MBTI category is ESTJ, another is INFP, and another is ENTP. Project managers can often benefit from knowing their team members' MBTI profiles by adjusting their management styles for each individual. For example, if the project manager is a strong N and one of the team members is a strong S, the project manager should take the time to provide more concrete, detailed explanations when discussing that person's task assignments. Project managers might also want to make sure that they have a variety of personality types on their team. For example, if all team members are strong introverts, it might be difficult for them to work well with other stakeholders who are often extroverts.

Many organizations use Wilson Learning's Social Styles Profile in team-building activities. Psychologist David Merril, who helped develop the Social Skills Profile, categorizes four approximate behavioral profiles, or zones. People are perceived as behaving primarily in one of four zones, based on their assertiveness and responsiveness:

- "Drivers" are proactive and task oriented. They are firmly rooted in the present, and they strive for action. Adjectives to describe drivers include pushy, severe, tough, dominating, harsh, strong-willed, independent, practical, decisive, and efficient.

- "Expressives" are proactive and people oriented. They are future oriented and use their intuition to look for fresh perspectives on the world around them. Adjectives to describe expressives include manipulating, excitable, undisciplined, reacting, egotistical, ambitious, stimulating, wacky, enthusiastic, dramatic, and friendly.
- "Analyticals" are reactive and task oriented. They are past oriented and strong thinkers. Adjectives to describe analyticals include critical, indecisive, stuffy, picky, moralistic, industrious, persistent, serious, expecting, and orderly.
- "Amiables" are reactive and people oriented. Their time orientation varies depending on whom they are with at the time, and they strongly value relationships. Adjectives to describe amiables include conforming, unsure, ingratiating, dependent, awkward, supportive, respectful, willing, dependable, and agreeable.

Figure 6-4 shows these four social styles and how they relate to assertiveness and responsiveness. Note that the main determinants of the social style are levels of assertiveness—if you are more likely to tell people what to do or ask what should be done—and how you respond to tasks—by focusing on the task itself or on the people involved in performing the task. For example, a driver is assertive in telling other people what to do and focuses on completing tasks. An amiable prefers to ask others what to do and focuses on pleasing people versus completing tasks.

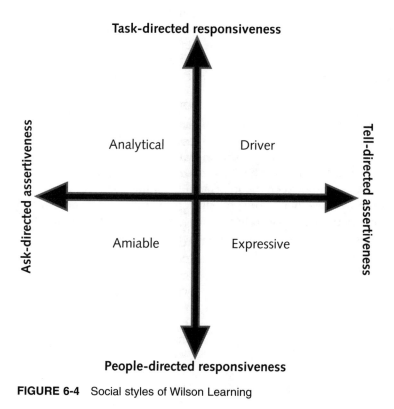

FIGURE 6-4 Social styles of Wilson Learning

Knowing the social styles of project stakeholders can help project managers understand why certain people may have problems working together. For example, drivers are often very impatient working with amiables, and analyticals often have difficulties understanding expressives. Project managers can use their facilitation skills to help all types of people communicate better with each other and focus on meeting project goals.

Reward and Recognition Systems

Another important tool for promoting team development is the use of team-based reward and recognition systems. If management rewards teamwork, it promotes or reinforces people to work more effectively in teams. Some organizations offer bonuses, trips, or other rewards to workers who meet or exceed company or project goals. In a project setting, project managers can recognize and reward people who willingly work overtime to meet an aggressive schedule objective or go out of their way to help a teammate. If teamwork is the essential goal, project managers should not reward people who work overtime just to get extra pay or because of their own poor work or planning.

Project managers must continually assess their team's performance. When they identify weaknesses in individuals or in the entire team, it's their job to find the best way to develop their people and improve performance.

Sample Team Performance Assessment

Project managers assess team performance in several different ways. As mentioned earlier, Kristin believed in management by wandering around, and she liked to have many short, informal discussions with various stakeholders, especially her project team members. She also observed them working alone and as a team, and assessed the quality of deliverables they produced. Kristin and other project managers at Global Construction also filled out performance appraisals for each team member once a year or when a project was completed.

Kristin also felt that it was important for people to assess their own performance and the performance of their teammates. She talked to each team member individually and the team as a group about this assessment because she knew that some people felt uncomfortable evaluating themselves or other people. She stressed that she had successfully used this approach in the past, and she would keep the information confidential. Her main goal was to help everyone work well together on the project. Table 6-5 is a sample of an informal questionnaire that Kristin periodically asked her project team members to fill out to assist in performance assessment. Kristin would discuss each person's assessment and take corrective actions as needed.

TABLE 6-5   Sample team performance assessment

Team Performance Assessment

August 1, 2007

Project Name: Just-In-Time Training Project
Individual Name: _____   **Project Manager:** Kristin Maur
Team Member Name: _____
Date: _____
  1. Using a scale of 0-100, assess how you think **the project team** is performing: _____
  2. Explain the rationale behind the above score.

  3. Using a scale of 0-100, assess how you think **you** are performing on this project: _____
  4. Explain the rationale behind the above score. What are your roles and responsibilities, and how
     well have you performed them?

  5. Briefly assess each team member's performance. If you had to give each person a score between
     0-100, what would it be?

  6. To compare individual contributions, if you had 100 points to allocate to your team, how would
     you allocate them?

  7. What suggestions do you have for improving team performance?

EXECUTING TASKS FOR PROJECT COMMUNICATIONS MANAGEMENT

Good communications management is also crucial to project execution. Information distribution is the main communications management task performed during project execution. The main output of this task is updating business processes.

Important Project Communications Concepts

Some project managers say that 90 percent of their job is communicating. Therefore, it is important to address important concepts related to improving project communications. Key concepts include formal and informal communications, nonverbal communications, using the appropriate communications medium, understanding individual and group communication needs, and the impact of team size on project communications.

Formal and Informal Communications

It is not enough for project team members to submit formal status reports to their project managers and other stakeholders and assume that everyone who needs to know that information will read the reports. In fact, many people may prefer to have a two-way conversation about project information rather than reading detailed reports, e-mails, or Web pages to try to find pertinent information. These people may want to know the people working on their projects and develop a trusting relationship with them, and so they use informal discussions about the project to develop these relationships. Therefore, project managers must be good at nurturing relationships through good communication. Many experts believe that the difference between good project managers and excellent project managers is their ability to nurture relationships and use empathic listening skills, as described earlier.

Nonverbal Communications

People make or break projects, and people like to interact with each other to get a true feeling for how a project is going. Research poses the theory that in a face-to-face interaction, 58 percent of communication is through body language, 35 percent through how the words are said, and a mere 7 percent through the content or words that are spoken. The author of this information (see *Silent Messages* by Albert Mehrabian, 1980) was careful to note that these percentages were specific findings for a specific set of variables. Even if the actual percentages are different in verbal project communications today, it is safe to say that it is important to pay attention to more than just the actual words someone is saying. Nonverbal communications, such as a person's tone of voice and body language, are often more important than the words being used.

Using the Appropriate Communications Medium

Table 6-6 provides guidelines from Practical Communications, Inc., a communications consulting firm, about how well different types of media—such as hard copy, phone calls, voice mail, e-mail, meetings, and Web sites—are suited to different communication needs. For example, if you were trying to assess commitment of project stakeholders, a meeting would be the most appropriate medium to use. A phone call would be adequate, but the other media would not be appropriate. Project managers must assess the needs of the organization, the project, and individuals in determining which communication medium to use, and when.

Additional media not included in this table include the use of Web logs or blogs, instant messaging, Webcasts, and live or delayed video. Global Construction was just starting to use several of these newer media.

TABLE 6-6   Media choice table

KEY: 1 = EXCELLENT   2 = ADEQUATE   3 = INAPPROPRIATE

HOW WELL MEDIUM IS SUITED TO:	Hard Copy	Phone Call	Voice Mail	E-Mail	Meeting	Web Site
Assessing commitment	3	2	3	3	1	3
Building consensus	3	2	3	3	1	3
Mediating a conflict	3	2	3	3	1	3
Resolving a misunderstanding	3	1	3	3	2	3
Addressing negative behavior	3	2	3	2	1	3
Expressing support/appreciation	1	2	2	1	2	3
Encouraging creative thinking	2	3	3	1	3	3
Making an ironic statement	3	2	2	3	1	3
Conveying a reference document	1	3	3	3	3	2
Reinforcing one s authority	1	2	3	3	1	1
Providing a permanent record	1	3	3	1	3	3
Maintaining confidentiality	2	1	2	3	1	3
Conveying simple information	3	1	1	1	2	3
Asking an informational question	3	1	1	1	3	3
Making a simple request	3	1	1	1	3	3
Giving complex instructions	3	3	2	2	1	2
Addressing many people	2	3 or 1*	2	2	3	1

Galati, Tess. *Email Composition and Communication (EmC2)*. Practical Communications, Inc. (*www.praccom.com*) (2001).

*Depends on system functionality

MEDIA SNAPSHOP

Although most projects do not use live video as a medium for sending project information, the technology is becoming more available and less expensive. You can reach many people at once using live video, and viewers can see and hear important information.

For example, Microsoft had been experimenting with its new conferencing product, Livemeeting. Anoop Gupta, a vice president of Microsoft's real-time collaboration group, says that one in every five face-to-face meetings can be replaced with Web conferencing tools, and Microsoft estimates that it will save $70 million in reduced travel for organizations worldwide in one year alone.[2]

continued

However, any live communication broadcast can also backfire, especially if millions of people are watching. In fact, one event, Janet Jackson's "wardrobe malfunction" during the 2004 Super Bowl in the United States, had a major impact on the entire broadcasting industry, causing television and radio stations to use several second delays to prevent offensive video or audio from reaching the airwaves. Reuters reported on September 22, 2004, that the Federal Communications Commission had officially voted to fine each of the 20 stations owned by the CBS television network $27,500 for violating indecency rules. The fine was the maximum allowed by law at the time, and Congress is considering legislation to increase the fine to as much as $500,000 per incident.[3]

Understanding Individual and Group Communication Needs

Many top managers think they can remediate project delays simply by adding people to a project. Unfortunately, this approach often causes setbacks because of the increased complexity of communications. In his popular book *The Mythical Man-Month,* Frederick Brooks illustrates this concept very clearly. People are not interchangeable parts. You cannot assume that a task originally scheduled to take two months of one person's time can be done in one month by two people. A popular analogy is that you cannot take nine women and produce a baby in one month!

In addition to understanding that people are not interchangeable, it is also important to understand individuals' personal preferences for communications. People have different personality traits, which often affect their communication preferences. For example, if you want to praise a project team member for doing a good job, an introvert might be more comfortable receiving that praise in private, whereas an extrovert might like everyone to hear about her good work. An intuitive person might want to understand how something fits into the big picture, whereas a sensing person might prefer to have more focused, step-by-step details. A strong thinker might want to know the logic behind information, whereas a feeling person might want to know how the information affects him personally, as well as other people. Someone who is a judging person might be very driven to meet deadlines with few reminders, whereas a perceiving person might need more assistance in developing and following plans.

Geographic location and cultural backgrounds also add to the complexity of project communications. For example, if project stakeholders are in different countries, it is often difficult or impossible to schedule times for two-way communication during normal working hours. Language barriers can also cause communication problems—for example, the same word may have very different meanings in different languages. Times, dates, and other units of measure are also interpreted differently. People from some cultures also prefer to communicate in ways that may be uncomfortable to others. For example, managers in some countries still do not allow workers of lower ranks or women to give formal presentations.

The Impact of Team Size on Project Communications

Another important aspect of information distribution is the number of people involved in a project. As the number of people involved increases, the complexity of communications increases because there are more communications channels, or pathways, through which people can communicate. The number of communications channels in relation to the number of people involved can be calculated as follows:

$$\text{number of communications channels} = \frac{n(n-1)}{2}$$

where n is the number of people involved.

For example, two people have one communications channel: $(2(2-1))/2 = 1$. Three people have three channels: $(3(3-1))/2 = 3$. Four people have six channels, five people have ten, and so on. You can see that as the number of people communicating increases, the number of communications channels increases rapidly. The lesson is a simple one: If you want to enhance communications, you must consider the interactions among different project team members and stakeholders. It is often helpful to form several smaller teams within a large project team to help improve project communications.

As you can see, information distribution involves more than creating and sending status reports or holding periodic meetings. Many good project managers know their personal strengths and weaknesses in this area and surround themselves with people who complement their skills. It is good practice to share the responsibility for project communications management with the entire project team.

Information Distribution and Updating Business Processes

Getting project information to the right people at the right time and in a useful format is just as important as developing the information in the first place. The communications management plan prepared during project planning serves as a good starting point for information distribution. During execution, project teams must address important considerations for information distribution, as described previously. The main output of information distribution is updating business processes through improved communications.

Sample Updates to Business Processes

Organizations have many different organizational process assets to help them improve business processes. Examples of these assets include various policies and procedures, guidelines, information systems, financial systems, management systems, lessons learned, and historical documents that help people understand, follow, and improve business processes.

As part of the Just-In-Time Training project, Kristin's team followed several existing business processes and provided new information to update some of them. For example, they used several communications media already well established at Global Construction, such as e-mail and project Web sites. Kristin's team also used several new technologies to enhance project communications and processes. Examples of these updated business processes include the following:

- Kristin and her team used instant messaging on a regular basis both within their team and with suppliers. Several of the people working on the project were in various parts of the world, so they found it very useful to use instant messaging.
- Several suppliers used Webcasts to communicate information in a more dynamic way without incurring travel expenses. The Webcasts included visuals, such as PowerPoint slides, along with audio and animation to point to and write in key information. There were several other interactive features available in the Webcasts, such as polling the audience and letting other people add their audio input.
- The Web-based courses that suppliers were developing for the project included discussion threads and an "Ask the Expert" feature, in which learners could ask specific questions of the instructor or experts within the company on various topics related to the course. The questions and their answers were automatically added to a database that future learners could access.
- Kristin kept her own personal project blog to document important events and lessons she was learning while managing the project. She had used blogs for personal communications in the past, such as documenting her last trip to Europe, but she had never used one in a work setting before. She found it very useful for personal reflection and knew it would help her write her final lessons-learned document for the project.

The project steering committee—pleased and fascinated with the success of these new communications media—asked Kristin to prepare guidelines on using them that employees could access on the corporate intranet after the project was completed. Kristin was glad to do so.

EXECUTING TASKS FOR PROJECT PROCUREMENT MANAGEMENT

Many projects include work performed by outside sources. The main executing tasks performed as part of project procurement include requesting seller responses and selecting sellers. Key outputs include procurement document packages, contracts, and contract management plans.

Requesting Seller Responses, Qualified Sellers Lists, and Procurement Document Packages

After planning for contracting, the next procurement management process involves choosing suppliers (sellers), sending appropriate documentation to potential sellers, and obtaining proposals or bids. Prospective sellers do most of the work in this process by preparing their proposals and bids, normally at no cost to the buyer. The buying organization is responsible for deciding how to approach sellers and providing required procurement document packages. A procurement document package generally includes a summary letter, a request for proposal or quote, and a contract statement of work, as described in Chapter 5.

Organizations can use several different methods to approach and select qualified sellers or suppliers:

- *Approaching a preferred supplier:* Sometimes, a specific supplier might be the number-one choice for the buyer. In this case, the buyer gives procurement information to just that company. If the preferred supplier responds favorably, the organizations proceed to work together. Many organizations have formed good working relationships with certain suppliers, so they want to continue working with them.
- *Approaching several qualified suppliers:* In many cases, several suppliers could meet an organization's procurement needs. The buying organization can send procurement information to those potential sellers and then evaluate the results. If it does not get the desired response, the buyer can either expand its list of potential sellers until it gets the desired response or revise its procurement plans.
- *Advertising to many potential suppliers:* In many cases, several suppliers may be qualified to provide the goods and services, and the buyer may not know who they are in advance. Advertising the procurement (on a Web site, in a trade journal, or by other means) and receiving proposals and bids from multiple sources often takes advantage of the competitive business environment. Increased globalization and virtual project teams have increased tremendously as organizations find suitable sellers around the globe. As a result of pursuing a competitive bidding strategy, the buyer can receive better goods and services than expected at a lower price.

Sample Qualified Seller List

The Just-In-Time Training project required goods and services from several different suppliers. Recall that the project involved training in four different areas: supplier management, negotiating skills, project management, and software application. The training also had to be provided in various delivery formats—instructor-led, Web-based, and CD-ROM. Kristin and her team used their knowledge of current training suppliers and researched additional ones. They were not sure if they should have different suppliers for each course or have a different supplier based on each delivery method.

As described in Chapter 5, because Global Construction was new to the concept of just-in-time training, the company decided to hire a consulting firm that both specialized in just-in-time training and worked with all types of training suppliers. The consulting firm then developed a qualified sellers list containing 30 potential sellers, as provided in Table 6-7. In addition to the list, the firm also provided a report with information on each seller, such as relevant products and services, backgrounds of senior management, and current customers. It also provided recommendations for developing partnerships with each seller. See Chapter 5 for the RFP and contract statement of work for this procurement.

TABLE 6-7 Sample qualified sellers list

Qualified Sellers List September 9, 2007			
Project Name: Just-In-Time Training Project			
Seller Name/ Web Site	**Areas of Expertise**	**Full-Time Staff**	**Reputation**
Company A www.coA.com	Construction industry, supplier management, project management	40	One of few training firms that specializes in training for the construction industry
Company B www.coB.com	E-learning, custom course development	100	Has many partnerships with other companies, reasonable prices
Company C www.coC.com	Project management, negotiating skills	10	Small firm but well respected; does instructor-led and e-learning
Etc.			

Selecting Sellers and Writing Contracts

After buyers receive proposals or bids, they can select a supplier or decide to cancel the procurement. Selecting suppliers or sellers, often called source selection, involves evaluating proposals or bids from sellers, choosing the best one, negotiating the contract, and awarding the contract. Several stakeholders in the procurement process should be involved in selecting the best suppliers for the project. Often, teams of people are responsible for evaluating various sections of the proposals. There might be a technical team, a management team, and a cost team to focus on each of those major areas. Often, buyers develop a **short list** of the top three to five suppliers to reduce the work involved in selecting a source. Reviewers often follow a more detailed proposal evaluation process for sellers who make the short list, often checking their references, requesting special presentations, or having them provide sample products.

It is customary to conduct contract negotiations during the source selection process. Sellers on the short list are often asked to prepare a best and final offer (BAFO). Expert negotiators often conduct these negotiations, especially for contracts involving large amounts of money. In addition, top managers from both buying and selling organizations often meet before making final decisions. The final output of the seller selection process is a contract. It is also appropriate on some projects to prepare a contract management plan to describe details about how the contract will be managed.

Sample Contract

As mentioned in Chapter 5, a contract is a mutually binding agreement that obligates the seller to provide the specified products or services, and obligates the buyer to pay for them. Chapter 5 also described the different types of contracts and provided sample clauses that can be included to address risks. The Just-In-Time Training project would include contracts with several different suppliers. Some might be short, fixed-price contracts, such as one for the consulting firm to develop a list of qualified sellers. Others might be much longer and involve fixed-price, cost-reimbursable, and unit-pricing aspects, such as a contract to develop and deliver several training courses in different formats.

Table 6-8 provides a sample of part of a contract or service agreement, as some contracts are called, that could be used to produce a qualified sellers list. Note the reference to exhibit A, the statement of work. (A sample was provided in Chapter 5 and sent out to prospective sellers as part of the procurement package.) This document should be modified based on the selected seller's proposal. There is also a reference to a schedule for the work, which the seller also prepared as part of the proposal. It is good practice to include a detailed statement of work and schedule as part of the contract to clarify exactly what work the seller will perform and when.

TABLE 6-8 Sample contract

Global Construction, Inc.
Service Agreement
August 10, 2007

Title of Work: Qualified Sellers List and Report

This is an Agreement made as of August 10, 2007 by ABC Training Consultants, 2255 River Road, Boston, MA (the Seller), and Global Construction, Inc., 5000 Industrial Drive, Minneapolis, M N (the Buyer).

THE SELLER AND THE BUYER AGREE THAT:

1. The Work: The Seller will create the Work as set forth in Exhibit A hereto. The Buyer will provide the Seller with the format and specifications in which each element of the Work is to be submitted. The Seller agrees to conform to such format and specifications.

2. Delivery of the Work: The Seller agrees to deliver to the Buyer the Work in form and content acceptable to the Buyer on or before the dates outlined in Exhibit B of this Agreement, time being of the essence to the Buyer.

3. Right to Terminate: If the Seller materially departs from the agreed-upon schedule or if the Work is not satisfactory to the Buyer (based on reviews of drafts, market conditions, and/or other criteria as determined by the Buyer), the Buyer may at its option:
   A. Allow the Seller to finish, correct, or improve the Work by a date specified by the Buyer;
   B. Terminate this Agreement by giving written notice to the Seller.

4. Payments: The Buyer will pay the Seller a fixed price of $5,000 upon accepted completion of the Work.

5. Exhibit: The following Exhibit is hereby incorporated by reference into this Agreement:
   Exhibit A: Statement of Work
   Exhibit B: Schedule

IN WITNESS WHEREOF, THE PARTIES HERETO HAVE EXECUTED THIS Agreement as a sealed instrument as of the date first above written.

Global Construction, Inc.	ABC Training Consultants
By: _____	_____
Date: _____	_____

CLOSING CASE

Kristin did her best to lead the team in executing the Just-In-Time Training project. Like most project managers, however, she faced several challenges. It was hard for Kristin to confront Jamie, a key project team member, about her poor performance. Kristin knew that it was best to address problems head on and come up with the best possible solution. Kristin and her team also had to determine how to address poor ratings for the prototype supplier management course. She was proud of the way they worked together to find the root cause of problems and take corrective actions. Understanding important quality, motivation, and communications concepts and using several tools and techniques helped ensure successful project execution.

Chapter Summary

Good execution is crucial to project success. Without it, the goods, services, and results planned from the project cannot materialize. This chapter summarizes the executing tasks and key outputs for project integration, quality, human resource, communications, and procurement management.

Executing outputs related to integration management includes deliverables, implemented solutions to problems, work performance information, and requested changes. Samples of these outputs are provided for the Just-In-Time Training project.

Executing outputs related to quality management includes recommended corrective actions and project plan updates. Samples of these outputs are provided for the Just-In-Time Training project.

Executing outputs related to human resource management includes staffing updates and team performance assessment. Samples of these outputs are provided for the Just-In-Time Training project. Project managers must also apply concepts related to motivation, influence, and effectiveness to lead people during project execution.

Executing outputs related to communications management consist of business process updates. Samples of these outputs are provided for the Just-In-Time Training project. Project managers must apply important concepts related to communications, such as formal and informal communications, nonverbal communications, the appropriate communications medium, individual and group communication needs, and the impact of team size on project communications.

Executing outputs related to procurement management includes procurement document packages and contracts. Samples of these outputs are provided for the Just-In-Time Training project.

Quick Quiz

1. *Fortune* summarized research showing that the main reason CEOs failed was due to
   _____ .

   a.   poor planning

   b.   poor execution

   c.   global competition

   d.   low stock prices

2. Which of the following is not an example of a soft skill?

   a.   leadership

   b.   motivation

   c.   team building

   d.   financial analysis

3. Most project sponsors would say that the most important output of any project is _____ .

   a. a satisfied customer/sponsor

   b. good financial results

   c. its deliverables

   d. good plans

4. Which conflict handling mode do successful project managers use most often?

   a. confrontation

   b. compromise

   c. smoothing

   d. forcing

5. _____ includes all of the activities related to satisfying the relevant quality standards for a project.

   a. Quality assurance

   b. Quality control

   c. Customer satisfaction

   d. ISO certification

6. _____ diagrams can assist in ensuring and improving quality by finding the root causes of quality problems.

   a. Pareto

   b. Mind map

   c. Fishbone or Ishikawa

   d. Affinity

7. Which of the following statements is false?

   a. The highest need in Maslow's pyramid is called self-actualization.

   b. Most people today prefer managers who follow Theory X versus Theory Y.

   c. Herzberg distinguished between motivating and hygiene factors.

   d. Projects are more likely to succeed when project managers influence team members by using work challenge and expertise.

8. Some project managers like to assess team performance by using a technique known as MBWA, which stands for _____ .

   a. management by wondering aloud

   b. management by wandering around

   c. measuring by work areas

   d. measuring by watching alertly

9. If a project team goes from three people to six, how many more communications channels are there?

    a. 3

    b. 6

    c. 9

    d. 12

10. A procurement document package generally includes all of the following except _____ .

    a. a short list

    b. a summary letter

    c. a request for proposal or quote

    d. a contract statement of work

Quick Quiz Answers

1. B; 2. D; 3. C; 4. A; 5. A; 6. C; 7. B; 8. B; 9. D; 10. A

Discussion Questions

1. Describe practices that should be followed in directing and managing project execution. Why are deliverables such an important output of project execution? What are some of the typical problems that project teams face during project execution?

2. What is quality assurance, and how does it affect project execution? What are some examples of recommended corrective actions that Kristin made during project execution? Do you agree with her decisions? Why or why not?

3. Why is human resource management so important during project execution? How does Maslow's hierarchy of needs affect motivation? What are some examples of motivators and hygiene factors, according to Herzberg? What are the three main categories in McClelland's acquired-needs theory? What is the difference between Theory X and Theory Y? What are the five steps in Tuckman's team-building model?

4. Why is communications management so important during project execution? What is the difference between formal and informal communications? Why are nonverbal communications so important? Why do communications become more complicated when team size increases?

5. What is involved in requesting seller responses and selecting sellers? How do project teams develop a list of qualified sellers? What are some of the main topics addressed in a contract or service agreement?

Exercises

1. Find an example of a large project that took more than a year to complete, such as a major construction project. Describe some of the tasks performed to execute the integration, quality, human resource, communications, and procurement aspects of the project. Write a one-page paper or prepare a short presentation summarizing your findings.

2. Take the Myers-Briggs Type Indicator (MBTI) test and research information on this tool. There are several Web sites that have different versions of the test available free, such as *www.humanmetrics.com*, *www.personalitytype.com*, and *www.keirsey.com*. Write a two-page paper describing your MBTI type and what you think about this test as a team-building tool.

3. Review the following scenarios, and then write a paragraph for each one describing what media you think would be most appropriate to use, and why. See Table 6-6 for suggestions.

   a. Many of the technical staff on the project come in between 9:30 and 10:00 a.m., while the business users always come in before 9:00 a.m. The business users have been making comments. The project manager wants the technical staff to come in by 9:00 a.m., although many of them leave late.

   b. Your company is bidding on a project for the entertainment industry. You know that you need new ideas on how to put together the proposal and communicate your approach in a way that will impress the customer.

   c. Your business has been growing successfully, but you are becoming inundated with phone calls and e-mails asking similar types of questions.

   d. You need to make a general announcement to a large group of people and want to make sure they get the information.

4. Develop your own scenarios for when it would be appropriate to use each of the five conflict-handling modes discussed in this chapter (confrontation, compromise, smoothing, forcing, and withdrawal). Document your ideas in a one- to two-page paper.

Team Projects

1. Your organization initiated a project to raise money for an important charity. Assume that there are 1000 people in your organization. Also, assume that you have six months to raise as much money as possible, with a goal of $100,000. List three problems that could arise while executing the project. Describe each problem in detail, and then develop realistic approaches to solving them in a two- to three-page paper or a fifteen-minute presentation. Be creative in your responses, and reference ideas discussed in this chapter. Remember that this project is run solely by volunteers.

2. You are part of a team in charge of a project to help people in your company (500 people) lose weight. This project is part of a competition, and the top "losers" will be featured in a popular television show. Assume that you have six months to complete the project and a budget of $10,000. You are halfway though the project, and morale is very low. People are also complaining about a lack of communication and support on the project. Although many people have been participating and have lost weight, many have plateaued or started gaining weight back. Identify four strategies you can implement to improve morale and communications, referencing some of the theories discussed in this chapter. Document your responses in a two- to three-page paper or a fifteen-minute presentation.

3. Using the information you developed in Team Project 1 or 2, role-play a meeting to brainstorm and develop strategies for solving problems with key stakeholders. Determine who will play what role (project manager, team member from a certain department, senior managers, and so on). Be creative in displaying different personalities (a senior manager who questions the importance of the project to the organization, a team member who is very shy or obnoxious).

4. Perform the applicable integration, quality, human resource, communication, and procurement executing tasks for one of the real projects your class or group developed in Chapter 1. Remember to address common problems, focus on deliverables, and practice good soft skills.

Companion Web Site

Visit the companion Web site for this text (*www.course.com/mis/pm/schwalbe*) to access:

- Lecture notes
- Interactive quizzes
- Template files
- Sample documents
- Guide to Using Microsoft Project 2003
- VPMi enterprise project management software
- More ideas for team projects, including real projects and case studies
- Links to additional resources related to project management

Key Terms

benchmarking — The process of generating ideas for quality improvements by comparing specific project practices or product characteristics to those of other projects or products within or outside of the performing organization.

cause-and-effect diagrams — Also called fishbone or Ishikawa diagrams, these diagrams can assist in ensuring and improving quality by finding the root causes of quality problems.

compromise mode — The conflict-handling mode that uses a give-and-take approach to resolve conflicts.

confrontation mode — The conflict-handling mode that involves directly facing a conflict using a problem-solving approach that allows affected parties to work through their disagreements.

empathic listening — The process of listening with the intent to understand by putting yourself in the shoes of the other person.

extrinsic motivation — A motivation that causes people to do something for a reward or to avoid a penalty.

forcing mode — The conflict-handling mode that involves exerting one's viewpoint at the potential expense of another viewpoint.

groupthink — The conformance to the values or ethical standards of a group.

intrinsic motivation — A motivation that causes people to participate in an activity for their own enjoyment.

Maslow's hierarchy of needs — A hierarchy that states that people's behaviors are guided or motivated by a sequence of needs (physiological, safety, social, esteem, and self-actualization).

mirroring — The matching of certain behaviors of the other person.

Myers-Briggs Type Indicator (MBTI) — A popular tool for determining personality preferences.

quality assurance — The activities related to satisfying the relevant quality standards for a project.

quality audit — A structured review of specific quality management activities that helps identify lessons learned, which could improve performance on current or future projects.

rapport — A relationship of harmony, conformity, accord, or affinity.

short list — A list of the top three to five suppliers created to reduce the work involved in selecting a source.

smoothing mode — The conflict-handling mode that de-emphasizes or avoids areas of differences and emphasizes areas of agreement.

synergy — The concept that the whole is equal to more than the sum of its parts.

Tuckman model — A model that describes five stages of team development (forming, storming, norming, performing, and adjourning).

withdrawal mode — The conflict-handling mode that involves retreating or withdrawing from an actual or potential disagreement.

End Notes

[1] Shadi Rahimi, "Bush Embarks on Tour to Survey Damage," *The New York Times* (September 2, 2005).

[2] Steve Lohr, "Ambitious Package to Raise Productivity (and Microsoft's Profit)," *The New York Times* (August 16, 2004).

[3] Reuters, "TV Stations Fined for Janet Jackson Breast Flash," *http://www.reuters.com/* (September 22, 2004).

CHAPTER 7

MONITORING AND CONTROLLING PROJECTS

LEARNING OBJECTIVES

After reading this chapter, you will be able to:

- List several tasks and outputs of project monitoring and controlling, and describe outputs common to all knowledge areas

- Discuss performing integration change control as part of project integration management and how to use earned value management

- Explain the importance of scope verification, scope control, and accepting deliverables

- Describe the schedule control process and schedule performance measurement tools, such as tracking Gantt charts

- Discuss tools and techniques to assist in cost control

- List the Seven Basic Tools of Quality, and provide examples of how they assist in quality control

- Explain the monitoring and controlling work done as part of project human resource management to help manage project teams and stake holders

- Summarize methods for performance reporting and managing stake-holders as part of project communications management

- Describe the risk monitoring and controlling process

- Explain how to monitor and control projects though good contract administration

Kristin worked closely with the project steering committee to monitor and control the Just-In-Time Training project. She knew that senior management was keeping a watchful eye on this project to ensure that it met its objectives and also addressed changing business needs. For example, since the project started, Global Construction had won several major construction projects and increased hiring by 10 percent. Therefore, there were more people than ever who needed the training the Just-In-Time Training project would provide. At their weekly meetings, Kristin, her team, and suppliers provided performance information and discussed changes that were required. The steering committee decided to have major suppliers report their progress directly to them as often as needed. They knew from past projects that to get the best results, it was important to develop a close relationship with suppliers and to monitor them as closely as internal employees. They also hoped to continue their partnerships with several suppliers to expand the training into other areas after this project was completed.

INTRODUCTION

Monitoring and controlling involves regularly measuring progress to ensure that the project is meeting its objectives and addressing current business needs. The project manager and other staff monitor progress against plans and take corrective action when necessary. This chapter summarizes the main tasks involved in monitoring and controlling projects, and provides examples of key outputs from this process group for the Just-In-Time Training project.

SUMMARY OF MONITORING AND CONTROLLING OUTPUTS

Table 7-1 summarizes key outputs of project monitoring and controlling by knowledge area, based on the *PMBOK® Guide*. Notice that every knowledge area is included. Also note that the table includes the category "All," which lists several outputs common to all the knowledge areas. Recall from Chapter 6 that these items can also be outputs of project execution, so examples of them are not repeated in this chapter.

TABLE 7-1   Summary of project monitoring and controlling outputs

Knowledge area	Key monitoring and controlling outputs
All	Requested changes, recommended corrective actions, updates to applicable plans and processes
Project integration management	Forecasts, approved change requests, corrective actions, preventive actions, defect repair, rejected change requests, validated defect repair, deliverables
Project scope management	Accepted deliverables

TABLE 7-1 Summary of project monitoring and controlling outputs (continued)

Knowledge area	Key monitoring and controlling outputs
Project time management	Performance measurements, forecasted completion time
Project cost management	Performance measurements, forecasted completion cost
Project quality management	Quality-control measurements
Project human resource management	Outputs under "All" category
Project communications management	Performance reports, resolved issues
Project risk management	Risk register updates
Project procurement management	Contract documentation

MONITORING AND CONTROLLING TASKS FOR PROJECT INTEGRATION MANAGEMENT

The main monitoring and controlling tasks performed as part of project integration management include monitoring and controlling project work and performing integrated change control. These are crucial tasks that must be done well to ensure project success.

Monitoring and Controlling Project Work

Project changes are inevitable, so it is important to develop and follow a process to monitor and control them. Monitoring and controlling project work includes collecting, measuring, and disseminating performance information. It also involves assessing measurements and analyzing trends to determine what process improvements can be made. The project team should continuously monitor project performance to assess the overall health of the project and identify areas that require special attention.

The project management plan, work performance information, performance reports, and change requests are all important inputs for monitoring and controlling project work. Key tools and techniques for performing this process include using a project management methodology, a project management information system, and expert judgment, as described earlier in this text. Another powerful technique is earned value management, which helps forecast future project performance.

Forecasting with Earned Value Management

Earned value management (EVM) is a project performance measurement technique that integrates scope, time, and cost data. Given a baseline, project managers and their teams can determine how well the project is meeting scope, time, and cost goals by entering actual information and then comparing it to the baseline. As defined in Chapter 4, a baseline is a starting point, a measurement, or an observation that is documented so that it can be used for future comparison. In earned value management, a baseline includes the following:

- Scope (WBS tasks)
- Time (start and finish estimates for each task)
- Cost information (cost estimates for each task)

Actual information includes whether or not a WBS was completed or approximately how much of the work was completed; when the work actually started and ended; and how much it actually cost to do the completed work. Some project teams do not define work using a WBS or have cost estimates for each task. Some project teams do not periodically enter actuals for scope, time, and cost information. If you do not have a good baseline or actual information, you cannot use earned value management.

In the past, earned value management was primarily used on large government projects. Today, however, more and more companies are realizing the value of using this tool to help control projects. Most project management software products, including Microsoft Project 2003, provide tables and reports for entering and viewing earned value information. See the *Guide to Using Microsoft Project 2003* on the companion Web site for detailed instructions on using this software for earned value management.

Earned value management involves calculating three values for each activity or summary activity from a project's WBS.

1. The **planned value (PV)** is that portion of the approved total cost estimate planned to be spent on an activity during a given period. The cost baseline for the Just-In-Time Training project included $5000 to be spent in month three on course development for supplier management training (see Figure 4-12 for the cost baseline). If the activity involved delivering a detailed course outine to be finished in one week for $5000, then the planned value (PV) for that activity that week would be $5000.

2. The **actual cost (AC)** is the total direct and indirect costs incurred in accomplishing work on an activity during a given period. For example, suppose it actually took one week and cost $6000 to create the detailed course outline because the hourly rate for the person doing the work was higher than planned. The actual cost (AC) for the activity would therefore be $6000.

3. The **earned value (EV)** is an estimate of the value of the physical work actually completed. It is based on the original planned costs for the activity and the rate at which the team is completing work on the activity to date. The **rate of performance (RP)** is the ratio of actual work completed to the percentage of work planned to have been completed at any given time. For example, suppose an activity is only half completed by the end of the week, when it should have been totally completed. The rate of performance for that activity that week would be 50 percent. In this example, the activity to develop a detailed course outline was totally completed at the end of the week, so the RP was 100 percent. Because the PV was $5000, the EV would also be $5000.

Note that you can use earned value management at either a detailed or a summary level. In other words, you can use a detailed WBS and its associated time and cost data (using level three, four, or whatever is the most detailed), or you can apply earned value at a higher WBS level, such as level one or two.

Table 7-2 summarizes the earned value information and also computes the cost and schedule variance and the cost and schedule performance indexes.

TABLE 7-2 Earned value calculations for one activity after one week

Activity	Week
Earned Value (EV)	$5000
Planned Value (PV)	$5000
Actual Cost (AC)	$6000
Cost Variance (CV)	–$1000
Schedule Variance (SV)	0
Cost Performance Index (CPI)	83.33%
Schedule Performance Index (SPI)	100%

The earned value calculations in Table 7-1 are carried out as follows:

$$EV = \$5000 \times 100\% = \$5000$$
$$CV = \$5000 - \$6000 = -\$1000$$
$$SV = \$5000 - \$5000 = 0$$
$$CPI = \$5000/\$6000 = 83.33\%$$
$$SPI = \$5000/\$5000 = 100\%$$

Table 7-3 summarizes the general formulas used in earned value management. Note that the formulas for variances and indexes start with EV, the earned value. Variances are calculated by subtracting the actual cost or planned value from EV, and indexes are calculated by dividing EV by the actual cost or planned value. You can use the indexes to forecast what it will cost and when the project will finish.

TABLE 7-3 Earned value formulas

Term	Formula
Earned Value (EV)	EV = PV to date × RP
Cost Variance (CV)	CV = EV – AC
Schedule Variance (SV)	SV = EV – PV
Cost Performance Index (CPI)	CPI = EV/AC
Schedule Performance Index (SPI)	SPI = EV/PV
Estimate at Completion (EAC)	EAC = BAC/CPI
Estimated Time to Complete	Original time estimate/SPI

NOTE

In general, *negative numbers for cost and schedule variance indicate problems in those areas.* Negative numbers mean the project is costing more than planned or taking longer than planned. Likewise, *CPI and SPI less than one or less than 100 percent indicate problems.*

Earned value calculations for all project activities (or summary level activities) are required to estimate the earned value for the entire project. Some activities may be over budget or behind schedule, whereas others may be under budget and ahead of schedule. By adding all of the earned values for all project activities, you can determine how the project as a whole is performing and forecast both when it will be completed and how much it will cost at completion.

The **budget at completion (BAC),** or the approved total budget for the project, can be divided by the cost performance index to calculate the **estimate at completion (EAC),** which is a forecast of how much the project will cost upon completion. Likewise, the approved time estimate for the project can be divided by the schedule performance index to calculate when the project will be completed. Earned value, therefore, provides an excellent way to monitor project performance and provide forecasts based on performance to date.

Sample Forecast Using an Earned Value Chart

You can graph earned value information to track project performance and to forecast when a project will be completed and for how much. Figure 7-1 shows an earned value chart for the Just-In-Time Training project. The budget at completion for the project was $1 million for this one-year project. The BAC point on the chart, therefore, is at twelve months and $1 million. The cost baseline had a total planned value of $689,500 at the end of six months. We can therefore plot the PV point after six months at that value. If we assume that the cumulative actual costs for all activities completed by the end of month six are $750,000 and the earned value is $700,000, we can plot those two points as well.

NOTE

The detailed numbers used to create this chart are provided in the Excel file named Figure 7-1 on the companion Web site.

You can also forecast when the project will be completed and what its final cost will be based on this information.

$$CPI = \$700,000/\$750,000 = .933333$$
$$SPI = \$700,000/\$689,500 = 1.015228$$
$$EAC = \$1000,000/.933333 = \$1,071,429$$
$$\text{New time estimate} = 12 \text{ months}/1.015228 = 11.82 \text{ months}$$

Notice that the EAC point is provided on the chart in Figure 7-1 at 11.82 months and at the cost of $1,071,429. Viewing earned value information in chart form helps you visualize how the project has been performing and forecasts both the end date and the total cost. For example, you can see the planned performance by looking at the planned value line. If the project goes exactly as planned, it will finish in 12 months and cost $1,000,000, as represented by the BAC point. Notice in the example that the actual cost line is always right on or slightly above the earned value line. When the actual cost line is right on or above the earned value line, costs are equal to or more than planned. The planned value line is pretty close to the earned value line, just slightly lower. This relationship means that the

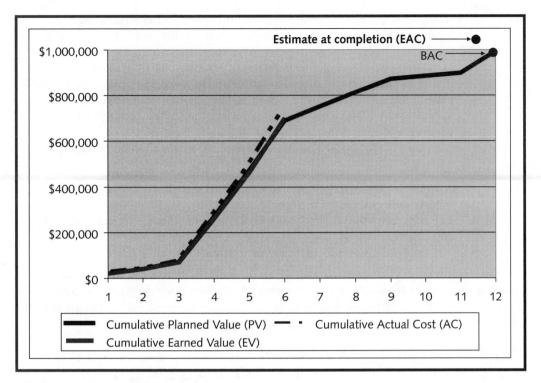

FIGURE 7-1   Sample earned value chart

project has been right on or slightly ahead of schedule the first six months. The forecasted completion date, therefore, is slightly earlier than planned while the forecasted total cost is slightly higher than planned.

If there are serious cost and schedule performance problems, senior management may decide to terminate projects or take other corrective action. The estimate at completion (EAC) is an important input to budget decisions, especially if total funds are limited. Earned value management is an important technique because when used effectively, it helps senior management and project managers evaluate progress and make sound management decisions.

Integrated Change Control

Integrated change control involves identifying, evaluating, and managing changes throughout the project's life cycle. The three main objectives of integrated change control are as follows:

1. *Influencing the factors that cause changes to ensure that changes are beneficial*: Changes can often be good for a project, so it is important to let everyone know that and focus on promoting changes that are beneficial. For example, changes that improve quality, reduce costs, save time, or improve stakeholder relationships are beneficial.
2. *Determining that a change has occurred*: To determine that a change has occurred, the project manager must know the status of key project areas at all

times. In addition, he must communicate significant changes to senior management and key stakeholders, who normally do not like surprises—especially unpleasant ones.

3. *Managing actual changes as they occur*: Managing change is a key role of project managers and their teams. It is important that project managers exercise discipline in managing the project to help control the number of changes that occur. Managers should focus on achieving project goals rather than putting out fires.

The project management plan provides the baseline for identifying and controlling project changes as follows:

- A section of the plan describes the work to be performed on a project, including key deliverables for the project and quality requirements.
- The schedule section of the plan lists the planned dates for completing key deliverables.
- The budget section provides the planned cost for these deliverables.

The project team must focus on delivering the work as planned. If the project team or someone else causes significant changes during project execution, project managers must formally revise the project management plan and have it approved by the project sponsor.

MONITORING AND CONTROLLING TASKS FOR PROJECT SCOPE MANAGEMENT

The main monitoring and controlling tasks performed as part of project scope management are scope verification and scope control. Key outputs are deliverables that are accepted by the customer. It is difficult to create a good project scope statement and WBS. It is often even more difficult to verify the project scope and minimize scope changes. Some project teams know from the start that the scope is very unclear and that they must work closely with the project customer to design and produce various deliverables. The project team must develop a process for scope verification that meets unique project needs. Careful procedures must be developed to ensure that customers are getting what they want and that the project team has enough time and money to produce the desired products and services.

Even when the project scope is fairly well defined, many projects suffer from **scope creep**—the tendency for project scope to grow bigger and bigger. There are many horror stories about projects failing due to scope creep. Even for fairly simple projects, people have a tendency to want more. How many people do you know, for example, who said they wanted a simple wedding or a basic new house constructed, only to end up with many more extras than they initially planned? In contrast, some projects also suffer from *not* delivering the minimum scope due to time or cost issues. A couple may have planned to go on a luxurious honeymoon until they saw how much the wedding cost, or a new homeowner may have settled for an unfinished basement in order to move in on time. These scenarios are similar to that of a project manager who must constantly cope with the triple constraint of balancing scope, time, and cost.

Scope Verification

Scope verification involves formal acceptance of the completed project scope by the project sponsor or designated stakeholders. This acceptance is often achieved through customer inspection and then sign-off on key deliverables. To receive formal acceptance of the project scope, the project team must develop clear documentation of the project's products and procedures, which the appropriate stakeholders can then evaluate for the degree of project completion and their satisfaction with the results.

The project scope statement, WBS dictionary, project scope management plan, and deliverables are the main inputs for scope verification. The main tool for performing scope verification is inspection. The customer, sponsor, or user inspects the work after it is delivered to decide if it is acceptable.

Sample of Accepted and Unaccepted Deliverables

The Just-In-Time Training project included many deliverables. Kristin, the project sponsor, the project steering committee, and other stakeholders—including employees taking the training courses—were all involved in verifying that deliverables were acceptable. Kristin worked closely with her project team and suppliers to make sure that deliverables were being developed correctly along the way. She knew that working closely with key stakeholders and reviewing progress was often the best way to ensure that final deliverables would be acceptable. Kristin knew from experience that foregoing draft reviews and delaying consultation with stakeholders until the final deliverable was ready often resulted in disaster.

Because Global Construction often worked with suppliers on projects, they had a formal process for verifying deliverables produced by suppliers. The project manager was responsible for signing off on their acceptance, as was the project sponsor. Table 7-4 provides a sample deliverable acceptance form. In this example, Kristin and Lucy, the project sponsor, document the fact that they do not accept the deliverable and provide feedback on what must be done to make it acceptable. Kristin did talk to the supplier about the changes required before accepting this particular deliverable—the course materials for the introductory supplier management course—but the supplier still did not deliver what was expected. The deliverable acceptance form provides formal documentation to ensure that deliverables meet project needs. In this case, because the particular deliverable was part of a contract, the supplier would not be paid until the deliverable was accepted.

Scope Control

You cannot control the scope of a project unless you have first clearly defined the scope and set a scope verification process in place. You also need to develop a process for soliciting and monitoring changes to project scope. Stakeholders should be encouraged to suggest beneficial changes and discouraged from suggesting unnecessary changes.

An example of successfully controlling scope comes from Northwest Airlines. The company developed a new reservation system in the late 1990s that took several years and millions of dollars to develop. They knew that users would request changes and enhancements to the system, so they built in a special function key for submitting change requests. They also allocated resources for specifically handling change requests by assigning three full-time programmers to handle them. Users made over 11,000 enhancement

TABLE 7-4   Sample deliverable acceptance form

Deliverable Acceptance Form

November 12, 2007

Project Name: Just-In-Time Training Project
Deliverable Name: Course materials for introductory supplier management course
Project Manager: Kristin Maur
Project Sponsor: Lucy Camarena

(We), the undersigned, acknowledge and accept delivery of the work completed for this deliverable on behalf of our organization. My (Our) signature(s) attest(s) to my (our) agreement that this deliverable has been completed. No further work should be done on this deliverable. If the deliverable is not acceptable, reasons are stated and corrective actions are described.

Name	Title	Signature	Date

1.   Was this deliverable completed to your satisfaction?   Yes ___   No _X_

2.   Please provide the main reasons for your satisfaction or dissatisfaction with this deliverable.

As stated in the contract statement of work, the course materials are not completed until all constructive feedback from the prototype course has been incorporated or the supplier has provided strong rationale as to why the feedback should not be incorporated. We requested that a new section be added to the course to cover issues related to working with suppliers in virtual settings. The final materials delivered did not include this new section or discuss why it was not added. We believe it was an oversight that can be corrected with a minimal amount of additional work.

3.   If the deliverable is not acceptable, describe in detail what additional work must be done to complete it.

The supplier will add a new section to the course on working with suppliers in a virtual setting. This section should take about thirty minutes of class time in a face-to-face or e-learning setting. This new section will follow the format and review process used for other topics in the course. We request delivery of the draft of this new section within one week and the final delivery within two weeks.

Contact's signature for resubmission of deliverable if found unacceptable: _____*Kristin Maur*_____ requests the first year the system was in use, which was much more than the three programmers could handle. The managers who sponsored the four main software applications had to prioritize the software enhancement requests and decide as a group what changes to approve. Given the time they had, the three programmers then implemented as many items as they could, in priority order. Although they only implemented 38 percent of the requested enhancements, these were the most important, and users were very satisfied with the system and process.

Another example of scope control is a practice some parents follow when their children get married. The parents provide a fixed budget for the wedding and honeymoon and let the young couple decide how to spend it. If the couple minimizes and controls the scope of the wedding, they can have extra money to pay off other debts or save for a down payment on a home. If they suffer from scope creep, they may not have any money for a honeymoon or become further in debt. This practice can be adapted to most business projects by providing incentives for workers to deliver the work as planned within time and budget constraints.

MONITORING AND CONTROLLING TASKS FOR PROJECT TIME MANAGEMENT

The main monitoring and controlling task performed as part of project time management is schedule control. Project managers often cite delivering projects on time (schedule control) as one of their biggest challenges, because schedule problems often cause more conflict than other issues. During project initiation, priorities and procedures are often most important, but as the project proceeds, especially during the middle and latter stages of a project, schedule issues become the predominant source of conflict.

Perhaps part of the reason schedule problems are so common is that time is easily and simply measured. After a project schedule is set, anyone can quickly estimate schedule performance by subtracting the original time estimate from the time actually expended. People often compare planned and actual project-completion times without taking into account the approved project changes. Time is also the variable with the least amount of flexibility. Time passes no matter what happens on a project.

Individual work styles and cultural differences may also cause schedule conflicts. For example, one dimension of the Myers-Briggs team-building tool that was described in Chapter 6 (Judgment/Perception, or J/P) deals with peoples' attitudes toward structure and deadlines. Some people (Js) prefer detailed schedules and focus on task completion. Others (Ps) prefer to keep things open and flexible. Different cultures and even entire countries have different attitudes about schedules. For example, some countries close businesses for several hours every afternoon to have siestas. Others observe religious or secular holidays during which little work is accomplished. Cultures may also have different perceptions of work ethic—some may value hard work and strict schedules, whereas others may value the ability to remain relaxed and flexible.

MEDIA SNAPSHOT

Planning and scheduling varied greatly for the 2002 Olympic Winter Games in Salt Lake City (see the Media Snapshot of Chapter 4) and the 2004 Olympic Summer Games in Athens, Greece. Many articles were written before the opening ceremonies of the Athens Games predicting that the facilities would not be ready in time. "With just 162 days to go to the opening of the Athens Olympics, the Greek capital is still not ready for the expected onslaught....By now 22 of the 30 Olympic projects were supposed to be finished. This week the Athens Olympic Committee proudly announced 19 venues would be finished by the end of next month. That's a long way off target."[1]

However, many people were pleasantly surprised by the amazing opening ceremonies, beautiful new buildings, and state-of-the-art security and transportation systems in Athens. For example, traffic flow, considered a major pre-Games hurdle, was superb. One spectator at the Games commented on the prediction that the facilities would not be ready in time, "Athens proved them all wrong....It has never looked better."[2] There were, however, several last-minute changes and many extra hours worked in the last few months before the games began. Costs exceeded $12 billion—*more than double the original budget.*[3] Many project managers and team members would have been more comfortable if the original plans had been followed, but Greek workers take pride in putting in major efforts near a deadline. The Greeks even made fun of critics by having construction workers pretend to still be working as the ceremonies began.

The goal of schedule control is to know the status of the schedule, influence the factors that cause schedule changes, determine whether the schedule has changed, and manage changes when they occur. A key output of schedule control is performance measurements.

Sample Schedule Performance Measurements

Earned value management, as described earlier, is a key tool for measuring schedule performance. Given the earned value and planned value, you can see how well the project team is meeting schedule goals and forecast when the project will be completed based on past schedule performance. Additional ways to measure schedule performance include:

- *Indicators:* Many senior managers like to focus on high-level color indicators of performance, such as green (on target), yellow (fair), and red (poor). They will oversee projects or tasks with red or yellow indicators much more closely than those with green indicators. Project management software offers color indicators as well as numerous reports to show schedule performance information. For example, Microsoft Project 2003 includes activity reports to show "should have started tasks" and "slipping tasks" to quickly identify problem areas. See the *Guide to Using Microsoft Project 2003* on the companion Web site for more information.
- *Milestone completion:* Experienced managers and buyers know that it is not enough to merely review indicators; they like to see the planned and actual completion dates of project milestones *and* the physical evidence that the work was actually completed. (See Chapter 4 for information on milestones.) For example, people having a house built often check on the physical progress to

make sure work is completed on schedule. Even though the contractor reports that key milestones are being completed, the buyer wants to see and review the work in person.

- *Worker morale and discipline:* Reviewing morale and work behavior is also a good way to measure schedule performance. If project team members are always working extra hours, the schedule might not be realistic. The project manager might need to negotiate a new schedule or request more resources. On the other hand, if workers are coming in late and leaving early while still producing quality work on time, the schedule might not be challenging enough. Project managers must empower team members to be responsible for completing work on time, yet they often have to use discipline to keep things on track and do what is in the best interest of the organization. (See Chapter 6 for information on motivating workers.)
- *Performance review meetings and tracking Gantt charts:* Another way to control project schedules is by holding periodic performance review meetings with management. The project steering committee for the Just-In-Time Training project held weekly meetings to make sure the project was meeting schedule and other goals. Project managers often illustrate progress with a **tracking Gantt chart**—a Gantt chart that compares planned and actual project schedule information. Many project managers believe that tracking Gantt charts are an excellent tool for tracking project schedule performance and reporting that information to stakeholders. Figure 7-2 provides a sample tracking Gantt chart that Kristin might use to measure schedule performance for a supplier. The tracking Gantt chart includes columns (hidden in Figure 7-2) labeled "Start" and "Finish" to represent actual start and finish dates for each task, as well as columns labeled "Baseline Start" and "Baseline Finish" to represent planned start and finish dates for each task. In this example, the project is completed, but several tasks missed their planned start and finish dates.

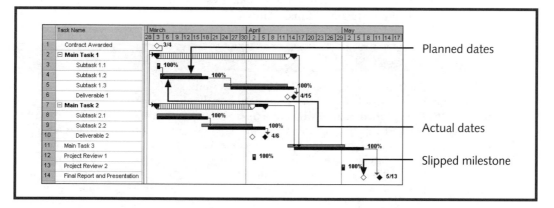

FIGURE 7-2 Sample schedule performance measurement using a tracking Gantt chart

To serve as a schedule performance measurement tool, a tracking Gantt chart uses a few additional symbols not found on a normal Gantt chart:

- Notice that the tracking Gantt chart in Figure 7-2 often shows two horizontal bars for tasks. The top horizontal bar represents the planned or baseline duration for each task. The bar below it represents the actual duration. Subtasks 1.2 and 1.3 illustrate this type of display. If the top and bottom bars are the same length and start and end on the same date, the actual schedule was the same as the planned schedule for that task. This scheduling occurred for Subtask 1.1, in which the task started and ended as planned on March 4. If the bars do not start and end on the same date, the actual schedule differed from the planned or baseline schedule. If the top horizontal bar is shorter than the bottom one, the task took longer than planned, as you can see for Subtask 1.2. If the top horizontal bar is longer than the bottom one, the task took less time than planned. A striped horizontal bar, illustrated by the bolded tasks named Main Tasks 1 and 2, represents the planned duration for those summary tasks. Recall from Chapter 4 that summary tasks are tasks that are decomposed into smaller tasks. The black bar adjoining the striped horizontal bar shows the progress for summary tasks. For example, Main Task 2 clearly shows that the actual duration took longer than what was planned.
- A white diamond on the tracking Gantt chart represents a slipped milestone. A **slipped milestone** refers to a milestone activity that was actually completed later than originally planned. For example, the last task provides an example of a slipped milestone because the final report and presentation were completed later than planned.
- Percentages to the right of the horizontal bars display the percentage of work completed for each task. For example, 100 percent indicates that the task is finished, whereas 50 percent indicates that the task is still in progress and is 50 percent completed.
- In the columns to the left of the tracking Gantt chart, you can display baseline and actual start and finish dates.

WHAT WENT RIGHT?

Canadian Imperial Bank of Commerce (CIBC) provides an excellent example of successfully controlling the schedule for a large information technology project in the banking industry. CIBC transformed 20,000 workstations in 1200 different financial branches in just one year. It created a Web-based tool to enable large, geographically dispersed teams to access information simultaneously. Each of the 1200 sites had 75 milestones to track, including the baseline, latest plan, and actual finish dates, resulting in 90,000 data points. According to Jack Newhouse, the company's director of application support, CIBC's Web-based tracking tool "was a critical component to success....Accurate, timely data was an invaluable management tool."[4]

Top management hates surprises, so the project manager must be clear and honest in communicating project status. By no means should project managers create the illusion that the project is going fine when, in fact, serious problems have emerged. When conflicts arise that could affect the project schedule, the project manager must alert top management and work with them to resolve the conflicts.

MONITORING AND CONTROLLING TASKS FOR PROJECT COST MANAGEMENT

The main monitoring and controlling task performed as part of project cost management is cost control. Cost control includes monitoring cost performance, ensuring that only appropriate project changes are included in a revised cost baseline, and informing project stakeholders of authorized changes to the project that will affect costs. The cost baseline, performance reports, change requests, and project funding requirements are inputs to the cost-control process. Outputs of cost control include project management plan updates, documentation of corrective actions, revised estimates for project completion, requested changes, and updates to organizational process assets, such as lessons-learned documents.

Several tools and techniques assist in project cost control:

- *Project management software:* Software packages, such as Microsoft Project 2003, have many cost-management features to help you enter budgeted costs, set a baseline, enter actuals, calculate variances, and run various cost reports.
- *Change-control system:* Projects should have a change-control system that defines procedures for changing the cost baseline. This cost-control change system is part of the integrated change-control system described earlier in this chapter. Because many projects do not progress exactly as planned, new or revised cost estimates are often required, as are estimates to evaluate alternative courses of action.
- *Performance review meetings:* These meetings can be a powerful aid for controlling project costs, just as they are for controlling schedules. People often perform better when they know they must report on their progress and are held accountable for their performance.
- *Earned value:* Another very important tool for cost control is earned value management, as described earlier.

Some projects leaders who encounter major problems, especially quality problems, blame those problems on poor cost control, as described in What Went Wrong? passage.

WHAT WENT WRONG?

Many people have heard about the problems with Boston's Big Dig project. Newspapers and Web sites showed the many leaks in the eight- to ten-lane underground expressway that took over 14 years and $14 billion to build. Did the project overseers cut corners to save time and money?

continued

Representative Stephen F. Lynch believes the answer to that question is yes, and that at some point, pressure to get the project done distracted Bechtel/Parsons Brinckerhoff from getting the project done right. "Under the pressure and scrutiny of a lot of people, they went back to look at areas where they could reduce cost in areas of material and time," said Lynch, a South Boston Democrat, in the aftermath of the Big Dig congressional hearing he brought to Boston on April 22, 2005. Pressure to finally speed up the costly, long-running project may explain why the new Artery tunnel is plagued by leaks. "As a casual observer, I am forced to conclude that the focus on the cost overrun and the schedule distracted attention from quality control issues on the Central Artery project," declared George J. Tamaro in written testimony to the Congressional Committee on Government Reform.[5]

MONITORING AND CONTROLLING TASKS FOR PROJECT QUALITY MANAGEMENT

The main project quality management task for monitoring and controlling is quality control. Key outputs include quality-control measurements, validated defect repair, and validated deliverables. Although one of the main goals of quality control is to ensure and improve quality, the main outcomes of this process are acceptance decisions, rework, and process adjustments.

- Acceptance decisions determine if the products or services produced as part of the project will be accepted or rejected. If they are accepted, they are considered to be validated deliverables. If project stakeholders reject some of the products or services produced as part of the project, there must be rework.
- Rework is action taken to bring rejected items into compliance with product requirements or specifications or other stakeholder expectations. Rework can be very expensive, so the project manager who excels at quality planning and quality assurance can reduce the need for rework.
- Process adjustments correct or prevent further quality problems. Based on the implementation of quality-control measurements, process adjustments often result in updates to the quality baseline, organizational process assets, and the project management plan.

Sample Quality-Control Measurements

Many different tools and techniques for performing quality control and developing control measurements are available. Some of these tools and techniques are also used for quality planning and assurance. The following seven tools are known as the Seven Basic Tools of Quality:

1. *Cause-and-effect diagrams*: As described in Chapter 6, cause-and-effect diagrams help you find the root cause of quality problems. Figure 6-2, repeated in this chapter as Figure 7-3, provides a sample cause-and-effect diagram that can be used to find the root cause of low course ratings for the Just-In-Time Training project.

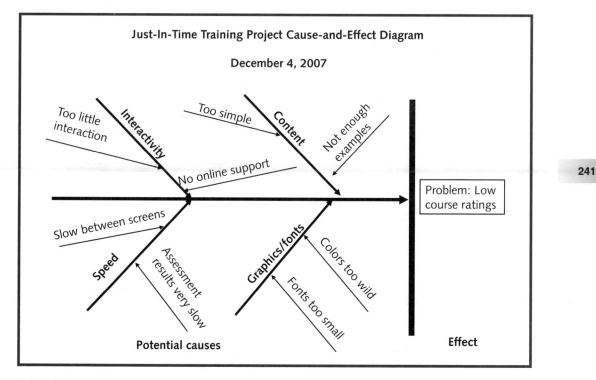

FIGURE 7-3   Sample cause-and-effect diagram

2. *Control charts:* A **control chart** is a graphic display of data that illustrates the results of a process over time. Control charts allow you to determine whether a process is in control or out of control. When a process is in control, any variations in the results of the process are created by random events. Processes that are in control do not need to be adjusted. When a process is out of control, variations in the results of the process are caused by nonrandom events. When a process is out of control, you need to identify the causes of those nonrandom events and adjust the process to correct or eliminate them. Figure 7-4 provides an example of a control chart for a process that manufactures 12-inch rulers. Assume that these are wooden rulers created by machines on an assembly line. Each point on the chart represents a length measurement for a ruler that comes off the assembly line. The scale on the vertical axis goes from 11.90 to 12.10. These numbers represent the lower and upper specification limits for the ruler. In this case, this would mean that the customer for the rulers has specified that all rulers purchased must be between 11.90 and 12.10 inches long, or 12 inches plus or minus 0.10 inches. The lower and upper control limits on the control chart are 11.91 and 12.09 inches, respectively. This means the manufacturing process is designed to produce rulers between 11.91 and 12.09 inches long. Looking for and analyzing patterns in process data is an important part of quality control. You can use control charts and the seven run rule to look for patterns in data. The seven run rule

states that if seven data points in a row are all below the mean, above the mean, increasing, or decreasing, then the process needs to be examined for nonrandom problems. In Figure 7-4, data points that violate the seven run rule are starred. Note that you include the first point in a series of points that are all increasing or decreasing. In the ruler-manufacturing process, these data points may indicate that a calibration device may need adjustment. For example, the machine that cuts the wood for the rulers might need to be adjusted, or the blade on the machine might need to be replaced.

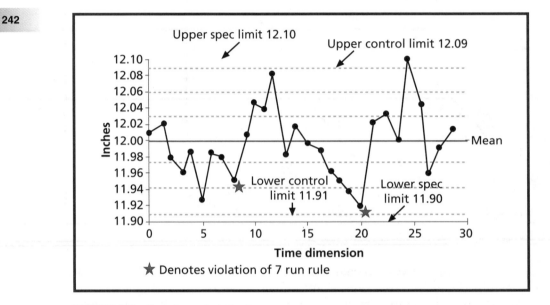

FIGURE 7-4 Sample control chart

3. *Run chart:* A run chart displays the history and pattern of variation of a process over time. It is a line chart that shows data points plotted in the order in which they occur. You can use run charts to perform trend analysis to forecast future outcomes based on historical results. For example, trend analysis can help you analyze how many defects have been identified over time to determine if there are trends. Figure 7-5 shows a sample run chart, charting the number of defects each month for three different types of defects. Notice that you can easily see the patterns of Defect 1 continuing to increase over time, Defect 2 decreasing the first several months and then holding steady, and Defect 3 fluctuating each month.

4. *Scatter diagram:* A **scatter diagram** helps show if there is a relationship between two variables. The closer data points are to a diagonal line, the more closely the two variables are related. Figure 7-6 provides a sample scatter diagram that the Just-In-Time Training project team might create to compare training participants' course evaluation ratings with their ages to see if there is a relationship. They might find that younger workers prefer the Web-based courses, for example, and make decisions based on that finding.

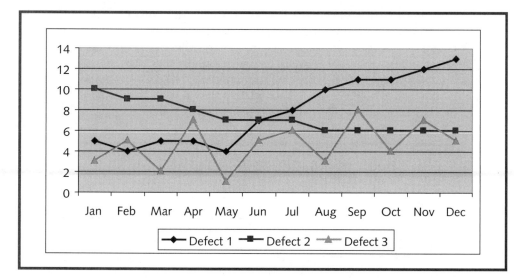

FIGURE 7-5 Sample run chart

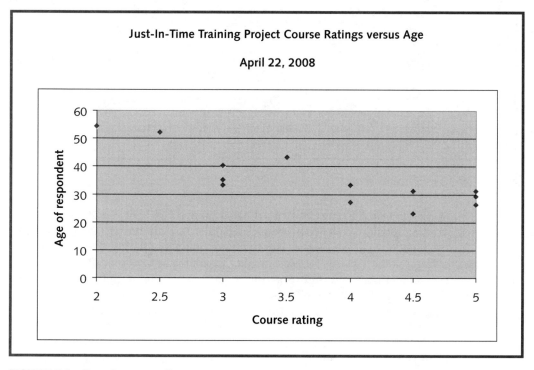

FIGURE 7-6 Sample scatter diagram

5. *Histograms:* A **histogram** is a bar graph of a distribution of variables. Each bar represents an attribute or a characteristic of a problem or situation, and the height of the bar represents its frequency. Chapter 5 provides a sample resource histogram in Figure 5-2, showing the number of people required for a project over time. The Just-In-Time Training project team created a histogram to show how many total complaints they received each month related to the project. Figure 7-7 shows the sample histogram.

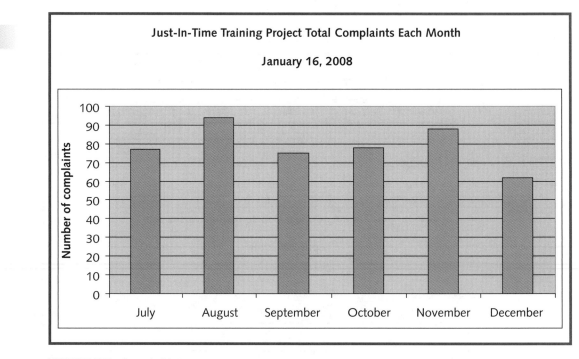

FIGURE 7-7 Sample histogram

6. *Pareto charts:* A **Pareto chart** is a histogram that can help you identify and prioritize problem areas. The variables described by the histogram are ordered by frequency of occurrence. Pareto charts help you identify the vital few contributors that account for most quality problems in a system. Pareto analysis is sometimes referred to as the 80/20 rule, meaning that 80 percent of problems are often due to 20 percent of the causes. Figure 7-8 is a sample Pareto chart that the Just-In-Time Training project team developed. They used it to help improve the quality of the information they provided about training courses on the corporate intranet. It shows the number of times people complained about the information on the intranet by category of complaint. Notice that the first two complaints account for a large percentage of the problems, so the team should focus on improving those areas to improve quality.

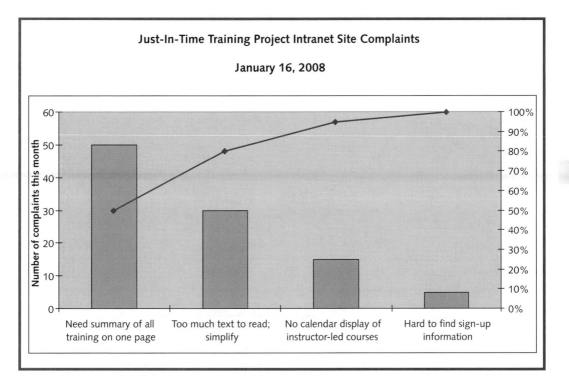

Just-In-Time Training Project Intranet Site Complaints

January 16, 2008

FIGURE 7-8 Sample Pareto chart

7. *Flowcharts:* **Flowcharts** are graphic displays of the logic and flow of processes that help you analyze how problems occur and how processes can be improved. They show activities, decision points, and the order of how information is processed. Figure 7-9 provides a simple example of a flowchart that shows the process Kristin's team used for accepting or rejecting deliverables.

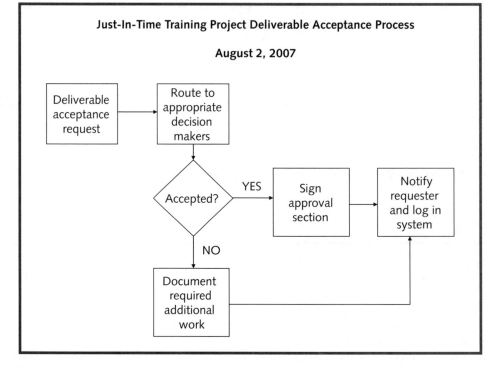

FIGURE 7-9 Sample flowchart

MONITORING AND CONTROLLING TASKS FOR PROJECT HUMAN RESOURCE MANAGEMENT

The main human resource management task performed as part of monitoring and controlling a project is managing the project team, which, of course, is no small task. After assessing team performance and related information, the project manager must decide if changes to the project should be requested, if corrective or preventive actions should be recommended, or if updates need to be made to the project management plan or organizational process assets. Project managers must use their soft skills to find the best way to motivate and manage each team member. Chapter 6 described many of these soft skills. The following sections describe tools and techniques to help manage project teams, and offer general advice on managing teams.

Tools and Techniques for Managing Project Teams

Several tools and techniques are available to assist in managing project teams:

- *Observation and conversation:* It is hard to assess how your team members are performing or how they are feeling about their work if you seldom see or discuss these issues. Many project managers, like Kristin, like to physically see and hear their team members at work. Informal or formal conversations about how a project is going can provide crucial information. For virtual workers, project managers can still observe and discuss work and personal issues via e-mail, telephone, or other communications media.

- *Project performance appraisals:* Just as general managers provide performance appraisals for their workers, so can project managers. The need for and type of project performance appraisals varies depending on the length of the project, the complexity of the project, organizational policies, contract requirements, and related communications. Even if a project manager does not provide official project performance appraisals for team members, it is still important to provide timely performance feedback. If a team member hands in sloppy or late work, the project manager should determine the reason for this behavior and take appropriate action. Perhaps the team member had a death in the family and could not concentrate. Perhaps the team member was planning to leave the project. The reasons for the behavior would have a strong impact on the action the project manager would take.

- *Conflict management:* Few projects are completed without any conflict. Some types of conflict are actually desirable on projects, but many are not. As described in Chapter 6, there are several ways to handle conflicts. It's important for project managers to understand strategies for handling conflicts and to proactively manage them.

- *Issue logs:* Many project managers keep an issue log (described in the next section) to document, monitor, and track issues that need to be resolved for effective work to take place. Issues could include situations in which people disagree, situations that need more clarification or investigation, or general concerns that need to be addressed. It is important to acknowledge issues that can hurt team performance and take action to resolve them. The project manager should assign someone to resolve each issue and assign a target date for resolution.

General Advice on Managing Teams

Effective project managers must be good team leaders. Suggestions for ensuring that teams are productive include the following:

- Be patient and kind with your team. Assume the best about people; do not assume that your team members are lazy and careless.
- Fix the problem instead of blaming people. Help people work out problems by focusing on behaviors.
- Establish regular, effective meetings. Focus on meeting project objectives and producing positive results.

- Allow time for teams to go through the basic team-building stages of forming, storming, norming, performing, and adjourning, as described in Chapter 6. Do not expect teams to work at the highest performance level from the start; moreover, not all teams will even reach the performing level.
- Limit the size of work teams to three to seven members to enhance communications.
- Plan some social activities to help project team members and other stakeholders become acquainted. Make the social events fun and not mandatory.
- Stress team identity. Create traditions that team members enjoy.
- Nurture team members and encourage them to help each other. Identify and provide training that will help individuals and the team as a whole become more effective.
- Acknowledge individual and group accomplishments.
- Take the additional actions necessary to work with virtual team members. If possible, have a face-to-face or phone meeting at the start of a virtual project or when introducing a virtual team member. Screen people carefully to make sure they can work effectively in a virtual environment. Clarify how virtual team members will communicate.

MONITORING AND CONTROLLING TASKS FOR PROJECT COMMUNICATIONS MANAGEMENT

The main communications management tasks performed as part of monitoring and controlling include performance reporting and managing stakeholders. Key outputs include performance reports, forecasts, and resolved issues.

Performance Reporting

Performance reporting keeps stakeholders informed about how resources are being used to achieve project objectives. Work performance information and measurements, forecasted completion dates, quality-control measurements, the project management plan, approved change requests, and deliverables are all important inputs to performance reporting. Two key outputs of performance reporting are performance reports and forecasts. Performance reports are normally provided as status reports or progress reports. Many people use the two terms interchangeably, but some people distinguish between them as follows:

- **Status reports** describe where the project stands at a specific point in time. Recall the importance of the triple constraint. Status reports address where the project stands in terms of meeting scope, time, and cost goals. Is work being accomplished as planned? How long did it take to do certain tasks? How much money has been spent to date? Status reports can take various formats depending on the stakeholders' needs.
- **Progress reports** describe what the project team has accomplished during a certain period. In many projects, each team member prepares a weekly or monthly progress report. Team leaders often create consolidated progress reports based on the information received from team members.

- **Forecasts** predict future project status and progress based on past information and trends. How long will it take to finish the project based on how things are going? How much more money will be needed to complete the project? Project managers can also use earned value management, as described earlier in this chapter, to answer these questions by estimating the budget at completion and the projected completion date based on how the project is progressing.

Stakeholders often review project performance information at status review meetings, such as the ones Kristin has with the project steering committee. Status review meetings are a good way to highlight important information, empower people to be accountable for their work, and have face-to-face discussions about key project issues. Many project managers also hold periodic status review meetings with their own team members to exchange important project information and motivate people to make progress on their parts of the project. Likewise, many senior managers, who are often part of a review board or oversight committee, hold status review meetings. At these meetings, several program and project managers must report overall status information to keep everyone abreast of important events and to learn from each other as well.

Unlike the managers found in Dilbert cartoons, most senior managers do want to review pertinent information at status review meetings and discuss problems, issues, and forecasts.

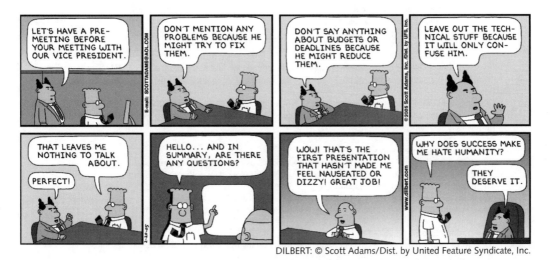

DILBERT: © Scott Adams/Dist. by United Feature Syndicate, Inc.

FIGURE 7-10   The shortest performance review meeting ever

Sample Performance Report

Table 7-5 provides a sample report that Kristin gave at a performance review meeting with the Just-In-Time Training project steering committee. Notice that the report references an earned value chart, similar to the one shown in Figure 7-1. Also notice the use of numbers that are of key interest to senior managers, such as the number of people trained to date and registered for courses. Also note the issues and suggestions and the project changes

Monitoring and Controlling Projects

section of the report. Performance review meetings should focus on addressing these items to ensure that projects succeed.

TABLE 7-5   Sample performance report

Progress Report

February 1, 2008

Project Name: Just-In-Time Training Project

Reporting Period: January 1 – February 1, 2008

Work completed this reporting period:
Held first negotiating skills course (instructor-led) with 20 participants
Held first supplier management executive course (instructor-led) with 17 participants
Held second supplier management introductory course (instructor-led) with 20 participants
Had 32 people begin the Web-based introductory supplier management course
Continued developing other Web-based courses
Prepared evaluations of all courses held to date

Work to complete next reporting period:
Hold first advanced supplier management course
Hold first project management course
Hold first software applications course

What's going well and why:
Participation in all courses is good. Every instructor-led course was full, except the supplier management executive course. All of the courses were advertised well, and we had more than enough people sign up for the classes. We put several people on the list for later courses after courses were filled in the registration system.
The average course ratings were above 3.8 on a 5.0 scale. Comments were generally very positive.
More people than expected started the first Web-based course. Development of new Web-based courses is going well.

What's not going well and why:
We did not fill the supplier management executive course, as planned. Three people could not attend at the last minute, and it was too late to get replacements. We will work on a policy to help prevent this problem in the future for all instructor-led classes.
We were surprised that so many people started the Web-based introductory supplier management course. We can handle the numbers, but we could have done a better job at forecasting demand.

Suggestions/Issues:
Develop a policy to handle people not being able to attend instructor-led courses at the last minute.
Try to do a better job at forecasting demand for Web-based courses.

Project changes:
No major changes to report. The earned value chart in Atch 1 shows planned value, actual cost, and earned value information to date. We are very close to our plans, running slightly ahead of schedule and a bit over budget.

Managing Stakeholders

Project managers must understand and work with various stakeholders while monitoring and controlling projects. In particular, they need to address how they will identify and resolve issues. An important tool that many project teams use is an issue log. An **issue** is a matter under question or dispute that could impede project success. An **issue log** is a tool used to document and monitor the resolution of project issues. It's important to resolve issues as soon as possible so that the project can proceed as planned.

Sample Issue Log

Table 7-6 shows part of an early issue log that Kristin and her team used to help document and manage the resolution of issues on their project. The issue log includes columns for the issue number, the issue description, the impact of the issue on the project, the date the issue was reported, who reported the issue, who the issue resolution was assigned to, the priority of the issue (High, Medium, or Low), the due date to report back on the issue, and comments related to the issue. Project managers can tailor the format of issue logs as needed. The project management software that Kristin's team used for the Just-In-Time Training project included an online issue log that could be sorted and filtered various ways. For example, Kristin always sorted issues by priority so that she could focus on high priorities. She also sorted them by who reported the issue and who was assigned to each to make sure that the appropriate people were making progress.

TABLE 7-6 Sample issue log

Issue Log

August 20, 2007

Project Name: Just-In-Time Training Project

Issue #	Issue Description	Impact on Project	Date Reported	Reported By	Assigned To	Priority (H/M/L)	Due Date	Status	Comments
1	Key project team member is not working out	Can severely hurt project because Jamie is our supplier management expert	Aug 2	Kristin	Kristin	H	Sep 2	Open	Working with Jamie and appropriate managers to find a replacement
2	IT staff that is performing survey is overallocated	Delaying the survey will delay the entire project because it is a critical task	Sep 26	Mohammed	Kristin	H	Aug 5	Closed	Paid overtime was approved
etc.									

MONITORING AND CONTROLLING TASKS FOR PROJECT RISK MANAGEMENT

Monitoring and controlling risks involves executing the risk management processes to respond to risk events. Recall from Chapter 5 that a risk event is a specific, uncertain event that may occur to the detriment or enhancement of the project. Executing the risk management processes means ensuring that risk awareness is an ongoing activity performed by the entire project team throughout the project. Project risk management does not stop with the initial risk analysis. Identified risk events may not materialize, or their probabilities of occurrence or impact may diminish or increase. Similarly, new risk events are normally identified as the project progresses. Newly identified risk events need to go through the same process of analysis and control as those identified during the initial risk assessment. A redistribution of resources devoted to risk management may be necessary because of relative changes in risk exposure.

Carrying out individual risk management plans involves monitoring risks based on defined milestones and making decisions regarding risks and their response strategies. It might be necessary to alter a strategy if it becomes ineffective, implement planned contingency activities, or eliminate a risk event from the list of potential risks. Project teams sometimes use **workarounds**—unplanned responses to risk events—when they do not have contingency plans in place.

Risk reassessment, risk audits, variance and trend analysis, technical performance measurements, reserve analysis, and status meetings or periodic risk reviews are all tools and techniques for performing risk monitoring and control. Outputs of this process include the following:

- Requested changes
- Recommended corrective and preventive actions
- Updates to the risk register, project management plan, or organizational process assets, such as lessons learned information that might help future projects

Sample Risk Register Updates

Recall from Chapter 5 that the number one risk event in the risk register for the Just-In-Time Training project at that time was a poor survey response. Because the project was now halfway completed, the risk register would have to change significantly. New risks would be identified and potential responses would change based on the current situation. Status of all risks would also be updated.

For example, halfway through the project, senior management informed Kristin that the company, Global Construction, Inc., was growing faster than expected, and they thought the number of people needing training would be higher than expected. This information resulted in the identification of several new risks related to the difficulty of accommodating this growth in trainees. For example, although the Web-based courses were the most popular and adding participants to them would be less expensive than adding to any other type of course, there was a risk that the discussion board would become unmanageable. People might waste time reading through hundreds of messages or just ignore this part of the course altogether. Kristin and her team, including suppliers for the Web-based courses, would need to develop potential responses to this risk and take action if it did occur.

Another risk related to employee growth might be the need to offer more instructor-led classes, which would result in increased costs to the project. As you can see, the risk register must be constantly updated as part of project monitoring and control.

MONITORING AND CONTROLLING TASKS FOR PROJECT PROCUREMENT MANAGEMENT

The main procurement management task performed to monitor and control projects is administering the contract. Administering the contract, or contract administration, ensures that the seller's performance meets contractual requirements. The contractual relationship is a legal relationship and, as such, is subject to state and federal contract laws. It is very important that appropriate legal and contracting professionals be involved in writing and administering contracts.

Several tools and techniques can help in contract administration:

- Formal contract change-control system
- Buyer-conducted performance reviews
- Inspections and audits
- Performance reporting
- Payment systems
- Claims administration
- Records management
- Information technology to support contract administration

A key output of contract administration is contract documentation. Contract documentation would include the contract itself along with requested unapproved contract changes and approved change requests. It is very important to document all changes to the contract and communicate those changes to all affected stakeholders. For example, if a supplier developing a course for the Just-In-Time Training project agreed to add a topic to the course at no extra cost, that agreement must be added to the contract to make it legal. Likewise, if Global Construction decided to add more than the agreed on number of instructor-led courses, it would need to update that information in the contract as well. Updates are often made by having both parties—the buyer and the seller—sign an addendum to the contract.

Project team members must be aware of the potential legal problems of their not understanding a contract. Changes must be handled properly for items under contract. Without understanding the provisions of the contract, a project manager might not realize that she is authorizing the contractor to do additional work at additional cost. Therefore, change control is an important part of the contract administration process.

It is critical that project managers and team members watch for constructive change orders. **Constructive change orders** are oral or written acts or omissions by someone with actual or apparent authority that can be construed to have the same effect as a written change order. For example, if a member of Kristin's project team has met with a supplier or contractor on a weekly basis for three months to provide guidelines for performing work, he can be viewed as an apparent authority. If he tells the contractor to redo part of a report that has already been delivered and accepted by the project manager, that action can be viewed as a constructive change order and the contractor can legally bill the buyer for the additional work. Likewise, if this apparent authority tells the contractor to skip parts of a critical review meeting in the interests of time, it would not be the contractor's fault if he missed important information.

Suggestions for Administering Contracts

The following suggestions help ensure adequate change control and good contract administration:

- Changes to any part of the project need to be reviewed, approved, and documented by the same people in the same way that the original part of the plan was approved.
- Evaluation of any change should include an impact analysis. How will the change affect the scope, time, cost, and quality of the goods or services being provided? There must also be a baseline against which to compare and analyze changes.
- Changes must be documented in writing. Project team members should document all important meetings and telephone calls.
- Project managers and their teams must stay closely involved with suppliers to make sure that their deliverables meet business needs and work in the organization's environment. Do not assume that work will run smoothly because you hired a reputable supplier. The buying organization needs to provide expertise as well.
- Have backup plans in case the procurement does not produce the desired results.

Chapter Summary

Monitoring and controlling involves regularly measuring progress to ensure that the project is meeting its objectives and addressing current business needs. The project manager and other staff monitor progress against plans and take corrective action when necessary. This chapter summarizes the monitoring and controlling tasks and key outputs for all nine knowledge areas.

Every knowledge area includes tasks and outputs to help monitor and control projects. Outputs common to all knowledge areas include requested changes, recommended corrective actions, and updates to applicable plans and processes.

Monitoring and controlling outputs related to integration management also include forecasts. Earned value management is a project performance measurement technique that integrates scope, time, and cost data. You can use it to forecast when a project will be completed and how much it will cost given past performance data.

Monitoring and controlling tasks related to scope management include scope verification and scope change control, and a unique output includes accepted deliverables. A sample form for verifying acceptance of deliverables is provided for the Just-In-Time Training project.

Monitoring and controlling outputs related to time, cost, and quality management include schedule control, cost control, and quality control. Unique outputs include performance measurements, forecasted completion, and quality-control measurements. Sample outputs are provided for the Just-In-Time Training project.

Monitoring and controlling outputs related to communications management include performance reports, forecasts, and resolved issues. Sample outputs are provided for the Just-In-Time Training project.

Monitoring and controlling outputs related to risk management include updating the risk register. Sample updates are provided for the Just-In-Time Training project.

Monitoring and controlling outputs related to procurement management include contract documentation. Suggestions are provided for administering contracts.

Quick Quiz

1. Which knowledge areas include tasks related to monitoring and controlling?
   a. project scope, time, cost, and quality management
   b. project integration, scope, time, cost, and quality management
   c. project human resource, communications, risk, and procurement management
   d. all nine knowledge areas

2. _____ is a project performance measurement technique that integrates scope, time, and cost data.
   a. Integrated change control
   b. Flowcharting
   c. Earned value management
   d. Forecasting

3. _____ involves formal acceptance of the completed project scope by the stakeholders.
   a. Scope creep
   b. Scope verification
   c. Deliverable acceptance
   d. Customer sign-off

4. _____ issues cause the most conflict over the life of projects.
   a. Change control
   b. Scope creep
   c. Cost
   d. Schedule

5. A _____ chart is a histogram that can help you identify and prioritize problem areas.
   a. Pareto
   b. control
   c. run
   d. scatter

6. When a process is out of control, variations in the results of the process are caused by _____ events.
   a. random
   b. nonrandom
   c. planned
   d. unplanned

7. Which of the following is not a tool or technique for managing project teams?
   a. observation and conversation
   b. issue logs
   c. performance appraisals
   d. control charts

8. _____ predict future project status and progress based on past information and trends.
   a. Forecasts
   b. Status reports
   c. Progress reports
   d. Histograms

9. _____ are unplanned responses to risk events.

    a. Contingencies

    b. Reserves

    c. Workarounds

    d. Overallocations

10. _____ change orders are oral or written acts or omissions by someone with actual or apparent authority that can be construed to have the same effect as a written change order.

    a. Constructive

    b. Contract

    c. Procurement

    d. Controlled

Quick Quiz Answers

1. D; 2. C; 3. B; 4. D; 5. A; 6. B; 7. D; 8. A; 9. C; 10. A

Discussion Questions

1. What is involved in monitoring and controlling projects? What outputs of monitoring and controlling are common to all knowledge areas?

2. Explain how earned value management helps you monitor project performance and forecast future cost and schedule information. What do you need to do to use earned value management?

3. What are the three main objectives of integrated change control?

4. What is the difference between scope verification and scope control? Why are both important to project success?

5. What are some of the tools and techniques for performing time, cost, and quality control? What are the Seven Basic Tools of Quality?

6. What are some of the tools and techniques for managing project teams? Summarize some of the advice typically given for managing teams. Which items do you think are most important?

7. Why is it important to keep the risk register up to date?

8. Why is it important to document contract changes? Why should project teams be watchful for constructive change orders?

Exercises

1. Find an example of a large project that took more than one year to complete, such as a major construction project. Describe some of the tasks performed to monitor and control the project. Write a one-page paper or prepare a short presentation summarizing your findings.

2. Given the following information for a one-year project, answer the following questions. Assume you have actual and earned value data at the end of the second month. Recall that PV is the planned value, EV is the earned value, AC is the actual cost, and BAC is the budget at completion.

   PV = $23,000

   EV = $20,000

   AC = $25,000

   BAC = $120,000

   a. What is the cost variance, schedule variance, cost performance index (CPI), and schedule performance index (SPI) for the project?

   b. How is the project progressing? Is it ahead of schedule or behind schedule? Is it under budget or over budget?

   c. Use the CPI to calculate the estimate at completion (EAC) for this project. Is the project performing better or worse than planned?

   d. Use the SPI to estimate how long it will take to finish this project.

   e. Sketch the earned value chart for this project, using Figure 7-1 as a guide.

3. Follow the steps for using Microsoft Project 2003 provided in the *Guide to Using Microsoft Project 2003,* pages A69–77, on the companion Web site for this text (*www.course.com/mis/ pm/schwalbe*). Open the data files as directed and then establish a baseline plan, create a tracking Gantt chart, and implement earned value management using this software. The data files are also provided on the companion site.

4. Assume you are working on a project to improve customer service. Create a Pareto chart based on the information in the following table. Use the Pareto chart template or sketch the chart by hand so that your resulting chart looks similar to Figure 7-8.

Customer complaints	Frequency/week
Customer is on hold too long	90
Customer gets transferred to wrong area or cut off	20
Service rep cannot answer customer's questions	120
Service rep does not follow through as promised	40

5. Using Appendix B and the detailed instructions on the companion Web site (as needed), run the Fissure simulation software. Summarize information from each of your workweek reports and print out the final earned value chart as well as any other information you think is valuable. Write a two- to three-page single-spaced report summarizing what you learned by using this simulation software.

Team Projects

1. Your organization initiated a project to raise money for an important charity. Assume that there are 1,000 people in your organization. Also, assume that you have six months to raise as much money as possible, with a goal of $100,000. List three problems that could arise while monitoring and controlling the project. Describe each problem in detail, and then develop realistic approaches to solving them in a two- to three-page paper or a 15-minute presentation. Be creative in your responses, and use at least one quality-control tool in your analysis. Remember that this project is run solely by volunteers.

2. You are part of a team in charge of a project to help people in your company (500 people) lose weight. This project is part of a competition, and the top "losers" will be featured in a popular television show. Assume that you have six months to complete the project and a budget of $10,000. You are halfway though the project, and morale is very low. People are also complaining about a lack of communication and support on the project. Although many people have been participating and have lost weight, many have plateaued or started gaining weight back. Create an issue log to document these and related issues. Also create a new entry for the risk register for this project. Document your responses in a two- to three-page paper or a 15-minute presentation.

3. Using the information you developed in Team Project 1 or 2, role-play a meeting to brainstorm and develop strategies for solving problems with key stakeholders. Determine who will play what role (project manager, team member from a certain department, senior managers, and so on). Be creative in displaying different personalities (a senior manager who questions the importance of the project to the organization, a team member who is very shy or obnoxious).

4. Create relevant monitoring and controlling documents, such as a performance report and issue log, for one of the real projects your class or group developed in Chapter 1, using the templates and samples in this chapter as guides. Present your results to the class.

Companion Web Sites

Visit the companion Web site for this text (*www.course.com/mis/pm/schwalbe*) to access:

- Lecture notes
- Interactive quizzes
- Template files
- Sample documents
- Guide to Using Microsoft Project 2003
- VPMi enterprise project management software
- More ideas for team projects, including real projects and case studies
- Links to additional resources related to project management

Key Terms

actual cost (AC) — The total direct and indirect costs incurred in accomplishing work on an activity during a given period.

budget at completion (BAC) — The approved total budget for the project.

constructive change orders — Oral or written acts or omissions by someone with actual or apparent authority that can be construed to have the same effect as a written change order.

control chart — A graphic display of data that illustrates the results of a process over time.

earned value (EV) — An estimate of the value of the physical work actually completed.

earned value management (EVM) — A project performance measurement technique that integrates scope, time, and cost data.

estimate at completion (EAC) — A forecast of how much the project will cost upon completion.

flowcharts — The graphic displays of the logic and flow of processes that help you analyze how problems occur and how processes can be improved.

forecasts — The reports that predict future project status and progress based on past information and trends.

histogram — A bar graph of a distribution of variables.

integrated change control — The process of identifying, evaluating, and managing changes throughout the project's life cycle.

issue — A matter under question or dispute that could impede project success.

issue log — A tool used to document and monitor the resolution of project issues.

Pareto chart — A histogram that can help you identify and prioritize problem areas.

planned value (PV) — That portion of the approved total cost estimate planned to be spent on an activity during a given period.

progress reports — The reports that describe what the project team has accomplished during a certain period.

rate of performance (RP) — The ratio of actual work completed to the percentage of work planned to have been completed at any given time.

scatter diagram — A diagram that helps show if there is a relationship between two variables.

scope creep — The tendency for project scope to grow bigger and bigger.

scope verification — The formal acceptance of the completed project scope by the project manager or designated stakeholders.

slipped milestone — A milestone activity that was actually completed later than originally planned.

status reports — The reports that describe where the project stands at a specific point in time.

tracking Gantt chart — A Gantt chart that compares planned and actual project schedule information.

workarounds — The unplanned responses to risk events.

End Notes

1   Fran Kelly, "The World Today—Olympic Planning Schedule behind Time," *ABC Online* (March 4, 2004).

2   Jay Weiner and Rachel Blount, "Olympics Are Safe but Crowds Are Sparse," *Minneapolis Star Tribune* (August 22, 2004), A9.

3   Reuters, "Olympics Bill Reportedly Passes $12 Billion," *MSNBC.com* (August 25, 2004).

4   Tom Chauduri and David Schlotzhauer, "So Many Projects, So Little Time," *PM Network* (October 2003): 58.

5   Joan Vennochi, "Time, Money, and the Big Dig," *Boston Globe* (April 26, 2005).

CHAPTER **8**

CLOSING PROJECTS AND BEST PRACTICES

LEARNING OBJECTIVES

After reading this chapter, you will be able to:

- List several tasks and outputs of project closing
- Discuss the process of closing a project performed as part of project integration management, and describe the contents of a customer acceptance/project completion form, final project report, and lessons-learned report
- Explain the process of contract closure performed as part of project procurement management, and describe the contents of a written notice of a closed contract
- List several best practices used in project management, and discuss how improving project management maturity can improve project performance

OPENING CASE

The Just-In-Time Training project was almost finished. Twenty instructor-led courses had been conducted over the past year, and a majority of Global Construction's employees took at least one Just-In Time course, most using the Web-based delivery option. Some senior managers were surprised at how quickly workers took to the Web-based courses and also pleased that many employees took the courses on their own time. Participants liked the interactive feedback and started networking more internally to improve productivity and collaboration. Employees provided excellent feedback on the new approach to training and suggested several new topics to be added to the list of training subjects. The project steering committee was looking forward to Kristin's final report and presentation on the project.

INTRODUCTION

Closing projects involves gaining stakeholder and customer acceptance of the final products and services, and bringing the project to an orderly end. It includes verifying that all of the deliverables are complete, and often includes a final presentation and report. For both projects that are completed and those that are canceled before completion, it is important to formally close the project and reflect on what can be learned to improve future projects. As philosopher George Santayana said, "Those who cannot remember the past are condemned to repeat it."

It is also important to plan for and execute a smooth transition of the project into the normal operations of the company. Most projects produce results that are integrated into the existing organizational structure. For example, Global Construction's Just-In-Time Training project will require staff to coordinate future training after the project is completed. Recall from Chapter 3 that the life-cycle cost estimate for the project included $400,000 each year for three years, or 40 percent of the total project cost, for work to be done after the project was completed. Before ending the project, Kristin and her team created a transition plan as part of the final report to integrate the new training into the firm's standard operations.

SUMMARY OF CLOSING OUTPUTS

Table 8-1 summarizes key outputs of project closing by knowledge area, based on the *PMBOK® Guide*. Notice that the first output listed is procedures for administrative and contract closure. Every project should have procedures to guide closure. Samples of closing procedures and other outputs produced in closing the Just-In-Time Training project are provided in this chapter.

TABLE 8-1 Summary of project closing outputs

Knowledge area	Outputs
Project integration management	Administrative and contract closure procedures Final products, services, or results Updates to organizational process assets
Project procurement management	Closed contracts Updates to organizational process assets

CLOSING TASKS FOR PROJECT INTEGRATION MANAGEMENT

The last task in project integration management is closing the project. To close a project, you must finalize all activities and transfer the completed or canceled work to the appropriate people. The main outputs of closing projects are as follows:

- *Administrative closure procedures:* It is important for project teams and other stakeholders to develop and follow a step-by-step process for closing projects. In particular, administrative closure procedures should define the approval process for all project deliverables. Chapter 7 provided a sample deliverable acceptance form used by Global Construction. The company also used a customer acceptance/project completion form to formally close the entire project, which will be shown later in this chapter.

- *Contract closure procedures:* Many projects involve contracts, which are legally binding agreements. Contract closure procedures describe the methodology for making sure that the contract has been completed, including both delivery of goods and services, and payment for them.

- *Final products, services, or results:* Project sponsors are usually most interested in making sure that final products, services, or results are delivered on schedule and within budget. A final project report and presentation are also commonly used during project closing. A sample table of contents from the Just-In-Time Training project's final report is provided in the next section, as well as part of the transition plan produced as part of the final report.

- *Updates to organizational process assets:* Recall from Chapter 6 that organizational process assets help people understand, follow, and improve business processes. Examples of organizational process assets include policies and procedures, guidelines, information systems, financial systems, management systems, lessons learned, and historical information. During project closing, the project team should update appropriate process assets, especially lessons learned. At the end of the Just-In-Time Training project, Kristin's team prepared a lessons-learned report, which will serve as a tremendous asset for future projects.

In closing the Just-In-Time Training project, Kristin and her team prepared a customer acceptance/project completion form, a final report and presentation, a transition plan (provided as part of the final report), and a lessons-learned report. Kristin also organized a project closure luncheon for the project team right after the final project presentation. She used the luncheon to celebrate a job well done.

Sample Customer Acceptance/Project Completion Form

As part of project closing, Global Construction had the project sponsor complete a customer acceptance/project completion form. Even if the project had been terminated, the sponsor would still have completed the form to signify the end of the project. Table 8-2 shows the form that was filled out for the Just-In-Time Training project. Note that this form refers to completion of the entire project, not just a specific deliverable. It should be completed and signed by the project sponsor.

TABLE 8-2 Sample customer acceptance/project completion form

Customer Acceptance/Project Completion Form
June 30, 2008

Project Name: Just-In-Time Training Project
Project Manager: Kristin Maur

I (We), the undersigned, acknowledge and accept delivery of the work completed for this project on behalf of our organization. My (Our) signature(s) attest(s) to my (our) agreement that this project has been completed. No further work should be done on this project.

Name	Title	Signature	Date
Lucy Camerena	Training Director	Lucy Camarena	June 30, 2008

1. Was this project completed to your satisfaction?   __X__ Yes _____ No

2. Please provide the main reasons for your satisfaction or dissatisfaction with this project.
The project met and exceeded my expectations. In my 15 years with this company, I have never seen workers so interested in training courses. Kristin effectively coordinated all of the people who worked on this project. We worked with a number of new suppliers, and everything went very smoothly.

3. Please provide suggestions on how our organization could improve its project delivery capability in the future.
One suggestion would be to try to improve our estimating and forecasting abilities. The project costs were slightly over budget, even with some reserve built in. The schedule buffer prevented the project from finishing late. We also need to improve the way we forecast the number of people who want to take courses. The demand for the Web-based courses was much higher than expected. Even though that was a pleasant surprise, it was still poor forecasting and caused extra work for project and support staff.

Thank you for your inputs.

Sample Final Report

Table 8-3 is the table of contents for the final project report for the Just-In-Time Training project (the cover page of the report included the project title, date, and team member names). Notice that the report includes a transition plan and a plan to analyze the benefits of the training each year. Also notice that the final report includes attachments for all the project management and product-related documents. Kristin knew the importance of providing complete final documentation on projects and that the project steering committee would expect a comprehensive final report on such an important project. The project team produced a hard copy of the final documentation for the project sponsor and each steering committee member, and placed an electronic copy on the corporate intranet with the other project archives. Kristin also led the team in giving a final project presentation, which summarized key information in the final project report.

TABLE 8-3 Sample table of contents for a final project report

---

Final Project Report
June 20, 2008

Project Name: Just-In-Time Training Project

1. Project Objectives
2. Summary of Project Results
3. Original and Actual Schedule
4. Original and Actual Budget
5. Project Assessment
6. Transition Plan
7. Training Benefits Plan

Attachments:

A. Key Project Management Documentation
   - Business case
   - Project charter
   - Project management plan
   - Performance reports

B. Product-Related Documentation
   - Survey and results
   - Summary of user inputs
   - Report on research of existing training
   - Partnership agreements
   - Course materials
   - Intranet site training information
   - Summary of course evaluations

Sample Transition Plan

As mentioned earlier, the life-cycle cost estimate for Global Construction's Just-In-Time Training project included $400,000 each year for three years for work to be done after the project was completed. The transition plan included information related to what work had to be done, by whom, and when. When developing a transition plan, the project team should work with managers in affected operating departments, and the contents of the plan should be tailored to fit the support needs of the project. Table 8-4 provides part of the transition plan for the Just-In-Time Training project.

TABLE 8-4 Sample transition plan

Transition Plan
June 20, 2008

Project Name: Just-In-Time Training Project

Introduction

The main goal of this project was to develop a new training program at Global Construction to provide just-in-time training to employees on key topics, including supplier management, negotiating skills, project management, and software applications. New courses were developed and offered in instructor-led, CD-ROM, and Web-based formats. These courses will continue to be offered at Global Construction for the next several years. This transition plan describes the work required to support these courses.

Assumptions

- Support for the just-in-time training will be handled by staff in affected operational departments, including the training, IT, HR, and contract departments.
- Funding for the required support is budgeted at $400,000 per year for three years. These funds will be used to pay staff in the operational departments supporting this project, experts providing information for courses, and suppliers providing training materials and courses.
- New course topics will be developed under a new project and are not part of this transition plan.

Organization

The Training Director, Lucy Camarena, will lead all efforts to support the Just-In-Time Training courses. Staff from the training, IT, HR, and contract departments will provide support as required. See the organizational chart provided in Attachment 1.

Work Required

The main work required to support the training developed from this project includes:

- Maintaining related information on the intranet site
- Handling course registration
- Determining the number of courses offered each year and when they will be offered
- Providing classrooms for the instructor-led training
- Coordinating with suppliers for all training courses
- Planning and managing the internal experts who provide some of the training and expert support for the courses
- Collecting course evaluation information and suggestions for changing the content or format of courses
- Reporting information to senior management on a monthly basis

See Attachment 2 for detailed information on the work required.

Schedule

See Attachment 3 for a draft schedule of work to be performed in the next year. The training director is responsible for scheduling and managing the work required to support the just-in-time training.

Sample Lessons-Learned Report

Instead of asking each member of the Just-In-Time Training project team and the project managers from the major supplier organizations to write individual lessons-learned reports, Kristin decided to use a technique she had read about in an article in which key stakeholders held a sticky-note party to document lessons learned. Instead of writing lessons learned in a traditional way, key stakeholders met, wrote down all of the lessons they had learned on sticky notes, and then posted them to the wall. It was an enjoyable way for everyone to get together and share what they had learned from the project. After they finished, Kristin summarized the inputs in a list that everyone could access on the project Web site. She also used the corporate template to prepare a short lessons-learned report for inclusion in the final documentation for the project, as shown in Table 8-5. Notice the question-and-answer format of the report, which is part of the lessons-learned template used for all projects done at Global Construction, Inc.

TABLE 8-5 Project lessons-learned report

<table>
<tr><td colspan="2" align="center">Lessons-Learned Report
June 20, 2008</td></tr>
<tr><td>Project Name:</td><td>The Just-In-Time Training Project of Global Construction Inc.</td></tr>
<tr><td>Project Sponsor:</td><td>Lucy Camarena</td></tr>
<tr><td>Project Manager:</td><td>Kristin Maur</td></tr>
<tr><td>Project Dates:</td><td>July 1, 2007–June 30, 2008</td></tr>
<tr><td>Final Budget:</td><td>$1,072,000</td></tr>
</table>

1. Did the project meet scope, time, and cost goals?

We did meet scope and time goals, but we had to request an additional $72,000, which the sponsor approved. We actually exceeded scope goals by having more people take training courses than planned, primarily the Web-based courses.

2. What was the success criteria listed in the project scope statement?

The following statement outlined the project scope and success criteria:
"Our sponsor has stated that the project will be a success if the new training courses are all available within one year, if the average course evaluations are at least 3.0 on a 1-5 scale, and if the company recoups the cost of the project in reduced training costs within two years after project completion."

3. Reflect on whether or not you met the project success criteria.

All of the new training courses were offered within a year, and the course evaluations averaged 3.4 on a 5.0 scale. We do not know if the cost of the project will be recouped within two years after completion, but the number of people who took the Web-based training courses far exceeded our expectations. Because the Web-based training is more cost-effective than the instructor-led training, we are confident that the costs will be recouped in less than two years.

4. What were the main lessons your team learned from this project?

The main lessons we learned include the following:
- Having good communication was instrumental to project success. We had a separate item in the WBS for stakeholder communications, which was very important. Moving from traditional to primarily Web-based training was a big change for Global Construction, so the strong communication was crucial. The intranet-site information was excellent, thanks to support from the IT department. It was also very effective to have different departments create project description posters to hang in their work areas. They showed creativity and team spirit.

TABLE 8-5   Project lessons-learned report (continued)

- Teamwork and supplier partnerships were essential. It was extremely helpful to take time to develop and follow a team contract for the project team and to focus on developing good partnerships with suppliers.
- Good planning paid off in terms of when plans were executed. We spent a fair amount of time developing a good project charter, scope statement, WBS, schedules, and so on. Everyone worked together to develop these planning documents, and there was strong buy-in. We kept the plans up to date and made key project information available for everyone on a secure Web site.
- Creativity and innovation are infectious: After departments had so much fun making their posters in their work areas, people picked up on the idea of being creative and innovative throughout the project. Everyone realized that training and learning could be enjoyable.
- The project steering committee was very effective, and it was extremely helpful to meet regularly with the committee. Having committee members from departments throughout the company was very important and helped promote the training created as part of this project.

5.   Describe one example of what went right on this project.

We were skeptical about hiring an outside consultant to help us develop a short list of potential suppliers for the training courses, but it was well worth the money. We gained a good deal of useful information very quickly, and the consultant made excellent recommendations and helped us develop partnerships that benefited us as well as our suppliers.

6.   Describe one example of what went wrong on this project.

The senior supplier management specialist assigned to the team at the beginning of the project was not a good fit. The project manager should have had more involvement in selecting project team members.

7.   What will you do differently on the next project based on your experience working on this project?

For future training projects, it would be helpful to line up experts and mentors further in advance. We underestimated the number of people who would take the Web-based courses, and participants liked the interactive features, such as getting expert advice and having a list of people willing to mentor them on various topics. We were scrambling to recruit people, and then had to figure out how to organize them in an effective manner.

CLOSING TASKS FOR PROJECT PROCUREMENT MANAGEMENT

The final process in project procurement management is closing the contract, or contract closure. **Contract closure** involves completion and settlement of contracts, and resolution of any open items. The project team should determine if all work required in each contract was completed correctly and satisfactorily. The team should also update records to reflect final results and archive information for future use.

Two tools to assist in contract closure are procurement audits and a records management system. **Procurement audits** are often performed during contract closure to identify lessons learned in the entire procurement process. Organizations should strive to improve all their business processes, including procurement management. A **records management system** provides the ability to easily organize, find, and archive procurement-related documents. It is often an automated system, or at least partially automated, because there can be a large amount of information related to project procurement.

Outputs from contract closure include updates to organizational process assets and closed contracts. Just as with administrative closure, updating organizational process assets under contract closure includes documentation, historical information, and lessons learned. To close contracts, the buying organization often provides the seller with formal written notice that the contract has been completed. Buyers might also consider the final payment to the seller as the contract closeout. The contract itself should include requirements for formal acceptance and closure.

Sample Written Notice of a Closed Contract

Table 8-6 provides an example of a formal letter that Global Construction sent to one of its sellers, ABC Training Consultants, to formally close out their contract. The contract, a service agreement in this case, included a clause that stated that written notice would be provided to formally close the contract. The seller in this particular example also requested that the buyer provide a short performance assessment as part of the closure letter. (See Table 6-8 in Chapter 6 to review the service agreement and Table 5-14 in Chapter 5 for the contract statement of work. Recall that the work had to be completed by September 9, 2007, for this contract.)

TABLE 8-6 Sample contract closure notice

Global Construction, Inc., Contract Closure Notice

September 16, 2007

As described in our service agreement (SA390-7), this letter provides formal notice that the work you were contracted to perform for Global Construction has been completed. ABC Training developed a qualified-sellers list containing 30 potential sellers and a report with one page of key information on each seller. Payment is being processed based on the invoice provided by ABC Training.

Kristin Maur, the project manager, has provided the following performance assessment for the work provided:

"We were very pleased with the work of ABC Training. Members of the firm were professional, knowledgeable, and easy to work with. Global Construction depended on ABC Training to develop a qualified sellers list for this important project, and we were extremely happy with the results. On a scale of 1 to 10, you earned a 10!"

Lawrence Scheller

By: Lawrence Scheller, Contract Specialist, Global Construction, Inc.

Date: September 16, 2007

BEST PRACTICES

Many organizations continue to struggle with project management. If you cannot manage projects well, you cannot manage programs or portfolios well either. People continue to try to understand the challenges of managing projects and question why there seem to have been few improvements in this important practice.

WHAT WENT WRONG?

When George Stephenson built a railway from Liverpool to Manchester in the 1820s, it was completed behind schedule and 45 percent over budget. In 2005, the reconstruction of Wembley Stadium, the home of English soccer, was threatened when the Australian developer of the site said it faced huge losses on the GBP 750 million (1.4 billion U.S. dollars) project. The cost of steel doubled in 2004, and labor costs were exceeding estimates as they worked to complete the stadium in time for the May 2006 FA Cup final.

One suggested reason why problems prevail is that project initiation gets separated from execution. Many projects are done by outside firms, and bidders competing for the work often make overly optimistic assumptions about costs and revenues. A study published in 2005 in the *Journal of the American Planning Association* examined 210 large rail and road projects in 14 different countries and found that forecasts of future passengers were wildly optimistic. For rail projects, the forecasts, on average, were 106 percent higher than the actual number of passengers, and one in eight forecasts were off by over 400 percent. For road projects, the miscalculations were more accurate, but were still optimistic by over 20 percent in more than half the cases. The article's authors—led by Bent Flyvbjerg, a professor at Denmark's Aalborg University—claim that the forecasts on similar projects are no more accurate now than they were 30 years ago.[1]

To prevent problems and improve project management, many people are attempting to discover and use best practices, such as developing more realistic estimates and forecasts. This text described how Global Construction used several good practices in managing its Just-In-Time Training project. What exactly are good or best practices? The following sections describe PMI's view of best practices from its Organizational Project Management Maturity Model (OPM3) publication, research results from Interthink Consulting's organizational project management baseline studies, information on best practices from the Ultimate Business Library, as well as a summary of best practices described in this text.

Figure 8-1 shows Dilbert's view of best practices and how he put them to use to buy everyone T-shirts.

DILBERT: © Scott Adams/Dist. by United Feature Syndicate, Inc.

FIGURE 8-1   Dilbert's view of best practices

Organizational Project Management Maturity Model (OPM3) Best Practices

The Project Management Institute (PMI) Standards Development Program published the Organizational Project Management Maturity Model (OPM3) in December 2003 to address the need to bridge the gap between organizational strategy and successful projects. OPM3 defines **organizational project management** as "the systematic management of projects, programs, and portfolios in alignment with the achievement of strategic goals."[2] OPM3 is a standard developed to provide a way for organizations to measure their organizational project management maturity against a comprehensive set of best practices. A **best practice** is "an optimal way recognized by industry to achieve a stated goal or objective."[3] OPM3 lists 586 best practices, which PMI says are achieved through developing and consistently demonstrating their supporting capabilities, as observed through measurable outcomes. **Capabilities** are incremental steps that lead to best practices, and **outcomes** are the results of applying capabilities. A **key performance indicator (KPI)** is a criterion used to determine whether the outcome associated with a capability exists, or the degree to which it exists.

OPM3 provides the following example to illustrate a best practice, capability, outcome, and key performance indicator:

- *Best practice:* Establish internal project management communities
- *Capability (one of four for this best practice):* Facilitate project management activities
- *Outcome:* Local initiatives, meaning the organization develops pockets of consensus around areas of special interest
- *Key performance indicator:* Community addresses local issues[4]

Best practices are organized into three levels: project, program, and portfolio. Within each of those categories, best practices are categorized by four stages of process improvement: standardize, measure, control, and improve. For example, the list that follows contains names and descriptions of several best practices listed in OPM3:

- Project best practices:
  - *Project initiation process standardization*—Project initiation process standards are established.
  - *Project plan development process measurement*—Project plan development process measures are established, assembled, and analyzed.
  - *Project scope planning process control*—Project scope planning process controls are established and executed to control the stability of the process.
  - *Project scope definition process improvement*—Project scope definition process problem areas are assessed, process improvement recommendations are collected, and process improvements are implemented.
- Program best practices:
  - *Program activity definition process standardization*—Program activity definition process standards are established.
  - *Program activity sequencing process measurement*—Program activity sequencing process measures are established, assembled, and analyzed.
  - *Program activity duration estimating process control*—Program activity duration estimating process controls are established and executed to control the stability of the process.
  - *Program schedule development process improvement*—Program schedule development process problem areas are assessed, process improvement recommendations are collected, and process improvements are implemented.
- Portfolio best practices:
  - *Portfolio resource planning process standardization*—Portfolio resource planning process standards are established.
  - *Portfolio cost estimating process measurement*—Portfolio cost estimating process measures are established, assembled, and analyzed.
  - *Portfolio cost budgeting process control*—Portfolio cost budgeting process controls are established and executed to control the stability of the process.
  - *Portfolio risk management planning process improvement*—Portfolio risk management planning process problem areas are assessed, process improvement recommendations are collected, and process improvements are implemented.

OPM3 and similar maturity models include questionnaires that help organizations determine their maturity levels in project, program, and portfolio management. A **maturity model** is a framework for helping organizations improve their processes and systems. A maturity model describes an evolutionary path of increasingly organized and systematically more mature processes. Many maturity models have five levels, with level one describing characteristics of the least organized or least mature organizations, and level five describing the characteristics of the most organized and most mature organizations. By improving their project, program, and portfolio management maturity and following best practices, organizations can improve business processes and business performance.

WHAT WENT RIGHT?

"Three years ago the board of Siemens launched a worldwide initiative to improve its project management. The German electronics group had worked out that half its turnover came from project-like work, and it calculated that if it could complete all of these projects on time and to budget, it would add EURO3 billion ($3.7 billion U.S. dollars) to its bottom line over three years. A key element of the scheme was the introduction of project managers to the company's sales teams to try and temper their more extravagant promises, a move that requires a careful balance between reining them in and killing the deal.

"Some companies have gone so far as to become more like project co-ordinators than producers of goods or services. The 'business-as-usual' bits of their operations have been outsourced, leaving them free to design and orchestrate new ideas. Nike, for instance, does not make shoes any more; it manages footwear projects. Coca-Cola, which hands most of the bottling and marketing of its drinks to others, is little more than a collection of projects, run by people it calls 'orchestrators.' Germany's BMW treats each new car 'platform,' which is the basis of new vehicle ranges, as a separate project. Meanwhile Capital One, a fast-growing American financial-services group, has a special team to handle its M&A 'projects.' For all these firms, project management has become an important competitive tool. Some of them call it a core competence. Good project management can certainly make a difference. BP's fortunes were transformed when it converted its exploration division, BPX, into a portfolio of projects, each of them more or less free from head-office control—a structure which the company describes as an 'asset federation.' Asset/project managers can no longer rely on head office for support. They are required to build their own self-sufficient teams."[5]

Interthink Consulting Research on Project Management Maturity

As discussed in the What Went Right? examples in Chapter 3, organizations have realized that following a project management methodology can lead to better project performance, lower costs for project management, and better value for stakeholders. Many people want to know how mature they need to be in following a methodology to reap the benefits.

Interthink Consulting Incorporated developed the Organizational Project Management (OPM) Baseline Study, which just completed its seventh year. This study provides a comprehensive overview of project management practices in organizations and industries worldwide, with over 600 participants. Part of the underlying thesis of the maturity model on which the OPM Baseline Study is based is that improved process capabilities will result in improved project delivery. Based on the 2004 study, there were definite relationships between maturity and project delivery. The study provides detailed results in several areas, such as maturity level, meeting budgets, schedules, customer satisfaction, and project goal attainment.

Figure 8-2 provides a graph from Interthink's 2004 OPM Baseline Study that compares project management process maturity with project goal attainment. Note that maturity is broken down into several categories, such as program initiation, project initiation, and project tracking. (See detailed study results from *www.interthink.ca*.)

"For projects that met their goals or exceeded them by a factor of 10% to 25% there is a slight but clear increase in overall maturity through the majority of the process capability areas. For the organizational capability areas, the increase in maturity is most clear in the areas of Risk Management and Organization. For projects that failed to exceed their goals, the indicated maturity in the majority of the process capability areas are relatively lower."[6]

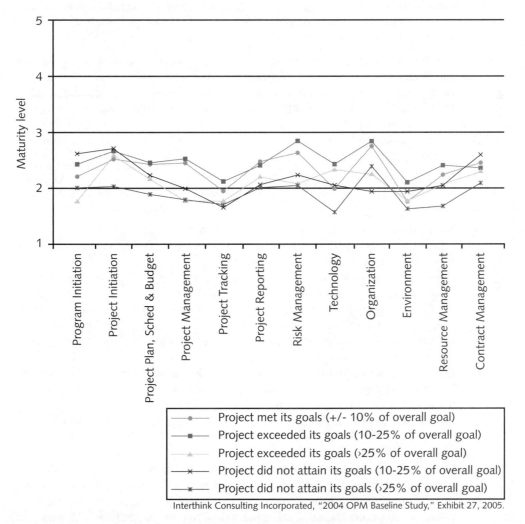

Interthink Consulting Incorporated, "2004 OPM Baseline Study," Exhibit 27, 2005.

FIGURE 8-2 Process maturity and project goal attainment

Ultimate Business Library Best Practices

In 2003, the Ultimate Business Library published a book called *Best Practice: Ideas and Insights from the World's Foremost Business Thinkers*. This book includes articles by well-known business leaders such as Warren Bennis (author of over 30 books on leadership, including *On Becoming a Leader*), Daniel Goleman (author of *Emotional Intelligence* and other works), and Thomas Stewart (editor of the *Harvard Business Review* and author of *Intellectual Capital: The New Wealth of Organizations*).

In the book's introduction, Rosabeth Moss Kanter, a professor at Harvard Business School and a well-known author and consultant, says that visionary leaders know "the best practice secret: Stretching to learn from the best of the best in any sector can make a big vision more likely to succeed."[7] Kanter also emphasizes the need to have measurable standards for best practices. Organizations can measure performance against their own past; against peers; and, even better, against potential. Kanter suggests that organizations need to continue to reach for higher standards. She suggests the following exercise regimen for business leaders who want to intelligently adapt best practices to help their own organizations:

1. Reach high. Stretch. Raise standards and aspirations. Find the best of the best and then use it as inspiration for reaching full potential.

2. Help everyone in your organization become a professional. Empower people to manage themselves through benchmarks and standards based on best practice exchange.

3. Look everywhere. Go far afield. Think of the whole world as your laboratory for learning.[8]

In addition, Robert Butrick, author of *The Project Workout*, wrote an article on best practices in project management for the Ultimate Business Library book. He suggests that organizations need to follow these basic principles of project management:

- Make sure your projects are driven by your strategy. Be able to demonstrate how each project you undertake fits your business strategy, and screen out unwanted projects as soon as possible.

- Use a staged approach. You can rarely plan a project in its entirety. Use progressive steps or stages to project planning, and use the same generic stages for all types of projects. Have gate reviews before starting each stage to revalidate a project and before committing more resources and funding for the project. Place high emphasis on the early stages of a project to reduce risks and decrease time to market.

- Engage your stakeholders. Ignoring stakeholders often leads to project failure. Be sure to engage stakeholders at all stages of a project, and encourage teamwork and commitment at all times.

- Ensure success by planning for it. To help projects succeed, the balance of power often needs to be tipped toward the project and away from line management.

- Monitor against the plan. Everyone working on projects must have guidance, training, and support in creating plans and making project-related decisions. Organizations must develop and follow control techniques for managing risks, issues, scope changes, schedule, costs, and project reviews. Monitoring and forecasting against a plan ensure that everyone is on the same page and prevent unwanted surprises.

- Manage the project control cycle. Monitoring should focus more on the future than on the past. Project managers must continuously check that the project plan is still fit for the purpose of the project and likely to deliver the business benefits on time. Project changes must be managed to ensure that only those enabling project benefits to be realized are accepted. Avoid the dangers of scope creep, and let stakeholders know that project benefits drive the scope.
- Formally close the project: Every project should be closed to make sure that all work ceases, that lessons are learned, and that remaining resources are released for other purposes.

MEDIA SNAPSHOT

Another view of best practices includes best places for people to work. For example, *Fortune* magazine lists the "100 Best Companies to Work For" in the United States every year. *Working Mother* magazine lists the best companies in the United States for women based on benefits for working families. The *Times Online* (*www.timesonline.co.uk*) provides the *Sunday Times* list of the "100 Best Companies to Work For," a key benchmark against which UK companies can judge their performance as employers. The Great Place to Work Institute, which produces *Fortune*'s "100 Best Companies to Work For," uses the same selection methodology for over 20 international lists, including "Best Companies to Work for" lists in all 15 countries of the European Union, Brazil, Korea, and a number of other countries throughout Latin America and Asia. Companies make these lists based on feedback from their best critics: their own employees. Quotes from employees often show why certain companies made the lists:

- "It is a friendly, courteous, caring hospital. We generally care about our co-workers and our patients. I can always get the help and support that I need to function in this hospital. This goes from the top all the way down to the cleaning people."
- "This is the best place I have ever worked. There's an open door policy. Every one is allowed to voice their opinion."
- "I get information about everything—profits, losses, problems. Relationships with people are easier here. It's more direct and open."[9]

Summary of Best Practices Mentioned in This Text

As you can see, understanding and applying best practices can help improve the management of projects, programs, portfolios, and entire companies. Several best practices were described throughout this text. Following is a brief summary of some of them:

- Determine how project, program, and portfolio management will work best in your own organization.
- Involve key stakeholders—including shareholders, customers, and employees—in making major decisions.
- Develop and follow a formal project selection process to ensure projects support business needs.

- Lay the groundwork for projects before they officially start.
- Separate projects by phases, such as a study phase project, when it makes sense to do so.
- Designate a project champion to provide high-level support and participate in key meetings.
- Assign a project manager from operations to lead projects that affect operations.
- Form a steering committee with key managers from various departments for projects that will cause major organizational change.
- Provide mentoring and training for project managers and other stakeholders.
- Document action items at meetings, and set the next meeting time.
- Document meeting minutes, focusing on key decisions and action items, and send them out quickly.
- Use more than one approach for creating cost estimates.
- Use formal supplier evaluation procedures to help select sellers.
- Include a detailed statement of work and schedule in contracts.
- Develop and follow a formal change-control process.
- Work with suppliers to ensure that deliverables are produced properly.
- Follow a deliverable acceptance process to verify project scope.
- Be clear and honest in communicating project status information, and share the responsibility for project communications with the entire project team.
- Formally close projects and share lessons learned.

CASE WRAP-UP

Kristin Maur stood in front of the project steering committee. She invited her whole team to give the final presentation as a team effort. Of course they had several challenges along the way, but overall, the project was a success. All the new training courses were offered within a year, and the course evaluations averaged 3.4 on a 5.0 scale, which exceeded the committee's goal of 3.0. More people took training courses than planned, primarily the Web-based courses. Because the Web-based training was more cost-effective than the instructor-led training, the team was confident that the costs of the Just-In-Time Training project would be recouped in less than two years, as projected. Kristin watched each team member summarize key project results, and she sensed the pride that everyone felt in a job well done.

Chapter Summary

Closing projects involves gaining stakeholder and customer acceptance of the final products and services, and bringing the project to an orderly end. It includes verifying that all of the deliverables are complete. This chapter summarizes the closing tasks and key outputs for project integration and procurement management.

Closing outputs related to integration management include administrative and contract closure procedures; final products, services, or results; and updates to organizational process assets. Sample closing documents for the Just-In-Time Training project include a final project report, lessons-learned report, and customer acceptance/project completion form.

Closing outputs related to procurement management include closed contracts and updates to organizational process assets. A sample written contract closure notice is provided for the Just-In-Time Training project.

Many organizations study and apply best practices to improve their ability to manage projects, programs, and portfolios. PMI developed the Organizational Project Management Maturity Model (OPM3) to help organizations assess and improve their organizational project management maturity. OPM3 lists 586 best practices organized by project, program, and portfolio management. Interthink Consulting Incorporated developed the Organizational Project Management (OPM) Baseline Study, which provides a comprehensive overview of project management practices in organizations and industries worldwide. The Ultimate Business Library published *Best Practices,* which provides advice on best practices to follow for managing projects and organizations in general. This text also describes several best practices in managing projects, programs, and portfolios.

Quick Quiz

1. Which knowledge areas include tasks related to closing?
    a. project scope, time, cost, and quality management
    b. project integration, scope, time, cost, and quality management
    c. project integration and procurement management
    d. all nine knowledge areas

2. Which of the following statements is false?
    a. Even though many projects are canceled before completion, it is still important to formally close any project.
    b. Closing includes verifying that all of the deliverables are complete.
    c. Closing often includes a final presentation and report.
    d. Closing does not include developing a transition plan.

3. Providing a list of project documentation, project closure documents, and historical information produced by the project in a useful format is part of _____ .
    a. updating organizational process assets
    b. administrative and contract closure procedures
    c. contract closure procedures
    d. lessons learned

4. Answering questions such as, "What will you do differently on the next project based on your experience working on this project?" is part of a _____ .

   a. lessons-learned report

   b. customer acceptance/project completion form

   c. written notice of contract closure

   d. transition plan

5. Contract closure involves completion and settlement of contracts and resolution of _____ .

   a. payments

   b. any open items

   c. performance issues

   d. legal matters

6. The _____ should include requirements for formal acceptance and closure of contracts.

   a. project management plan

   b. procurement management plan

   c. contract itself

   d. contract management plan

7. A _____ is an optimal way recognized by industry to achieve a stated goal or objective.

   a. benchmark

   b. key performance indicator

   c. capability

   d. best practice

8. The Project Management Institute published the _____ in December 2003 to address the need to bridge the gap between organizational strategy and successful projects.

   a. Organizational Project Management Maturity Model (OPM3)

   b. Best Practices Report

   c. *PMBOK® Guide*

   d. Organizational Project Management Report

9. Organizations can measure performance against their own past; against peers; and, even better, against _____ .

   a. profits

   b. potential

   c. revenues

   d. the future

10. Which of the following is not a basic principle of project management from Ultimate Business Library's *Best Practice*?

   a. Make sure your projects are driven by your shareholders' suggestions.

   b. Use a staged approach.

   c. Engage your stakeholders.

   d. Ensure success by planning for it.

Quick Quiz Answers

1. C.; 2. D; 3. A; 4. A; 5. B; 6. C; 7. D; 8. A; 9. B; 10. A

Discussion Questions

1. What is involved in closing projects? Why should all projects be formally closed?

2. What are the main closing outputs created as part of integration management? Why is it important to create a final project report, presentation, and lessons-learned report?

3. What are the main closing outputs created as part of procurement management?

4. Why should organizations identify and use best practices? What are the main categories of best practices developed as part of OPM3? What does research from Interthink Consulting Incorporated show about the relationship between process maturity and project performance? What are some of the best practices mentioned in Ultimate Business Library's *Best Practice*? What additional best practices were suggested in this text?

Exercises

1. Find an example of a large project that took more than a year to complete, such as a major construction project. Describe some of the tasks performed to close the project. Write a one-page paper or prepare a short presentation summarizing your findings.

2. Using the lessons-learned template on the companion Web site (*www.course.com/mis/pm/schwalbe*), write a lessons-learned report for a project you worked on. If you cannot think of one, interview someone who recently completed a project and write a lessons-learned report on that project.

3. Review the best practices or basic project management principles presented in this chapter. Select any two of them and write a one- to two-page paper describing how each practice could help improve project management. Develop examples of how they could be applied to real project situations.

Team Projects

1. Your organization is about to complete a project to raise money for an important charity. Assume that there are 1,000 people in your organization. Also, assume that you had six months to raise as much money as possible, with a goal of $100,000. With just one week to go, you have raised $92,000. You did experience several problems with the project, which you described in Chapter 7. Using that information and information you prepared in other chapters related to this project, prepare a two- to three-page paper or 15-minute final presentation for the project. Be creative in your responses.

2. You are part of a team in charge of a project to help people in your company (500 people) lose weight. This project is part of a competition, and the top "losers" will be featured in a popular television show. Assume that you had six months to complete the project and a budget of $10,000. The project will end in one week, so you and your team are busy closing out the project. Prepare a lessons-learned report for the project, using information from your responses to this exercise in previous chapters as well as your creativity to determine what the final outcome was for the project.

3. Using the information you developed in Team Project 1 or 2, role-play the final project meeting, at which you present the final presentation to key stakeholders. Determine who will play what role (project manager, team member from a certain department, senior managers, and so on). Be creative in displaying different personalities (a senior manager who questions the importance of the project to the organization, a team member who is very shy or obnoxious).

4. Create a final project presentation and lessons-learned report for one of the real projects your class or group developed in Chapter 1, using the templates and samples in this chapter as guides. Present your results to the class.

Companion Web Site

Visit the companion Web site for this text (*www.course.com/mis/pm/schwalbe*) to access:

- Lecture notes
- Interactive quizzes
- Template files
- Sample documents
- Guide to Using Microsoft Project 2003
- VPMi enterprise project management software
- More ideas for team projects, including real projects and case studies
- Links to additional resources related to project management

Key Terms

best practice — An optimal way recognized by industry to achieve a stated goal or objective.[3]

capabilities — The incremental steps that lead to best practices.

contract closure — The completion and settlement of contracts, and resolution of any open items.

key performance indicator (KPI) — A criterion used to determine whether the outcome associated with a capability exists, or the degree to which it exists.

maturity model — A framework for helping organizations improve their processes and systems.

organizational project management — The systematic management of project, programs, and portfolios in alignment with the achievement of strategic goals.[2]

outcomes — The results of applying capabilities.

procurement audits — Reviews often performed during contract closure to identify lessons learned in the entire procurement process.

records management system — A tool that provides the ability to easily organize, find, and archive procurement-related documents.

End Notes

[1] Mary Evans, "Overdue and Over Budget, Over and Over Again," *Economist.com* (June 9, 2005).

[2] Project Management Institute, Inc., Organizational Project Management Maturity Model (OPM3) Knowledge Foundation (2003), p. xiii.

[3] Ibid., p. 13.

[4] Ibid., p. 15.

[5] Evans, "Overdue and Over Budget."

[6] Mark E. Mullaly, "2004 Organizational Project Management Baseline Study Results Overview," (*http://www.interthink.ca/*) (2005).

[7] Ultimate Business Library, *Best Practice: Ideas and Insights from the World's Foremost Business Thinkers,* Cambridge, MA: Perseus Publishing, 2003, p. 1.

[8] Ibid., p. 8.

[9] Great Place to Work Institute, Best Companies Lists (*www.greatplacetowork.com*) (June 2005).

APPENDIX **A**

RESOURCES

INTRODUCTION

This appendix summarizes resources you can use to expand your understanding of project management. It describes information provided on the companion Web site and presents a list of additional sites with useful information. You can also go to the author's Web site (*www.kathyschwalbe.com*) to access these and other resources.

COMPANION WEB SITE (WWW.COURSE.COM/MIS/PM/SCHWALBE)

The companion Web site for this text includes the following:

- Links to the references mentioned in this appendix.
- *A Guide to Using Microsoft Project 2003*, a 105-page document that includes detailed instructions on using this powerful software package. It includes an overview of Microsoft Project 2003 and sections on using it for project scope, time, cost, human resource, and communications management. It includes 75 figures and hands-on steps to help you feel comfortable using the world's most popular project management software. There are also four exercises to help you apply your new skills. The CD included with this text provides a 120-day trial edition of Project 2003 Professionals. You can also download a free 60-day trial version from *www.microsoft.com* or order a CD kit.
- Project 2003 data files mentioned in *A Guide to Using Microsoft Project 2003*, contained in one compressed file.
- Instructions for accessing and using a 120-day trial for up to five users of VPMi, a Web-based enterprise project management software product from Virtual Communications Services (VCS). This software automates project, program, and portfolio management and includes Microsoft Project integration.
- Detailed instructions for using Fissure's project management simulation software.
- Template files mentioned in this text. See the section on template files in this appendix for more information.
- The project Web site and all the sample documents (over 50 of them) from the Just-In-Time Training project mentioned throughout this text.
- Lecture notes for each chapter created in Microsoft PowerPoint.
- Interactive test questions for each chapter.
- A link to the author's site (*www.kathyschwalbe.com*).
- A link to the publisher's site (*www.course.com*).

TEMPLATE FILES

As mentioned throughout this text, using templates can help you prepare various project management documents, spreadsheets, charts, and other files. Table A-1 lists the template name, table or figure number where it is used in the text, the filename, and the application software used to create it. Be careful to enter information into the templates carefully, and feel free to modify the templates to meet your particular project needs. You can download the files in one compressed file from the companion Web site or the author's site. You must have the application software to use the templates.

TABLE A-1   Templates available for download on the companion Web site

Template name	Table/figure reference	Application software
Payback period chart	Figure 2-6	Excel
Weighted scoring model	Figure 2-7	Excel
Stakeholder analysis	Table 3-3	Word
Business case	Table 3-4	Word
Busienss case financials	Figure 3-2	Excel
Project charter	Table 3-5	Word
Kick-off meeting agenda	Table 3-6	Word
Preliminary scope statement	Table 3-7	Word
Team contract	Table 4-2	Word
Project management plan	Table 4-3	Word
Scope management plan	Table 4-4	Word
Scope statement	Table 4-5	Word
WBS	Table 4-6	Word
WBS dictionary entry	Table 4-7	Word
Activity list and attributes	Table 4-8	Word
Milestone list	Table 4-9	Word
Activity resource requirements	Table 4-10	Word
Project schedule	Figure 4-9	Project
Cost estimate	Figure 4-11	Excel
Cost baseline	Figure 4-12	Excel
Quality management plan	Table 5-2	Word
Quality metrics	Table 5-3	Word

TABLE A-1   Templates available for download on the companion Web site (continued)

Template name	Table/figure reference	Application software
Quality checklist	Table 5-4	Word
Project organizational chart	Figure 5-1	PowerPoint
RACI chart	Table 5-5	Excel
Resource histogram	Figure 5-2	Excel
Staffing management plan	Table 5-6	Word
Communications management plan	Table 5-7	Word
Project Web site	Figure 5-3	FrontPage
Risk management plan	Table 5-8	Word
Probability/impact matrix	Figure 5-5	PowerPoint
Risk register	Table 5-9	Excel
Make-or-buy analysis	Table 5-11	Word
Procurement management plan	Table 5-12	Word
Request for proposal	Table 5-13	Word
Contract statement of work	Table 5-14	Word
Supplier evaluation matrix	Figure 5-7	Excel
Milestone report	Table 6-2	Word
Change request	Table 6-3	Word
Cause-and-effect diagram	Figures 6-2 and 7-3	PowerPoint
Team roster	Table 6-4	Word
Team performance assessment	Table 6-5	Word
Qualified sellers list	Table 6-7	Word
Contract	Table 6-8	Word
Earned value chart	Figure 7-1	Excel
Deliverable acceptance form	Table 7-4	Word
Run chart	Figure 7-5	Excel
Scatter diagram	Figure 7-6	Excel
Histogram	Figure 7-7	Excel
Pareto chart	Figure 7-8	Excel
Flow chart	Figure 7-9	PowerPoint

TABLE A-1   Templates available for download on the companion Web site (continued)

Template name	Table/figure reference	Application software
Performance report	Table 7-5	Word
Issue log	Table 7-6	Excel
Customer acceptance-project completion form	Table 8-2	Word
Final project report table of contents	Table 8-3	Word
Transition plan	Table 8-4	Word
Lessons learned report	Table 8-5	Word
Contract closure notice	Table 8-6	Word

USEFUL PROJECT MANAGEMENT SITES

Thousands of Web sites provide useful information related to project, program, and portfolio management. This brief listing highlights just a few useful sites, which provide many links to other sites. You can easily link to these sites from the companion Web site for this text, and you can also search the Internet to find other useful sites.

Professional Societies

- *Project Management Institute (www.pmi.org)*: This site includes lots of information related to project management, Project Management Professional (PMP) certification, project management seminars and conferences, and so on. Students throughout the world can join PMI at deep discounts. As a member, you receive a free copy of the PMBOK® Guide, subscriptions to the monthly PM Network magazine and quarterly PM Journal, and access to online member resources.
- *Students of Project Management (www.studentsofpm.org)*: This virtual group, sponsored by PMI, supports students studying project management.
- *International Association of Project and Program Management (www.iappm. org)*: This site includes information about the Certified Portfolio Managers (CPM) certification and other services provided by this international professional society for project and program managers.
- *Association for Project Management (www.apmgroup.co.uk)*: This UK-based professional society provides an accreditation, certification, and examination body for key elements of best practice in program, project, and risk management.
- *American Society for the Advancement of Project Management (www.asapm. org)*: This competency-based credentialing organization advocates effective project management practice throughout all organizations.
- *Australian Institute of Project Management (www.aipm.com.au)*: This professional group was organized in 1976 to promote and progress the profession of project management in Australia.

Sites with Project Management Articles

- Chief Project Officer (*www.cpo.com*)
- Gantthead.com (*www.gantthead.com*)
- Project Management Boulevard (*www.pmblvd.com*)
- Project Management Control Tower (*www.4pm.com*)
- Project Management Forum (*www.pmforum.org*)
- ProjectNet (*www.projectnet.co.uk*)
- Projects @ Work (*www.projectsatwork.com*)
- The Center for Business Practices (*www.cpbonline.com*)
- The International Research Network on Organizing by Projects (*www.irnop.org*)
- The Project Manager's Resource Center (*www.allpm.com*)
- The Tenstep Project Management Process Methodology (*www.tenstep.com*)

FISSURE PROJECT MANAGEMENT SIMULATION

INTRODUCTION

Many people enjoy using simulation software to help them learn. This appendix briefly describes Fissure's project management simulation demo, which is included on the CD-ROM that accompanies this text. Fissure (*www.fissure.com*) is a Project Management Institute (PMI) Registered Education Provider (REP) that specializes in training in the following fields: project management, software management, leadership, and organizational change. Fissure has used an expanded version of this simulation tool to help thousands of people learn how to apply various project management concepts.

You can access more detailed instructions for using this simulation, including several screen shots and suggestions on how to use it in various learning settings, from the companion Web site (*www.course.com/mis/pm/schwalbe*). This simulation uses many of the concepts, tools, and techniques described throughout this text. You should be familiar with at least Chapters 1 through 7 before running the simulation. Feel free to consult the text to reinforce your understanding of some of the topics included in the simulation.

INTRODUCTION TO FISSURE'S SIMULATION SOFTWARE

Fissure's project management simulation software is based on the SimProject Alliance Prototype project. The demo version of the simulation software bundled with this text includes a fairly simple, 11-week project consisting of only seven tasks and 10 potential team members. Fissure estimates that it takes about 3–4 hours to run the demo simulation. Contact Fissure (*www.fissure.com* or 1-877-877-6333) for more information on their advanced project simulation, which includes 22 tasks and 30 potential team members, as well as other products and services.

Table B-1 describes the project. A similar description of the project is provided in the project definition document included in the References section of the simulation software:

TABLE B-1 Simulation project information

Description:
The Alliance Prototype project represents a strategic effort to augment the sales and marketing capabilities of Uniworld with an e-commerce equipped Web site. This Web site is needed to help Uniworld regain its global market dominance. To validate this objective and to gain a better understanding of Web site deployment, the company has budgeted $40,000 for the development of a prototype Web site. Marketing has stated that it needs this prototype site to be fully demonstratable within 11 weeks to make a determination to proceed with a fully functional site.

Deliverables:
The Alliance Prototype project will provide hardware and software required for establishing an e-commerce Web site that will demonstrate the feasibility of developing a fully fuctional site that will be capable of taking product orders and generating product fulfillment. The deliverables for this project are the demonstration Web site, the site documentation, and a recommended product architecture.

Performance:
The Alliance Prototype Web site will be accepted upon successful completion of the customer acceptance test with no more than seven known defects, which will represent an estimated Meant Time To Failure (MTTF) of five days. Furthermore, no known defects can be present that can cause potential system failure or major loss of functionality. The Web site must be capable of demonstrating the feasibility of handling a peak load of 2000 hits per hour without appreciable degradation in system response.

To participate in this simulated project, you are expected to read about the company, project, and people available to work on this project. You plan your project and make typical project decisions each week, such as when to assign staff, when to hold meetings, and when to send staff to various training opportunities. You run your project a week at a time, analyzing your results each week, referring to your weekly reports, and making your decisions for the next week. As you run the simulation each week, you are presented with communications from people within the company, team members, or other stakeholders related to the project. You choose how to respond to these communications, and all the decisions you make impact how your project progresses. You can close the simulation at any time and save your work, if desired. You can also run the simulation as many times as you like, and the results vary based on your decisions.

INSTALLING AND LAUNCHING THE SIMPROJECT SIMULATION

Before you begin working with the simulated project, you need to install the simulation software.

To load the simulation software:

1. Insert the Fissure Project Management Simulation Demo CD-ROM into your CD-ROM drive. This CD-ROM is attached to the inside back cover of this text.
2. Click the **Start** button on the taskbar, and then click **Run**.
3. In the Run dialog box, click **Browse**. Click the **Look in list arrow** and select

the drive letter associated with your computer's CD-ROM drive. Double-click the **SimProject Demo** icon, and then click **OK**.

4. Follow the installion instructions. The installation takes about 1-2 minutes, and you will need to restart your computer before running the simulation software.

TIP

It is recommended that you use Microsoft Windows 2000 Professional or XP to run the simulation software. If you have any technical problems, contact Course Technolgy's Support Services at *www.course.com/support.*

After installation is complete, you can launch SimProject and take a tour.
To launch SimProject and take a tour:

1. Click the **Start** button on the taskbar, select **Programs**, and then select **SimProject.**
2. Move your mouse to the right to click on **SimProject**
3. Click on the **green parrot** in the upper right of your screen. Your screen should resemble Figure B-1. The green parrot, Peedy, is your project assistant and guide for using the simulation tool. Notice the other main pictures or reference buttons on the screen: References, Planning, Staffing, Team Interaction, Stakeholders, Reports, and Work Week 1. Click **Yes** to explore the software.

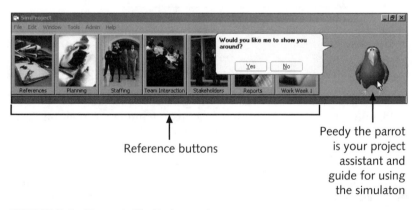

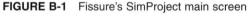

Reference buttons

Peedy the parrot is your project assistant and guide for using the simulaton

FIGURE B-1   Fissure's SimProject main screen

RUNNING THE SIMPROJECT SIMULATION

To familiarize yourself with the simulation software, Peedy shows you what each reference buttons gives you access to (References, Planning, Staffing, Team Interaction, Stakeholders, Reports, and Work Week 1) and explains the basic process for running the simulation. The simulation includes audio, and it also displays the text so that you can see what Peedy is saying. Listen closely to the instructions, but you can run them again as needed. Also don't be surprised to hear Peedy making sleeping sounds in the background if you open the simulation tool and then neglect it!

Among the last elements Peedy describes are the items available under the Reports button, such as the earned value graph, as shown in Figure B-2. See Chapter 7 for more information on earned value management.

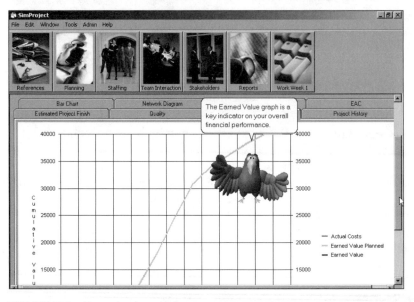

FIGURE B-2   Earned value graph

After you complete Peedy's tour, you can begin the project.

To start running your project:

1. Click the **Reference** button to read important reference information.
2. Click the **Planning** button to enter your resource planning information for Week 1. Figure B-3 shows the initial Planning screen. Several tabs are available from this screen to allow you to enter and view information related to the budget, resources, risks/opportunities, education, and stakeholder relations. Be sure to enter all the appropriate planning information, and check to make sure your budget does not exceed the approved budget. *The detailed version of this appendix on the companion Web site provides many more sample screen shots to guide you through the planning process.*
3. *Before* you run the simulation for that week, update your plan, including staffing, training, education, and stakeholder interactions for the week. Select the display of your resource plan and then click the **Staffing** button to see your

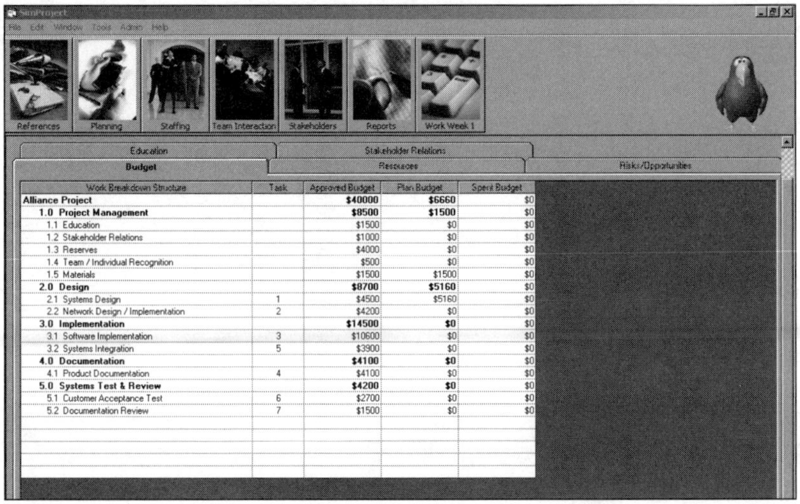

FIGURE B-3 Planning screen

resource plan in the background as you make your weekly staffing decisions. Decisions you need to make each week before "running" the simulation for the week include the following:

- *Staffing*: Select individuals you want to add to your team or remove from your team. Note that there is a "quick look" button to your resource plan located in the lower-left corner of the window.
- *Task assignments*: Assign individuals to work on specific tasks and request overtime. Within the assignment window is a useful "quick look" button for glancing at your resource plan to facilitate your planning.
- *Team meetings*: Select the day, the duration, and the topic(s) for meetings.
- *Individual conferences*: Select the individual, the day, the duration, and the topic(s).
- *Training*: Select the individual or team and the specific training.
- *Recognition*: Select the individual or team and the recognition.
- *Stakeholder relations*: Select the stakeholder and the interaction.

4. To run the simulation for the week, click **Work Week**. This indicates the number of the project week you are running. As you run the week's simulation, you are presented with communications from various sources. Read the communications carefully and choose your response. The decisions you make prior to running each week's simulation and the decisions you made in earlier weeks determines the results you see for the project. At the completion of each week, a report of the week's decisions and results is displayed. This report can be printed, and it is also viewable via the History tab within the Reports screen. Figure B-4 provides an example of the Work Week report. This report was run without entering any new planning information for Week 1 in the simulation. *Before* running the Work Week report, make sure you enter all planning information.

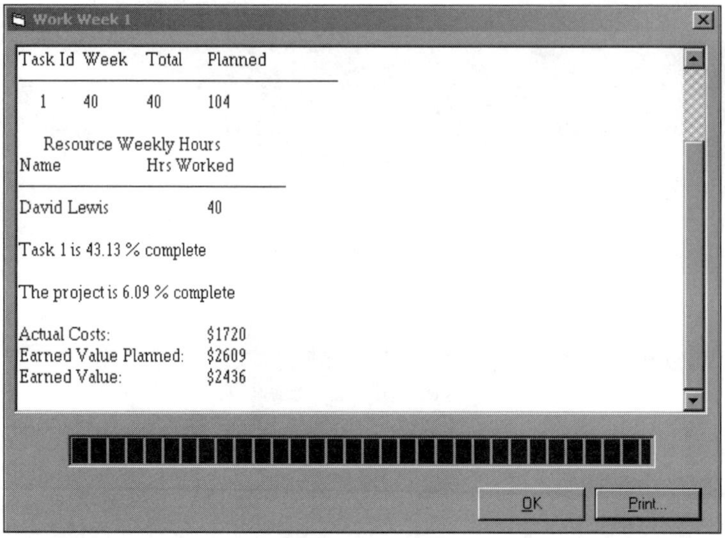

FIGURE B-4 Sample work week report

5. Click **Reports** to review various project management reports to help you assess your current project status each week. Reports include the following:
    - *Bar chart*: Displays a Gantt chart showing a project timetable and task status or progress
    - *Network diagram*: Shows task dependencies/sequences
    - *Project performance index (PPI)*: Shows the percentage of the budget spent/the percentage of the project complete
    - *Estimate at completion (EAC)*: Provides an estimate for the cost of the project at completion assuming that the project performance continues at the same pace
    - *Estimated project completion*: Provides an estimate for the time when the project will be complete assuming that the project performance continues at the same pace
    - *Quality*: Shows the number of open defects reports
    - *Earned value*: Displays a comparison of planned value, actual cost, and earned value
    - *Project history*: Provides a report of each week's decisions and results

Look at each report carefully each week and use them to help make your weekly decisions. Don't forget to keep your plans, especially your resource plan, updated. Any of this information can be printed at any time. Review the results of your simulation. Did you do a good job managing the project? What did you learn by running the simulation? You might want to run the simulation more than once to practice your project management skills.

activity attributes Information that provides schedule-related information about each activity, such as predecessors, successors, logical relationships, leads and lags, resource requirements, constraints, imposed dates, and assumptions related to the activity.

activity list A tabulation of activities to be included on a project schedule.

activity-on-arrow (AOA) approach or the arrow diagramming method (ADM) A network diagramming technique in which activities are represented by arrows and connected at points called nodes to illustrate the sequence of activities.

actual cost The total direct and indirect costs incurred in accomplishing work on an activity during a given period.

analogous estimates or top-down estimates The estimates that use the actual cost of a previous, similar project as the basis for estimating the cost of the current project.

balanced scorecard A methodology that converts an organization's value drivers to a series of defined metrics.

baseline A starting point, a measurement, or an observation that is documented so that it can be used for future comparison; also defined as the original project plans plus approved changes.

benchmarking The process of generating ideas for quality improvements by comparing specific project practices or product characteristics to those of other projects or products within or outside of the performing organization.

best practice An optimal method of performing a task that is recognized by a specific industry because it effectively achieves a stated goal or objective.

bid A document prepared by sellers providing pricing for standard items that have been clearly defined by the buyer.

blogs The easy-to-use journals on the Web that allow users to write entries, create links, and upload pictures, while allowing readers to post comments to particular journal entries.

bottom-up estimates Cost estimates created by estimating individual activities and summing them to get a project total.

budget at completion (BAC) The approved total budget for the project.

burst An event that occurs when two or more activities follow a single node on a network diagram.

business case A document that provides justification for investing in a project.

capabilities The incremental steps that lead to best practices.

cash flow Benefits minus costs, or income minus expenses.

cause-and-effect diagrams Also called fishbone or Ishikawa diagrams, these diagrams can assist in ensuring and improving quality by finding the root causes of quality problems.

champion A senior manager who acts as a key proponent for a project.

checklist A list of items to be noted or consulted.

closing processes The actions that involve formalizing acceptance of the project or phase and bringing it to an orderly end.

communications management plan A document that guides project communications.

compromise mode The conflict-handling method that uses a give-and-take approach to resolve conflicts.

conformance to requirements The process of ensuring that the project's processes and products meet written specifications.

confrontation mode The conflict-handling method that involves directly facing a conflict using a problem-solving approach that allows affected parties to work through their disagreements.

constructive change orders Oral or written acts or omissions that are written by someone with actual or apparent authority that can be construed to have the same effect as a written change order.

contingency plans The predefined actions that the project team will take if an identified risk event occurs.

contingency reserves or **contingency allowances** The funds held by the project sponsor that can be used to mitigate cost or schedule overruns if unknown risks occur.

contract closure The completion and settlement of contracts, and resolution of any open items.

contract statement of work (SOW) A description of the work that is to be purchased from an outside vendor.

contracts The mutually binding agreements that obligate the seller to provide the specified products or services, and obligate the buyer to pay for them.

control chart A graphic display of data that illustrates the results of a process over time.

cost baseline A time-phased budget that project managers use to measure and monitor cost performance.

cost-reimbursable contract A contract that involves payment to the seller for direct and indirect actual costs.

crashing A technique for making cost and schedule trade-offs to obtain the greatest amount of schedule compression for the least incremental cost.

critical path The series of activities that determine the *earliest* time by which the project can be completed; it is the *longest* path through the network diagram and has the least amount of slack or float.

critical path method (CPM) or **critical path analysis** A network diagramming technique used to predict total project duration.

deliverable A product or service produced or provided as part of a project.

dependency or **relationship** The sequencing of project activities or tasks.

directives The new requirements imposed by management, government, or some external entity.

discount factor A multiplier for each year based on the discount rate and year.

discount rate The rate used in discounting future cash flows.

discretionary dependencies The dependencies that are defined by the project team.

duration The actual amount of time spent working on an activity *plus* elapsed time.

earned value (EV) An estimate of the value of the physical work actually completed.

earned value management (EVM) A project performance measurement technique that integrates scope, time, and cost data.

effort The number of workdays or work hours required to complete a task.

empathic listening   The process of listening with the intent to understand by putting yourself in the shoes of the other person.

estimate at completion (EAC)   A forecast of how much the project will cost upon completion.

executing processes   The actions that involve coordinating people and other resources to carry out the project plans and produce the deliverables of the project.

external dependencies   The dependencies that involve relationships between project and nonproject activities.

extrinsic motivation   A motivation that causes people to do something for a reward or to avoid a penalty.

fallback plans   The plans that are developed for risks that have a high impact on meeting project objectives, and are put into effect if attempts to reduce the risk are not effective.

fast tracking   A schedule compression technique where you perform activities in parallel that you would normally do in sequence.

fitness for use   The ability of a product to be used as it was intended.

fixed-price or **lump-sum contract**   A type of contract that involves a fixed price for a well-defined product or service.

flowcharts   Graphic displays of the logic and flow of processes that help you analyze how problems occur and how processes can be improved.

forcing mode   The conflict-handling mode that involves exerting one's viewpoint at the potential expense of another viewpoint.

forecasts   Reports that predict future project status and progress based on past information and trends.

Gantt charts   A standard format for displaying project schedule information by listing project activities and their corresponding start and finish dates in a calendar format.

groupthink   The conformance to the values or ethical standards of a group.

histogram   A bar graph of a distribution of variables.

initiating processes   The actions that begin or end projects and project phases.

integrated change control   Identifying, evaluating, and managing changes throughout the project's life cycle.

internal rate of return (IRR)   The discount rate that results in an NPV of zero for a project.

intrinsic motivation   A motivation that causes people to participate in an activity for their own enjoyment.

issue   A matter under question or dispute that could impede project success.

issue log   A tool used to document and monitor the resolution of project issues.

key performance indicator (KPI)   A criterion used to determine whether the outcome associated with a capability has been reached, or the degree to which it has been reached. Quantifiable measurements, agreed to beforehand, that reflect progress made toward achieving specific outcomes.

kick-off meeting   A meeting held at the beginning of a project so that stakeholders can meet each other, review the goals of the project, and discuss future plans.

leader   A person who focuses on long-term goals and big-picture objectives, while inspiring people to reach those goals.

make-or-buy analysis   The process of estimating the internal costs of providing a product or service and comparing that estimate to the cost of outsourcing.

manager   A person who deals with the day-to-day details of meeting specific goals.

mandatory dependencies   The dependencies that are inherent in the nature of the work being performed on a project.

Maslow's hierarchy of needs A hierarchy that states that people's behaviors are guided or motivated by a sequence of needs (physiological, safety, social, esteem, and self-actualization).

maturity model A framework for helping organizations improve their processes and systems.

merge A situation when two or more nodes precede a single node on a project network diagram.

methodology A plan that describes how things should be done to manage a project.

metric A standard of measurement.

milestone A significant event on a project.

mirroring The act of imitating or matching the physical behaviors of the person to whom you are talking.

monitoring and controlling processes The actions taken to measure progress toward achieving project goals, monitor deviation from plans, and take corrective action.

Myers-Briggs Type Indicator (MBTI) A popular tool for determining personality preferences.

net present value (NPV) analysis A method of calculating the expected net monetary gain or loss from a project by discounting all expected future cash inflows and outflows to the present point in time.

network diagram A schematic display of the logical relationships among, or sequencing of, project activities.

node The starting and ending point of an activity on an activity-on-arrow network diagram.

opportunities Chances to improve the organization.

opportunity cost of capital The return available by investing the capital elsewhere.

organizational project management The systematic management of project, programs, and portfolios in alignment with the achievement of strategic goals.

outcomes The results of applying capabilities.

parametric modeling A technique that uses project characteristics (parameters) in a mathematical model to estimate project costs.

Pareto chart A histogram that can help you identify and prioritize problem areas.

payback period The amount of time it will take to recoup, in the form of net cash inflows, the total dollars invested in a project.

phase A distinct stage in project development.

planned value That portion of the approved total cost estimate planned to be spent on an activity during a given period.

planning processes The actions that involve devising and maintaining a workable scheme to ensure that the project meets its scope, time, and cost goals as well as organizational needs.

portfolio A collection of projects or programs and other work that are grouped together to facilitate effective management of that work to meet strategic business objectives.

precedence diagramming method (PDM) A network diagramming technique in which boxes represent activities.

problems Undesirable situations that prevent the organization from achieving its goals.

process A series of actions directed toward a particular result.

procurement audits Reviews often performed during contract closure to identify lessons learned in the entire procurement process.

program A group of projects managed in a coordinated way to obtain benefits and control not available from managing them individually.

Program Evaluation and Review Technique (PERT) A network analysis technique used to estimate project duration when there is a high degree of uncertainty about the individual activity duration estimates.

program manager The person who provides leadership and direction for the project managers heading the projects within a program.

progress reports (PV) Reports that describe what the project team has accomplished during a certain period.

project A temporary endeavor undertaken to create a unique product, service, or result.

project buffer The additional time added to a project schedule before a project's due date to account for unexpected factors.

project charter A document that formally recognizes the existence of a project and provides a summary of the project's objectives and management.

project cost management The processes required to ensure that a project team completes a project within an approved budget.

project human resource management Making effective use of the people involved with a project.

project integration management The process of coordinating all the project management knowledge areas throughout a project's life cycle.

project management The application of knowledge, skills, tools, and techniques to project activities to meet project requirements.

project management knowledge areas The competencies that are key to success as a project manager, including management of scope, time, cost, quality, human resources, communications, risk, procurement, and project integration.

project management office (PMO) An organizational entity created to assist project managers in achieving project goals.

project management plan A document, which is a deliverable for the project integration management knowledge area, used to coordinate all project planning documents and to help guide a project's execution and control.

project management process groups The progression from initiating activities to planning activities, executing activities, monitoring and controlling activities, and closing activities.

Project Management Professional (PMP) The certification provided by the Project Management Institute (PMI) that requires documenting project experience, agreeing to follow the PMI code of ethics, and passing a comprehensive exam.

project management tools and techniques The methods available to assist project managers and their teams; some popular tools in the time-management knowledge area include Gantt charts, network diagrams, critical-path analysis, and project management software.

project manager The person responsible for working with the project sponsor, the project team, and the other people involved in a project to meet project goals.

project organizational chart A graphic representation of how authority and responsibility are distributed within the project.

project portfolio management The grouping and managing of projects and programs as a portfolio of investments that contribute to the entire enterprise's success.

project quality management Processes undertaken to ensure that the project will satisfy the stated or implied needs for which it was undertaken.

project scope management The process of defining and controlling what work is or is not included in a project.

project sponsor The person who provides the direction and funding for a project.

project time management   The process required to ensure timely completion of a project.

proposal   A document in which sellers describe what they will do to meet the requirements of a buyer.

quality   The totality of characteristics of an entity that bear on its ability to satisfy stated or implied needs.

quality assurance   The activities related to satisfying the relevant quality standards for a project.

quality audit   A structured review of specific quality management activities that helps identify lessons learned, which could improve performance on current or future projects.

RACI charts   A type of resource histogram that shows Responsibility, Accountability, Consultation, and Informed roles for project stakeholders.

rapport   A relationship of harmony, conformity, accord, or affinity.

rate of performance (RP)   The ratio of actual work completed to the percentage of work planned to have been completed at any given time.

records management system   A tool that provides the ability to easily organize, find, and archive procurement-related documents.

Request for Proposal (RFP)   A document used to solicit proposals from prospective suppliers.

Request for Quote (RFQ)   A document used to solicit quotes or bids from prospective suppliers.

required rate of return   The minimum acceptable rate of return on an investment.

resource histogram   A column chart that shows the number of resources required for or assigned to a project over time.

responsibility assignment matrix (RAM)   A matrix that maps the work of the project as described in the WBS to the people responsible for performing the work.

return on investment (ROI)   (Benefits minus costs) divided by costs.

risk   An uncertainty that can have a negative or positive effect on meeting project objectives.

risk events   The specific, uncertain events that may occur to the detriment or enhancement of the project.

risk register   A document that contains results of various risk management processes, often displayed in a table or spreadsheet format.

root cause   The real or underlying reason a problem occurs.

scatter diagram   A diagram that helps show if there is a relationship between two variables.

scope baseline   The approved project scope statement and its associated WBS and WBS dictionary.

scope creep   The tendency for project scope to grow bigger and bigger.

scope management plan   A document that includes descriptions of how the team will prepare the project scope statement, create the WBS, verify completion of the project deliverables, and control requests for changes to the project scope.

scope statement   A document used to develop and confirm a common understanding of the project scope.

scope verification   Formal acceptance of the completed project scope by the project manager or designated stakeholders.

short list   A list of the top three to five suppliers created to reduce the work involved in selecting a source.

slack or float   The amount of time an activity may be delayed without delaying a succeeding activity or the project finish date.

slipped milestone A milestone activity that was actually completed later than originally planned.

smoothing mode The conflict-handling mode that de-emphasizes or avoids areas of differences and emphasizes areas of agreement.

staffing management plan A plan that describes when and how people will be added to and taken off a project.

stakeholder analysis A document that provides information on key stakeholders to help manage relationships with them.

stakeholders The people involved in or affected by project activities.

standard A document that describes best practices for what should be done to manage a project.

status reports Reports that describe where the project stands at a specific point in time.

strategic planning The process of determining long-term objectives by analyzing the strengths and weaknesses of an organization, studying opportunities and threats in the business environment, predicting future trends, and projecting the need for new products and services.

SWOT analysis Analyzing strengths, weaknesses, opportunities, and threats.

synergy The concept that the whole is equal to more than the sum of its parts.

team contract A document created to help promote teamwork and clarify team communications.

template A file with a preset format that serves as a starting point for creating various documents so that the format and structure do not have to be re-created.

three-point estimate An estimate that includes an optimistic, most likely, and pessimistic estimate.

time-and-materials contract A type of contract that is a hybrid of both fixed price and cost-reinbursable contracts.

tracking Gantt chart A Gantt chart that compares planned and actual project schedule information.

triggers The indicators or symptoms of actual risk events.

triple constraint The balancing of scope, time, and cost goals.

Tuckman model A model that describes five stages of team development (forming, storming, norming, performing, and adjourning).

weighted scoring model A technique that provides a systematic process for basing project selection on numerous criteria.

withdrawal mode The conflict-handling mode that involves retreating or withdrawing from an actual or potential disagreement.

work breakdown structure (WBS) A deliverable-oriented grouping of the work involved in a project that defines the total scope of the project.

work breakdown structure (WBS) dictionary A document that describes detailed information about each WBS task.

work package A task at the lowest level of the WBS.

workarounds Unplanned responses to risk events.

INDEX

Q

R